SIERRA BRAVO

BOOKS BY LES ROBERTS

Milan Jacovich Mysteries
Pepper Pike
Full Cleveland
Deep Shakeer'
The Cleveland Connection
The Lake Effect
The Duke of Cleveland
Collision Bend
The Cleveland Local
A Shoot in Cleveland
The Best-Kept Secret
The Indian Sign
The Dutch
The Irish Sports Pages
King of the Holly Hop
The Cleveland Creep
Whiskey Island
Win, Place or Die
(with Dan S. Kennedy)
The Ashtabula Hat Trick
Speaking of Murder
(with Dan S. Kennedy)

Dominic Candiotti Novels
*The Strange Death of
Father Candy*
Wet Work

Saxon Mysteries
*An Infinite Number
of Monkeys*
Not Enough Horses
A Carrot for the Donkey
Snake Oil
Seeing the Elephant
The Lemon Chicken Jones

Stand-Alones
The Chinese Fire Drill
Sheehan's Dog
The C.I.
An Only Child
Sierra Bravo

Novella
A Carol for Cleveland
(later made into a play by
Eric Coble for the Cleveland
Play House holiday season)

Short Stories
The Scent of Spiced Oranges

Non-Fiction Memoir
We'll Always Have Cleveland

LES ROBERTS

SIERRA BRAVO

Down & Out Books
3959 Van Dyke Road, Suite 265
Lutz, FL 33558
DownAndOutBooks.com

Cover design by JT Lindroos

ISBN: 1-64396-388-0
ISBN-13: 978-1-64396-388-4

To Kyndle,
You'll always be in my heart

CHAPTER ONE

Depending on your point of view, Monday can be the best day of the week, or the worst.

Best because if you're lucky, you have a regular job, you get two weekend days to relax, to not think about your work, to do something enjoyable, or at least take on a home-related task like cleaning out the garage or raking the leaves, and now on Monday you're rested and ready to tackle the real world once more.

Worst because being back at the job, pecking at the ground like a hungry chicken, trying to make a buck and not considering anything else until Friday night eventually comes around and you can peel off your work clothes, dig out your sweatpants, T-shirts and flip flops, and count the freedom hours until you must put on the uniform of the day again, whether a subdued gray suit, boots and canvas pants, or a true uniform like the one Sierra Bravo wore to her job—a dark blue uniform, with a gold name badge, spit-shined shoes, medals, a Glock at her hip, and silver stars on the shirt collar to indicate she was the Chief of Police of Sundown Beach, California.

She'd been hired nine months earlier by city manager and lawyer, Chris Fornadel, who helped her out of a scrape or two back when she was a patrol cop in a small town in San Bernardino County, and put in a good word for her with the Sundown Beach City Council that has the final say on hiring and firing. Sundown Beach is south of L.A. and north of San Diego, an upscale community with beautiful Southwestern Tex-Mex houses of all sizes and shapes, a shopping and dining area, and a large, classy library. Downtown, the heart of the city spread over several blocks in a neighborhood collectively called Seaview, though it was a mile inland of the Pacific Ocean.

The city council was made up of three members. Two of them liked Sierra Bravo, appreciating the job she was doing running a small, efficient police department. One, though, had no use for her at all, which didn't bother Sierra in the slightest. She wasn't a political person. She loathed the one-upmanship part of police work and disliked how *being* a chief made her political herself, whether she wanted to be or not.

She entered the precinct parking lot on Sassafras Road, a stupid name for a street borrowed from a street of the same name in nearby San Diego. Quietly, she quietly drifted into the reserved space, her name and rank painted on a serious-looking sign. In the ranks, there were no assistant chiefs or deputy chiefs, as the town was a bit too small.

She wriggled out of the car, leaving her gold-braided cap on the passenger seat. She never wore that cap unless it was to a formal occasion, believing she looked ridiculous in any hat resembling a comic costume out of a musical by Gilbert and Sullivan.

When she arrived at her desk, one of her officers, Nancy Flower, stuck her head in the door, beaming as usual. Flower, Sierra thought, was an odd name for a police officer—but then Sundown Beach was no crime-ridden town like Chicago, Detroit or Oakland, so it didn't matter if an attractive, married female officer named Flower was also a "tough" cop.

"Morning, Chief," Nancy Flower said. "Coffee?"

"Thanks, maybe later." A coffeeholic, Sierra preferred getting it herself. She didn't feel like the President of the United States, or a CEO of a Fortune 500 Company—picking out an underling to get her a cup of coffee. She was just a cop who could walk thirty steps down the hall for her own coffee. The precinct was twice as big as it needed to be, well-designed and stocked with several big computers in every room to contact any other police department in the country, and evidence lockers designed so the fewer people touched the clues the better.

There were only four "holding cells," as prisoners were rarely kept overnight but shipped off to nearby Long Beach, several miles north. A spacious workout room had all the commercial health club amenities, and was frequently in use, before or after a shift. There were two detective rooms, but no detectives on staff. Two dozen uniformed officers worked there full time, including three sergeants, one for each shift.

The only thing not included in the recently built department was a shooting range. The cops drove up to Long Beach for target practice, but the trip was time-consuming, and few of them were expert marksmen.

Officer Flower had a slim stash of reports in her hand, which she laid on Bravo's desk. "Not much here. It was a quiet weekend."

"It's always a quiet weekend." Sierra thumbed through the reports. Drunk driving, speeding, fender-benders—none of which seemed a major disaster in the making.

Then she found the name of Dylan Zack—a seventeen-year-old high school senior stopped for reckless driving just before one o'clock on a Sunday morning—and the traffic officer found a too-large stash of weed tucked under the front seat. Trouble.

Not that young Zack was a serial killer, enraged maniac, or drug kingpin. He was the son of Kenneth Zack, Sundown Beach's wealthiest citizen—a hedge fund manager who truly believed he and his family were better, richer, more important, and far more entitled than anyone else. Ken Zack was best pals with City Councilwoman Danielle Micaela Tokes.

Tokes was successful in her own right, a prestigious realtor and a board member of several Southern California corporations. Unfortunately, in many cases, women who fought hardest for their positions of power often would bend over backwards to keep other females from climbing closer to the top, which might have been why, from the beginning, Tokes viewed Sierra Bravo as her archenemy.

Sierra checked her wristwatch, despite the large hanging clock on the wall right in front of her, with its old-fashioned schoolroom tick that sounded sixty times each minute. She knew she could make a fuss and have it removed, but she had more important things to do at her job.

She sighed. Seven minutes past nine. She soon would get an angry call from Tokes any time now, complaining that the son of her BFF, Kenneth Zack, was being harried and persecuted because he was rich.

Being hassled for wealth was one thing, Sierra thought. Whining about a traffic bust and for carrying marijuana because one is an arrogant little snot-nose far more privileged to everything than the rest of the world is quite another.

F. Scott Fitzgerald wrote, "The rich are different from you and me." Sierra Bravo, who'd been born and raised one tiny step above poverty, had read *The Great Gatsby* five times, and believed that quote, even though with each reading—several years apart—she changed her mind about Jay Gatsby or those around him. Love them, hate them, pity them, view them with contempt—that was the terrific thing about *The Great Gatsby*; the masterpiece changed the view of those who spend their entire lives thinking about fictional characters on New York's Long Island Sound.

Now Sierra *needed* a cup of coffee.

She had her own mug with *Chief* emblazoned on it, along with a circle of silver stars, a welcoming gift from the police officers who worked for her, even though most had not met her. At first, she was not beloved. She was still new to Sundown Beach and had irritated some local cops who felt they deserved the chief's status she'd hijacked from them. But the mug was on her desk the morning she arrived, wrapped with a large red ribbon, a sign of respect she appreciated.

She filled the mug with black coffee. For twenty-five years, ever since her teens, she'd never put sugar or cream in her coffee. It ruined the taste and texture—like sucking on a hot, wet marshmallow that never got elegantly browned at a campfire.

Sergeant Griffin Parrish appeared at Sierra's elbow. In his early fifties and sitting out eight months until he could retire, Griff was the only black police officer on the force, in a seaside town in which only four percent of its full-time citizens were people of color. He was easy-going—the local children loved him. First suspicious of a woman hired to run the department, he'd grown to believe Sierra Bravo deserved the gold badge.

"Chief," he said, "there's a guy out front demanding to see you."

"Demanding? I hate the sound of that word. Demanding, eh? He should be thrilled to talk to you, Griffin. You're a sergeant."

"He wouldn't tell me his problem. He insists he has to talk to the chief of police."

"Is he pissed off?"

"No," Parrish said, "more like—very disturbed."

"Can I drink my coffee first?"

He looked over his shoulder toward the front desk he manned every day and shook his head. "He seems anxious."

"Monday, Monday," Sierra murmured, sipping her coffee and then quickly sucking in a cooling breath. "Damn, that's *hot!*" She headed back to her office. "Count to ninety, and then bring him in."

She watched Griff move down the hallway. She'd miss him when he retired. Wise, resourceful, a thoughtful cop—and paternal about his chief. He was a childless widower, and his protection of Sierra was good for both of them. Sierra, with no family to speak of, no friends, and no lover, was relieved knowing good cops like Parrish had her back.

Back in her office, she blew on her coffee to cool it, and just had time to adjust her star-spangled shirt collar as Griff ushered Walter Lyons in. She'd never heard of Walter Lyons before. He was in his late forties, five foot eight, dumpy, and tired-looking. Sierra figured he hadn't exercised since he was in high school and forced to go to gym class every day. His suit—no particular shade or color—was inexpensive and his tie extremely dull.

"Thank you for seeing me, Chief," he said.

"Have a seat, Mr. Lyons. What can I do for you that Sergeant Parrish can't?"

"It's kind of a weird story. I really don't know where else to turn."

"Do you have a problem?"

Lyons was suffering from dry mouth, desperately licking his lips so he could speak more easily, and he looked at her coffee cup with longing.

"Can we have the sergeant bring you some coffee, too, Mr. Lyons?"

"I'm too concerned to worry about coffee," he said, "even though this has nothing to do with me."

"Nothing to do with you? Then why are you here?"

"It's—well, let me start from the beginning."

Sierra nodded, knowing that when anyone started from the beginning, the story would be longer than an eleven-hundred-page Stephen King novel—and few people spoke as clearly as Stephen King writes.

"Yesterday," Lyons said, "Sunday afternoon—I went to the movies—the big theater right here in Sundown Beach."

Sierra shook off the beginnings of a shudder. If it had been another horrifying mass shooting in a movie theater less than a mile from where she sat, she would have heard about it immediately. But most of the time, the Sundown multiplex was family-friendly, and almost as safe as a church. She queried, "Were you alone?"

He nodded. "My wife isn't into super action movies, like I am—they're loud, violent, and just one punch can send someone crashing through a brick wall and come bouncing back without a mark on them."

Oh please, Sierra thought, *don't recount the whole plot of the movie.*

Lyons continued, "Those films are my fantasy world—I'm no superhero. It was two and a half hours long. When it was over, I figured it was time to make a pit stop."

"Are you telling me some gay guy hit on you in the men's room?"

"Oh, no—nothing like that. As I said, this isn't about me." He cleared his throat as she sat back in her chair. "This is a multiplex theater. Lots of different movies play there. Kid movies, action movies, romances—you know."

Sierra impatiently tapped her fingers on the desk. "I'm not much of a movie-goer," she said. "I don't have the time."

"This isn't about movies." Walter Lyons grew more nervous by the moment, and she realized it was her fault. Many civilians felt awkward and uncomfortable speaking to a police officer. Maybe it was the cop garb and the badge.

And the gun.

"It's a roomy men's john," Lyons went on, "about eight urinals, six sinks, maybe four stalls—because there were quite a few guys in there. After I took—after I finished my—business at the urinal, I went to one of the sinks to wash my hands."

Lyons waited a beat for Bravo to urge him to continue. Was he expecting praise for washing his hands after a pee? The moment turned awkward. At length she said, "And?"

"Well, in the mirror, I see a guy walk into the men's room." He took a deep breath. "With a little girl, about eleven years old."

That got Sierra sitting up straight in her chair. "What?"

"Yes, ma'am. They marched right in."

"An eleven-year-old girl in a men's restroom?"

Lyons nodded. "They walked the whole length of the bathroom, down to the farthest stall. The man went in, but he didn't close the door—and the child stood right outside."

Mental pictures assaulted Sierra from all sides, leaving a copper taste in her mouth. She hated to ask, "What was he doing in there that she was watching him?"

"I don't know, Chief. She was looking around—but I didn't want to stare at her." Lyons's cheeks flamed pink. "Our eyes met for a second or two, though."

"Did she look strange in some way? Scared?"

"I don't think so. She just looked—I don't know—sad, maybe."

"Or resigned?"

Lyons nodded slowly. "Good guess."

Sierra said. "Was it father and daughter? Did the two look anything alike?"

He crinkled up his nose. "Not really."

"Okay, so what did you do about it?"

Lyons looked blank. "What was I supposed to do? I couldn't approach him in the men's room."

True, Sierra thought. Women chat with other women in public restrooms all the time, but men are very cautious about talking to strangers in a similar situation.

"I sure wouldn't approach the little girl," Lyons added quickly. "That'd make me seem perverted."

"Did you notify the police?"

Lyons took in a quick breath and held it for a moment, wishing he'd not visited the Chief's office in the first place. Eventually he said, "No. I was too upset."

"Did you follow them out to the parking lot to see what car they got into, and maybe read and remember the license plate?"

"N-no. I was too flustered to do—anything. I just went home."

"I see."

"I told my wife about it last night, and she said I should come here and tell you."

Sierra Bravo ground her teeth together in irritation, and the bones at each side of her jaw jumped. She pulled a legal pad toward her. "What did the man look like?"

"Around my age. Five foot nine, maybe, and sort of thick. He was bulky—maybe muscular—like he worked at some sort of job like construction, or warehousing." Lyons ran his hand over his own head. "Oh yeah, he had a crewcut."

"A military cut?"

"I can't tell. Lots of people who aren't in military service have short cuts, too."

"What was he wearing?"

Lyons frowned, thinking. "A kind of dress shirt, open collar—blue with stripes of some sort—I think he had a white T-shirt under it. And he wore a sweater—-an Argyle sweater."

Sierra thought only Ivy Leaguers wore Argyle sweaters any-more, especially with a striped shirt. She said, "You're doing fine. Pants?"

Walter Lyons closed his eyes for a quarter of a minute, then shook his head. "I don't look at men's pants. But I don't think it was jeans—or dress pants, either."

"Khaki slacks? Like Dockers?"

"I couldn't tell what brand they were."

"Of course not. Color of the pants?"

"I can't remember. Light-colored, probably."

Sierra thought that narrowed it down to half the males in Southern California. "What about the child? What did she look like?"

Lyons ran two fingers inside his collar, grateful he wore a jacket because the underarms of his shirt were soaked. "I tried not to look at her—to embarrass her or anything."

"Any description?'"

"Well—she was white. Caucasian."

Sierra tried to suck back her annoyance, but it found its way into her impatient tone. "Is there anything else?"

"Brown hair, cut kind of short. Not fat, but not skinny, either. I don't think she was an adolescent yet."

"What was she wearing?"

He ran a trembling hand through his thinning hair. In another five years, his head would be bare. "Not a skirt or dress—she was wearing long pants and a long-sleeved T-shirt—gray or dark green or something. She was carrying a jacket, but I couldn't tell you what it looked like." He floundered. "Just—an ordinary-looking kid."

Sierra thought hard before her next question. "Might the child have been mentally challenged? Or physically challenged, for that matter?"

"I don't think so. Like I said, I tried not to look at her."

"All right, then. About eleven years old?"

"Ten or eleven, yeah."

"No younger?"

"No, she was a few inches under five feet tall."

"I know grown women whore aren't even five feet tall. Did she have any particular ethnic look? Italian? Irish? Jewish? Arabic?"

Walter Lyons shook his head. "California. That's about it."

Bravo reached for her coffee cup. "There was no crime committed."

"No crime?"

"Taking a pre-adolescent child into an opposite gender restroom is odd," Sierra said, "especially if the child didn't need to use it, since the women's restroom is about six steps away. But I'm not sure it's a crime."

"But in women's rooms," Lyon said, "they always go into the stalls and close the door before—exposing themselves." He blushed and ducked his head. "I guess you know that. In a men's room, you're standing at the urinal with your dick in your hand..." His eyes bulged, and he put two fingers over his mouth. "Penis, I mean." His cheeks turned rosy red. "I'm sorry—I didn't mean to gross you out."

"I've heard the word before. I'm a cop, not a nun."

Lyons was relieved. "This whole thing was weird."

"If weird was a criminal offense, the whole world would be a ghost town."

Silence for a moment as Lyons fidgeted with the knot on his tie and tried patting away the sweat on his forehead with his hand. Then he said, "I'm sorry I bothered you. I didn't know who else to talk to."

"It was no bother," she said, standing. "Next time you're concerned, call someone right away, get a license plate number—or something. As it is, I have nothing to go on."

"My fault," Walter Lyons said. "It's just—we have a nine-year-old daughter at home, and—things like this upset me."

Sierra took a moment to process that. "Do you have problems with your daughter?"

That got Lyons breathing more heavily. "No, no! Nothing like that! Really! She's a good girl, does good in school…"

"That's good to hear."

"She's—pretty much organized. I mean, she's happy. She's not—loving right now, but kids that age can't stand being kissed or hugged. When she was littler, about three to six years old, she was a real hugger."

"Sounds like you have a nice family."

"We try."

Sierra fiddled with her ballpoint pen. She hadn't written much down. At length, she said, "Thank you for coming in, anyway, Mr. Lyons—and if anything else upsets you, feel free to contact the department. You take care, now."

She sat quietly after Lyons left, shoulders slumping, as if he carried an impossibly heavy load around his neck. Was he telling the truth? If so, there wasn't much the police could do about it—a waste of time and money investigating a crime that wasn't a crime. It might *be* a felony or a misdemeanor, to take a child into the public restroom of the opposite sex. Sierra hadn't faced this problem before. But Walter Lyons was only a witness—and whatever else went on in that men's room on a crowded Sunday, there was no sexual abuse of a child.

Not there, anyway.

Nevertheless, it chewed at her liver. The mistreatment of a little girl, even a passive one, was digging at her insides, trying to get out.

She swallowed the rest of her cooling coffee and headed out for some more.

"Nancy," she said to Flower, "I need a favor."

"More coffee?"

"No. Walter Lyons, who was just in here, says he lives in Sundown Beach. See if you can find out where he works."

"Maybe he's a drug kingpin?" Nancy Flower said, smiling. "Runs an entire network of crack cocaine distributors right here?"

"Drug kingpins dress better than he does. All of them have bodyguards, and sleazy hookers follow them everywhere." She refilled her coffee mug, looking for Parrish, who was always where he was supposed to be—at the front desk.

Near the front door, she said, "Griff, you've been in this department longer than God. Do you recall any children who've gone missing in the last ten years?"

"Just about everything happened here, except a race riot or a terrorist attack. Yeah, I think a few kids have gone missing."

"Look it up for me, would you?"

"Sure, no problem. How fast do you want it?"

"The day before yesterday," Sierra Bravo said.

The only difference between public schools in Sundown Beach and many in the rest of the country was that children dressed better. Within the city limits, resident poverty was unknown, and the mean income of local families was close to two hundred thousand bucks, so for the most part, they dressed their kids in Los Angeles elegance. That's what Sierra thought as she strode toward the office of a recently built middle school. In other places, a uniformed cop would strike fear in the hearts of kids who figured it was their turn to get hauled down to the po-po store—but in sleepy Sundown Beach, pupils regarded cops with mild annoyance or tolerant amusement. The financially comfortable parents had enough money and prestige to protect their progeny from all but the worst trouble they might get into.

The women at desks in the outer school office—salaries on

the low side—didn't look as well-turned out as the students. They wore straight skirts, plain white blouses, and cardigan sweaters of different *blah* shades that had seen better days.

The one nearest the door looked up. "Can I help you with something, Officer?"

Officer. Sierra wondered if the clerk had noticed the silver stars on her collar, or if she thought all cops wore them. She tried not to glower. "I'm Chief of Police Bravo. I'd like to talk to the principal."

"*You're* the chief of—" The clerk blushed in surprise. "Oh—I didn't know. The principal is out of town for three days. Can the vice principal be of assistance?"

"I'll never know unless I talk with her."

"It's a him. He's rather busy this morning."

"So am I," Bravo said, and subtly pointed to her gold badge.

Feeling insulted and put-upon, the woman arose, sniffed angrily, and disappeared behind an inner office door. The other two clerks continued their work, pretending Sierra was invisible.

While she waited, she read the notes and announcements stuck on a large cork board mounted opposite the desk. Most were for teachers and office staff, having little to do with the children. One teacher was approaching her sixtieth birthday, and the plea for funds for a big cake and flowers had been copied onto bright scarlet paper.

Finally, the clerk emerged, disliking the Chief of Police for no particular reason, and indicated Sierra should enter the inner office.

The man behind the desk stood as she entered. "Good morning, Chief. I'm Chet Quigley—assistant principal." He gestured at a chair on Sierra's side of the desk. "Make yourself comfortable."

As she sat down, Chester Quigley suddenly found himself *uncomfortable.* Sierra Bravo was a very attractive woman, despite her authoritarian uniform. Tall, willowy, with bright blue eyes that were twin exclamation points, and a pert nose that crinkled when she smiled. Quigley subtly glanced at her left hand for a wedding ring that wasn't there. In his position, he rarely met pretty single women. None ever walked into his office before.

But stunning as she was, this top cCop scared the hell out of him.

"I hope there's no trouble," he said at last. "We have a good group of kids here."

"No trouble, Mr. Quigley. How long have you worked here?"

"Fourteen years—eight as an English and art teacher, six as vice principal. And I still teach art sometimes, too."

She nodded. "According to police records, about seven years ago, a little girl who went to this school vanished without a trace."

His smile dimmed considerably. "I couldn't forget that. Caitlin Killian. She was in my art class." He furrowed his brow. "Were you the chief of police at that time?"

"No, I came to Sundown Beach recently." She shifted on the unforgiving chair, not remembering any school she'd ever been in that had a chair one might consider snug. It had probably been designed for third graders. "How old was Caitlin?"

"Ten," he said. "She left school at the usual time and started for home. She usually walked by herself—she didn't have many friends."

"Why was that?"

"She was a nice child, but—different than most of the others. Creative, imaginative, and most other girls that age didn't really—understand her." Chet Quigley shrugged sadly. "Young girls can be bullies. Caitlin was friendly, generous, and giving."

"Was her disappearance because of bullying?" Sierra said, all at once alert.

"I don't think so. The girls here aren't that bad. We discuss bullying in class all the time, to make sure. No, Caitlin left school and headed home. That's the last anyone saw of her." Quigley seemed sad. "That's the worst thing that ever happened here."

"The Sundown Beach police worked on it?"

"Yes—police from San Diego, too—and lots of volunteers showed up and combed the wooded areas nearby for her. But she was gone."

"Are her parents still in the area?"

"No. It's common. When married couples lose a child to death, or an unexplained disappearance, after a while, the marriage breaks up. That's what happened with Caitlin Killian's parents. Two years after she was gone, they got divorced and moved away. The last I heard, Caitlin's mother is in Arkansas. I don't remember where the father went. He was actually the stepfather, as he married the mother when Caitlin was about five years old. He's probably somewhere outside California now."

Stepfather, Sierra Bravo thought, and she felt the hair on her arm stand up straight beneath her uniform. "Are there any other children in this school having problems at home? Being—abused or anything?"

Quigley's shoulders lifted and fell. "I can't be sure. We keep an eagle eye out for bruises, depression, or even fear. You know, changes in their behavior. But I didn't notice anything, and no one reported it to me."

"How about any kids who are overprotected? Kids that can't go anywhere out of their parents' gaze for even a minute."

He smiled. "Helicopter moms. They hover. They drive their kids to school every day, pick them up at night, take them to their sports activities or dancing or music lessons, work as class volunteers so they can keep their eye on them. A helicopter mom is a full-time job—no meal breaks, no sick days, and no two-week vacations every year."

"When I was a kid, there were no helicopter moms."

"You're right. We'd get to and from school by ourselves, and we'd stay outside and play until it was time to go home and wash up for dinner."

"What about," Sierra said, "helicopter *fathers?*"

"Not all that usual—but there are some, sure."

"Are you a helicopter father, Mr. Quigley?"

He shook his head. "There's only one requirement for that kind of job—you must have a kid over which to hover."

"You have no children of your own?"

"Nope. No wife, either. Being a father is scary, even for me. It's easier to watch over four hundred of them than to take care of one."

"Are any of the Sundown Beach kids home-schooled?"

"There are a few in town. I don't know their names, but the parents report to the school supervisor's office."

"What if they don't?" Sierra asked. "What if they keep their kids home all the time to educate them and don't tell anyone about it?"

"That's illegal." Chet Quigley cocked his head to one side. "Why these questions?"

"I can't discuss it. I will say that as far as we know, no crime has been committed."

"Then why are you investigating? Is that what you're doing right now?"

"Just being prepared," Sierra said.

"Like the Boy Scouts?"

"I was never a Boy Scout—or a Girl Scout, either. Those mint cookies are horrible." She stood. "I appreciate your taking the time to talk to me, Mr. Quigley."

"You're always welcome here," he said, standing up, too. Then his smile was close to a leer, and he added, "You can investigate *me* anytime."

"Cute," she said, and her glance withered him.

"Sorry, just trying to get a smile out of you. Whatever it is you're investigating, I hope it works out well for you."

When she was behind the wheel of her car, she took out a notebook and scribbled *Chester Quigley.* She didn't know why—but often cops have hunches, like eating a potato and realizing much later there was a tiny piece they hadn't digested along with the others.

***

Sierra Bravo and Griff Parrish lunched at a Lebanese restaurant in the Seaview shopping district as they did at least twice a week, since almost everything on the menu was more or less healthy, some of it even vegan. The waitstaff—none from Lebanon, but local young people—knew Sierra and Griff by their first names.

Parrish studied other diners as he wolfed down a baba ganoush wrap. "I'm lucky. I work in a city where so many good-looking women have time for a leisurely lunch in here."

"That's because their husbands make lots of money," Sierra said. "But this Walter Lyons from this morning? I don't think he's one of our town's movers and shakers."

Parrish nodded. "I never heard of him."

"I'll want to talk to him some more."

"Why?"

Sierra hitched up her right shoulder. "He reported sighting a little girl in a public men's room with an adult male. Lyons has a little girl of his own at home."

"Oh, hell, Chief. Is this another one of those rabid complaints about transgenders using the restroom they feel better in rather than following what their birth certificate says? Laws against that have stirred up everyone in this country one way or another." He thought about it. "Parents are scared trannies will sexually attack kids in restrooms. As far as I know, that's never happened anywhere."

"This wasn't a little boy who dresses like a little girl, at least from what Lyons said."

Griffin nodded. "And no child would march into a public men's room in drag and try to rape a grown man on a crowded afternoon. But it's pretty weird for a guy to have a little girl follow him into the john."

"It might be nothing," Sierra said, and then added, "It probably is."

"Then why bother, Chief?"

"I just—need to take a closer look."

"Need? You're not even investigating a criminal case."

"I'm not sure what I'm investigating—just poking around a little."

"Why make it your business?" Parrish asked.

"Maybe there was something wrong with the girl mentally. Maybe they were father and daughter, which also legalizes it, though I find that extremely peculiar. But according to Lyons, she didn't look anything like him."

Parrish became defensive. "I don't look like my father, either."

"You're right," Sierra said, eyes twinkling. "I've met your father. He's handsome and sexy—and you don't look a damn bit like him. Ah, I don't know, Griff, but it bothers the crap out of me. Why did the girl stand at the open stall door while he did whatever he was doing in there?"

"There could be a logical explanation."

"There are a lot of things that have no logical explanation—religion, for one, and a hell of a lot of people believe in it. On faith."

"Yeah," Parrish argued, "but you haven't even seen this little girl."

"And nobody's ever seen Jesus, but a gazillion faithful swear he's there."

"I'd worry more about Councilperson Tokes," Parrish reminded her. "The son of her best buddy in town, Ken Zack, got busted last night for speeding, and he had a stash of weed under the seat."

"Tokes hates my guts. What else is new?"

"She'll be all over your face about wiping that arrest off the books."

"I can deal with her," Sierra said.

"She wants your head on a pike. If you're looking for a crime you don't even know happened, it leaves you vulnerable." Parrish shook his head. "You're making a big deal out of nothing, Chief."

"If it's not nothing to me, then it's something." Sierra took a swig of iced tea. "Ever been to that movie theater? There must be at least ten employees there at the same time—taking tickets, popping fake-butter popcorn, selling Diet Pepsi and outrageously expensive candy. If it were your kid, wouldn't you ask some female employee to keep an eye on her for about two minutes while you had to pee?"

"Sure. And the ladies' room is a few steps away. You could ask a woman going in there if she'd watch the kid. Lots of middle-aged women go to movies, more than younger kids who'd just as soon play video games as watch a flick."

"How many women go to the movies by themselves, especially in Sundown Beach? They either have husbands with them, or some other woman friend."

"Chief," Parrish said kindly, "you deal with speeders, drunkards and pickpockets—and rarely a mom-and-pop-store stick-up. You have to make nice with the mayor and kiss the butts of the city cCouncil. Why waste time about something that could be nothing?"

"*Could* is the operative word."

"Shoulda-woulda-coulda," Griffin said. "Then I'm with you, no matter what."

She bumped her fist against his. "It's good to have good cops working with me. It makes me feel more secure."

Sundown Beach was a suburban city, and most of its college grad residents worked in L.A. and drank cocktails, ate in top restaurants, bought designer clothes, and drove late-model cars that were never *seen* in Sierra Bravo's old stomping grounds in another state where she'd been born and raised.

Sundown Beach was a good place to live, if one could afford it. There were very few serious police problems, few violent criminal acts, and hardly anyone threw trash in the street or let their dogs run free to bite a neighbor. The Chief looked around, caught the eye of their waitress, and mimed signing the check.

Sierra said, "I'll drop you off at the station, Griff. I have another stop to make."

"Where're you going, Chief?"

"To the movies," Sierra said.

CHAPTER TWO

The multiplex movie house is south of Sundown Beach, set so far back from the east-west highway that if you didn't know it was there, you'd never get to see a film at all.

There were only eight cars in the parking lot. No big movie crowd jammed into the spacious lobby on an early Monday afternoon, but the popcorn maker still crackled away, as Sierra Bravo spoke to the vacant-looking girl behind the ticket counter—a recent high school graduate, too young to vote, and not nearly old enough to publicly drink a beer.

"I'm Police Chief Bravo," she said, pointing to her badge. "Is the manager in?"

Sierra's appearance jolted the girl from her boredom. "Yes, ma'am," she said. She picked up the phone and punched out two numbers. "The chief of police is here to see you, Josh." Pause. Then, annoyed, "I don't *know* what it's about." She listened a few moments more, then hung up. "Please come inside," she said. "He'll be out in a minute."

"Thanks." Sierra walked into the large lobby and stood near the popcorn machine. She loved popcorn, but stopped eating it at theaters years before because they cooked it in fake butter. It also got stuck in her teeth. A twentyish man from the office approached her, wearing the same management-produced type of shirt worn by the ticket-seller, and a pinned-on name tag that said JOSH—MANAGER. He was the old-timer of the group—

probably all of twenty-four and still battling a troubled teenage complexion.

"What can I do for you, Officer?"

Officer again. Sierra wondered if people saw Colin Powell in his four-star general uniform would simply say, *"Hi, soldier?"* She leaned against the counter. "Were you on duty around four o'clock yesterday afternoon?"

Josh nodded. "I'm the day manager."

"Did you notice a man, maybe forty-five, stocky, with a graying crew cut, and had with him a little girl about ten years old?"

Josh grinned. "There were at least twenty father-daughter combos like that in here yesterday—to see the new Pixar feature. I paid no attention unless there was a problem."

"I'm not sure there was a problem," Sierra continued, "except this man took her into the relatively crowded men's room when the movie was over with."

"Eew!"

It amused Sierra that if a mother took an eleven-year-old son into the ladies' room, few of the women would make much of a fuss, probably because they did what they came to do behind closed stall doors where no one could see them. But the men, standing openly at urinals, would all freak out if a female of *any* age, even a toddler, interrupted what they were doing. Obviously, Josh was no exception.

"Did anyone ever asked an employee to keep an eye on a child while they went to the john?"

His deep inhale expanded his skinny chest. "I'm not the toilet monitor, Officer I don't follow who goes to the bathroom. If it happened to one of the employees," he said with more than a touch of self-importance, "they wouldn't tell me. It's not that big a deal."

It probably wouldn't have been a big deal back when Sierra was a kid. Growing up in Mansfield, a small-to-medium-sized city between Cleveland and Columbus, she managed to play outside, unsupervised, every day, and walked almost everywhere. She'd often hang around downtown with some of her girlfriends, mostly in the independent drugstore where they could stand at the rack and read comic books and teen magazines, and their parents really didn't worry about where they were, who they were with, or what they did until it was time for them to come home and wash up for supper. There were child molesters back then, too, but rarely did anyone give it a thought unless they lived in a big dangerous city.

That was then. This is now.

"That's *Chief,* Josh," she said. "Not *Officer.* Do you still have the surveillance DVD's from yesterday?" Bravo asked, "both in the lobby and out in the parking lot?"

Josh shifted nervously from one foot to another. His relatively low-paying job gave him a flashy title, and pathetic power over minimum-wage employees barely younger than he—but faced with a high-level cop wearing the glittering displays of rank, he was petrified that he might lose his job altogether. "We don't have cameras here."

That gave Chief Bravo pause. There were cameras *everywhere.* Video cameras watch you on most business-oriented streets, in shops and public places like movie theaters and big-box stores like Walmart and Target, and even in gas stations and convenience stores—everywhere except public restrooms. Pick your nose, scratch your ass, spit on the sidewalk, or try a hold-up with or without a gun, and *somebody* knows about it, but take a tinkle and you're all but invisible.

This theater was owned by a national chain of movie houses. Sierra removed her notebook from her hip pocket. "Who's the regional manager around here?"

Young Josh really looked frightened. "He's in Berkeley," he stammered. "That's our west coast headquarters."

"Does he have a name in Berkeley?"

"Stanley Meyer. He doesn't get down here all that often, though."

"Maybe not," Sierra said, writing down the name, "but I'd like to chat with him about the need for security cameras in a big movie chain. As for you, young man—keep your eyes open when kids are running around, and if anything like this happens again, make sure you find out who they are—or get a license plate number you can report to the police. Are we clear?"

In the parking lot, Sierra Bravo took a better look around. It was almost empty at the moment, but yesterday afternoon, a Sunday, families and children and couples had made it fairly crowded. Rarely would any employee watch to see what car someone who might or might not have done a bad thing drives off.

When she got back to police headquarters, Nancy Flower was waiting for her.

"You've been busy," Flower said, a fistful of message slips clutched in one hand.

"One of those hours I was eating lunch. Are those complaints that nobody else in the department can handle?"

"Hmm, let's see." Flower recited the names on each of the slips. "Danielle Tokes. Ken Zack. Danielle Tokes. A library clerk— someone was smuggling rental DVDs out of the library. Danielle Tokes. Danielle Tokes. Danielle—"

"All that shit in two hours? Tokes must've put my number on her fast call list."

Flower suggested, "Return it. When I tell her you're not here, she gets nastier."

Sierra raised one eyebrow. "Get nasty back at her."

"Great idea, Chief. I have time open to do that—at three o'clock in the afternoon next *never!*"

Chief Bravo took the phone memos from her. "If I'm on the call with her for more than three minutes, set off the fire alarm so she hears the siren." In her office, her hand hovered above the phone until she picked it up resentfully and dialed.

"I've been calling you all morning!" Danielle Tokes snarled. "What were you doing that you were too busy to answer?"

"I figured," the Chief said, "that if your house were on fire, or a terrorist gang was invading your home, you'd have reported it to any police officer who answered the phone. As for me—I had business elsewhere."

"Business?" Tokes made the word obscene. "Need I remind you I'm your boss?"

"You're not my boss, Ms. Tokes. Unless you're a police officer with a higher rank and authority than mine, or the state Attorney General, you're sure as hell not my boss! Okay, here I am. Talk to me, because I have other things to do."

Tokes took a while harrumphing and clearing her throat. Finally, she said, "Dylan Zack was harassed by the police last night."

"He was stopped for speeding, he was stoned, and an illegal amount of ganja was found in his car. I wouldn't call that harassment."

"What's ganja?"

Sierra Bravo closed her eyes, leaning her chin on one hand propped up by an elbow. "Weed," she recited as though reading the United States Constitution to a three-year-old. "Grass, reefer, marijuana, Mary Jane, dope, hashish, cannabis—and let's not forget shit." She looked up toward the ceiling for sustenance. "I know you've never heard any of those words before."

"I've heard some of them."

"You must live an interesting life, Ms. Tokes."

"I'm trying to say to you that Dylan's just a kid."

"A kid, whacked out and driving a sixty-thousand-dollar car that can kill a human being as easily as an adult could."

Phone silence crackled like a campfire, Danielle Tokes's angry breathing a counterpoint. Then she said, as though she had a tooth cavity but no novocain, "Ken Zack is my friend—a really important person. I won't bore you with the good things he's done for Sundown Beach—donations, city council advisements—"

"Then don't. My job is to enforce laws on the books—laws people like you and Mr. Zack caused to be written in the first place. Fixing a kid's parking ticket is one thing, but reckless driving under the influence is something else altogether."

"You could've let him go with a warning," Tokes persisted.

"I didn't make the arrest. When an officer stops a reckless driver, the decision is his and his alone to decide what to do about it. Once the citation is written, it's on the books forever. And since there were illegal drugs in the car, we kept him here for several hours until his father drove down and paid a fifty-dollar fine to take him home."

"And what if his father hadn't paid the fifty dollars?"

"Then," Sierra said, "the kid goes to Long Beach and stays in a cell until someone comes to bail him out."

"That's not fair!"

"It's only fair for poor people and minorities? But if the son of a wealthy, powerful citizen is involved, all of a sudden it's not fair anymore. Have I got that right?"

"That's goddamn insulting!"

"I'm sorry. What was so insulting?"

More heavy Tokes breathing. Then: "Which cop wrote that ticket in the first place?"

"I'll tell you if you want, but he won't tear that citation up. I'll forbid him to."

Danielle's voice rose in frustration. "You'll send Dylan Zack to prison for a minor offense?"

"Don't be ridiculous! He's not going to prison. There's a big difference between a local jail and a prison—and I doubt very much if Dylan will do time in either one. A fine? Probably—and I'm sure Daddy pays it for him. Hours of community service work? It won't kill Dylan. And I'm sure Mr. Zack has a dozen attorneys at his fingertips who can take care of this in court."

Shocked—*shocked.* "Are you suggesting Ken Zack bribe a judge?"

"I didn't suggest anything." The falafel pocket Sierra had for lunch was kicking off heartburn, and she fought to avoid groaning. "I don't give a damn what happens in court. That's not my job—and you wanting me to run my department your way pisses me off."

"Let's see how pissed off you are when your contract comes up for renewal!" Tokes blustered.

"I won't be in this job until I'm ninety years old, anyway. Good day, Ms. Tokes."

Hanging up in the middle of a Tokes reply, emotions pulled Sierra several ways. She didn't like civilians deciding what police should and should not do, especially when it comes to the very rich and their money-empowered children. Besides, the entire business Walter Lyons dumped on her desk that morning had made her head throb.

She also realized that in all the conversations she'd had with Danielle Tokes, the woman had never used her first or last name, nor even her title. Possibly subconsciously, but Sierra doubted it. For her, it was crossing the red line when someone dislikes someone else so much that they refuse to say their name.

Inhaling deeply and releasing the air slowly, she tapped her fingernails on the top of her desk, too late realizing she really needed a manicure.

The main Anaheim Police Department is right in the middle of downtown, in a high-rise building that is also home, on the higher floors, to Criminal Court. Sierra Bravo, standing on the sidewalk and looking up, wasn't impressed with tall buildings—she'd been in other cities many times—but compared to the pocket-sized police department in Sundown Beach, Anaheim was a different experience. Even in uniform with the silver stars and the gold-decorated police cap—Why do uniforms mix gold and silver, anyway?—she felt like a small-timer seeing a busy city in full throttle for the first time.

She identified herself and stated her business to one of the guards downstairs, so she didn't have to pass through the archway that would register any metal on her body. Her ID was enough. Otherwise, considering all she wore strapped at her waist—her weapon, handcuffs, two-way radio, plus the throwaway gun she holstered around her right ankle and a sharpened nail file in her left shoe, she would have had to practically undress.

The elevator took her up to the floor where the Vice Squad was installed.

"Not many police officers visit here unless they're part of my crew," Lieutenant Lil Kendall said. Her office was small, and crowded—and even though she was only five feet seven inches tall, she seemed too large for the space. "To tell you the truth, Chief Bravo, it grosses them out. There are sex crimes committed in this town you haven't even dreamed of." She waved to the stacks of folders on her desk and atop the file cabinets. "You wouldn't want to look at those photos. They're worse than anything you'd see in a slice-and-dice horror movie. Trust me."

"I thought you busted hookers and johns."

"I wish that was all." In her late forties, with broad shoulders and buzz-cut ginger hair, Lil Kendall was the head of Anaheim Vice. Her reputation was spotless, and she was well known for the strong stomach and indomitable emotions that had kept her in her job for the past seven years. Most officers lasted eighteen months in Vice before begging to be transferred to another squad. They all had nightmares every night.

"I have about twenty minutes to spare before I have to go upstairs for a meeting," Kendall said. "What's going on in your wealthy suburb you need to tell me about?"

"This is weird, Lieutenant, because I can't do anything about it. A complete stranger dumped it on my doorstep this morning, and I wanted to run it by you."

The lieutenant sat behind her desk, pushing some files to one side. "I'm listening."

Sierra sat opposite her and told the story pretty much the way Walter Lyons had. When she finished, Kendall was quiet for a bit. Then she said, "It's none of your business, Chief. You don't know if a crime was committed at all. You didn't see it happen. You have the slimmest of descriptions of the man and the child. Worse, your witness or whoever the hell he is could be making this up."

"I know all that. But it bothers me—a lot."

"Why is that?"

Bravo didn't answer at once. She discreetly checked her collar with her fingertips to ensure the silver stars were still there. At length she said, "It just does. Can you help me?"

Lieutenant Kendall studied her visitor. There was something personal that Sierra Bravo chose not to answer. Well, what the hell, she thought. She turned to her desk and punched a few keys on her computer, then frowned as she studied what she'd found. "It happens, Chief," she said, "but it's usually one-on-one. Someone kidnaps a child—females ten times more often than males. They're flown to some Third-World country to work sixteen hours a day in a factory or a rice paddy. Some are sold as sex slaves. Some are simply kidnapped. You remember the Ariel Castro situation in Cleveland? He abducted three young girls and kept them chained up in his house for more than a decade."

"How could I forget?"

Kendall nodded. "Sometimes in foreign countries and even here in the good old USA—and this is as disgusting as it gets—it's the girls' own parents who turn them out to sell themselves on the street or sell them to a sex trafficker. Most often, they're forced into prostitution, making money for an international organization. Billions of dollars change hands every year. The kids are shipped all over the world—to Uzbekistan, Libya, Romania, Cambodia, some ratty neighborhood in Rio de Janeiro—anywhere."

"Anywhere men pay good money to fuck children," Sierra said bitterly.

"The girl in the theater might be from some Third-World country where poverty is a way of life, and wound up turning tricks in Sundown Beach, even though she barely spoke English."

"Jesus."

"But it might all be innocent. The man might be her own father."

"Why did he take her into the men's room with him, then?"

"I can't think of a reason. But you have nothing to go on except a witness who didn't see a crime happen, either."

"So, what should I do, Lieutenant?"

The head of Anaheim Vice looked at her wristwatch, pushed herself away from her computer and rose. "Go home, Chief, have some wine, get laid, and forget what bothers the shit out of you."

"Forgetting isn't on my bucket list," Sierra said, "nor, sadly, is getting laid. May I contact you again if I need to?"

"Sure. After all, that's *my* business."

As she moved toward the door, Sierra suppressed a shudder while walking by those files with photographs that freaked her out, even if she hadn't looked at any of them.

Driving westward during late afternoon rush hour, frustrated drivers zoomed all around her. The setting sun was right in her eyes. She was further distracted by what the vice squad lieutenant had suggested—to ignore an incident she hadn't even seen. Major crime was never much of a factor in Sundown Beach.

Sierra's home was a spacious condo on the second floor of a complex four minutes from the sea. Pouring a white wine, she took a shower, donned skinny jeans and a tank top before cooking up some pasta and eating it out on the deck. There wasn't much view from the balcony, but the cool breeze helped blow away some of the day's problems.

Not all of them.

The theater incident tormented her gut. As a child, she was regularly abused and loathed her father ever since. She'd not corresponded with him for the past eighteen years. But in those days, that was a normal childhood for too damn many kids—and it hadn't changed much since.

But that nameless little girl was not physically punished at the movie theater, and if a visit to a men's bathroom was traumatic, Walter Lyons would have noticed confusion or even fear.

Resigned was the word Lyons had used to describe her expression. Was a public men's john an everyday occurrence for a little girl? If so, what else in her existence would make the child compliant and submissive?

Momentarily, Sierra felt \she should have taken a job in some bigger city rather than Sundown Beach, where horrific things happened as sure as the sun arose each day. But that would have made her hard, tough, unbending—and as insecure about herself as everyone else on the planet.

Rising from her deck chair as though she were two hundred pounds heavier, she went inside and thumbed through the sheaf of papers she'd brought home until she located the name and address of Walter Lyons, which she'd copied when Nancy Flower found it that morning.

She clutched her cellphone for too long before tapping in the Lyons home number, waiting through four rings until a child answered.

"Lyons Residence," the little girl parroted, "Olivia speaking."

"Hello, Olivia," Sierra said. "Is your daddy home?"

The little girl put the phone down to summon her father. *Olivia*—a favored given name for American female children in the twenty-first century.

Walter Lyons' voice sounded unfamiliar on the phone, but Sierra had only spoken to him once, ten hours earlier.

"Mr. Lyons, might I drop by your house for a few minutes this evening?"

A slight gasp found its way through the phone connection. "What for?"

"To talk further about the incident yesterday."

"In my home?"

Sierra Bravo brushed her hair back from her forehead. "At the moment, I can't put this case on the police blotter, Mr. Lyons— it's unofficial. It's better not to talk at headquarters. I won't take more than fifteen minutes of your time. Please."

He took twenty seconds to say, "Well..."

It was a short drive from her condo to Walter Lyons's home. West of downtown, many homes are quite elegant—but frame houses in this particular neighborhood look very much like they do in almost any older municipality—solidly lower-middle class, with the outdoor property self-tended rather than hiring an expensive landscaper to come in every week to mow the lawn, plant flowers and pluck weeds.

She parked in front of the house—no driveway but a garage peeked out from the backyard, accessible only from the alley, which meant either Olivia was driven to and from school every day, or taken to the bus. Perhaps she was home-schooled. Sierra wanted to know all these things—and wasn't sure why.

Grace Lyons opened the door, wearing thigh-length light blue shorts and a sleeveless white blouse, her hair pinned up close to her head, her eyes a watery brown. Her only makeup was nominal lipstick. She and Walter were plain-looking people who found each other and were trying to keep it together.

"You're chief of police?" she stammered, somewhat taken aback. "I thought you'd be in uniform."

"I'm off-duty right now. This is unofficial—so far. May I come in?"

Grace stepped aside and Sierra moved past her and into the living room, as there was no entryway or central hall in which to pause. Olivia, the little girl, was sprawled out on the floor in front of the TV, watching *Despicable Me 2.* She had big brown eyes, and light brown hair caught up in one thick pigtail. She was prettier than either of her parents.

She tore her eyes from the screen to study this new arrival. "Hello," she said.

"Hello, Olivia. I'm Sierra."

"Hi, Sierra. Wanna watch this movie with me?"

"Maybe later," Sierra said. "I came by to talk with your daddy for a little bit."

"You're missing a good movie, then." Olivia pointed an index finger at Sierra before turning back to her entertainment.

"Walter will be down shortly," Grace Lyons said. "Won't you sit down?"

Sierra tried not to frown. "Is there someplace else we could talk?" she asked, her sidelong glance at the child unmistakable.

"Oh!" Grace was flummoxed once more. "Uh—we have a little patio out back. We can sit out there." Helpless, she added, "There are mosquitoes, though—especially in the early evening."

Sierra followed Grace Lyons out into what there was of the backyard. Small to begin with, at least half the yard was paved to accommodate the Lyons parking their cars in the detached garage. The patio, as Grace had referred to it, was as big as a two-person prison cell, but four outdoor chairs crowded around a small wrought-iron table. Grace lit a citronella candle, then held a chair out so Bravo could sit.

"Ms. Lyons, I'm assuming Walter told you the same story he told me."

Grace shook her head eagerly. "Oh, yes. We were both upset about it."

"Anyone with a child would be upset. Does Olivia go to public school here?"

Grace's hand fluttered up to the top button of her blouse as though it had a mind of its own. "Uh—no. We send her to private school." She named a locally famous private school in Laguna Beach that charged an arm and a leg to educate their child each year. Walter Lyons worked for the county at a modest salary, as Sierra understood it, and from her appearance and demeanor, Grace was probably a relatively low-paid worker. How could they afford to send Olivia to a blue ribbon school? And if so, why wasn't she doing her Monday evening homework instead of watching an animated movie on a DVD in her living room?

Walter Lyons came out through the back door, waving Sierra back in her chair as she stood. "Relax, Chief," he said. "This is informal, right?" He chuckled, discomfited. "Unless you have a warrant."

"No chance of that, Mr. Lyons. I want to go over a few things with you, if that's okay? And Ms. Lyons, I'd appreciate it if you stayed, too."

Walter sat down. "I told you the whole story this morning." He wore a short-sleeved white shirt and a pair of purple shorts, exposing too much of his flabby white legs and thighs. In her lifetime, Sierra Bravo had seen few men who looked good wearing shorts. Walter didn't make the cut.

"I'll try not to take up too much of your time."

He nodded and sat down timorously, reaching to cover Grace's hand with his own.

"You said there were ten other men in that theater restroom when these two people walked in."

"Well, I didn't count heads. *Approximately* ten men. Should I have used that word?"

"If there were that many men, and they all saw the same thing you saw—how come none of the others did anything about it?"

"Did anything?"

"Confront the man with the little girl. Notify the theater manager. Report it to the police like you did."

"Oh," Walter said.

"Maybe they didn't notice," Grace Lyons offered.

"I doubt if men at urinals would miss a little girl wandering in."

"The urinals face a wall, so they might not have noticed. They probably didn't want to get involved," Walter said.

"*You* did, though."

"I was across the room, washing my hands and looking into a mirror. It would've been hard for me to miss."

"It was important to you," Sierra Bravo said, "or you'd have ignored it, too." She glanced at the back door and lowered her voice. "You have a little girl of your own."

"We love her very much," Grace Lyons said, which Sierra thought peculiar. Most mother love was unspoken.

"Let's think about it again," Sierra said. "in case something new occurs to you. Your description of the little girl was great, Walter. Now let's concentrate on the man."

Walter turned both palms upward. "If you say so."

Intense, Sierra leaned toward him. "When they came in, *how* did the man look. Proud, like he was showing the girl off?"

"Uh—no. It wasn't like he was boasting or anything."

"Not strutting?"

"No."

"Was he embarrassed? Or apologetic?"

Walter rubbed his face. "He wasn't apologizing, either, as far as I could tell."

"Did he make eye contact with anyone?"

"When they first came in, I only saw them through the mirror."

"When did you start looking at them without the mirror?"

"When they headed down to the last stall in the men's room, it got my attention."

"No eye contact?"

"Not with him. He went right into the stall."

"No eye-to-eye with her?"

Walter Lyon hesitated for too long a moment. "She and I did look at each other for no more than three seconds."

"And she seemed resolved?"

"I'm not even sure what that word means," Walter Lyons said. "She seemed like she didn't want to be there, but she couldn't do anything about it, so she accepted it."

"And you don't know what he was doing in the stall while she waited outside?"

"No." He blinked his eyes hard. "You make me feel like I did something wrong."

"Not at all, Mr. Lyons. You're a witness—my only witness."

"Well—"

"Did she know what he was doing in there?"

"She wasn't looking in at him." He squirmed in the chair, annoyed. "What do you think people do when they go into toilet stalls?"

"Many things besides using the john—like vomiting, sniffing coke, or injecting oneself with an illegal drug. And if the child wasn't his relative, he wouldn't let her run around alone in the theater lobby. Where was she looking when not making contact with you?"

"I don't know!" Lyons' tone grew sharp. "I'm just reporting this. Don't turn me into some sort of pervert!" He stood quickly, stomping toward the back door. "God, I hate this! I goddamn *hate* this! I could kick myself in the ass for coming to see you in the first place. Leave us *alone!*"

The kitchen door was on a spring, which was the only reason Walter Lyons couldn't slam it as hard as he wanted to.

The two women were momentarily quiet. Then Grace said, "I'm so sorry, Chief Bravo. Walter is sensitive sometimes, especially when it comes to—little girls."

"Why is that, Ms. Lyons?"

"Olivia." She lowered her voice to a whisper. "She's adopted, you know."

"I didn't know," Sierra said.

"When she was two and a half years old."

"I see."

Grace Lyons touched Sierra softly on the wrist. "It wasn't easy for a long time. We tried raising her safely and quietly. Before we found her through a state adoption agency, she'd been— molested."

Sierra Bravo tried ignoring the burning that flared up in her throat and threatened to turn into vomit. She bit the inside of her cheek. "A toddler?"

Ms. Lyons nodded, closing her eyes to staunch the tears that were ready to come. "She's probably forgotten about it—she was too young. But you can see why Walter is so upset about the safety of little girls. That's why he contacted you, because we both couldn't sleep last night." She stood up. "I'll have to ask you to leave." She pointed to a small gate at the side of the property. "You can go through there—I don't want you and Walter getting into it again if you leave through the house."

Sierra drove home slowly in the twilight. Her head throbbed. She knew that, like Walter, she wouldn't get much sleep tonight, either.

CHAPTER THREE

Chris Fornadel was at his sleek, classy, upscale penthouse office above the Seaview shopping center. A managing law partner, he enjoyed a corner office with both northern and eastern views. All his clients had yearly incomes of at least eight figures, without the decimal point. Each morning he ran two miles in the more rural stretches of Sundown Beach before returning to his mini-mansion to don a fifteen-hundred dollar "lawyer suit," one of several in various colors and patterns. He had an attractive wife in her thirties, with two athletic sons approaching puberty, and a sex fashion-model girlfriend from Dana Point he'd visit at least twice a week. He lived a relatively good life.

Sundown Beach is a good place to be a lawyer.

As his career progressed, however, he'd squeezed in some not-so-rich clients he found more pleasant, which is how he became friends with Sierra Bravo when she'd been policing in a small mid-California town about eight years earlier. She ran into trouble when she arrested a town councilman for selling crack at the high school where his daughter attended. When the councilman insisted that Sierra be fired and actually run out of town, a friend of a friend told Sierra about Chris Fornadel in Sundown Beach.

Fornadel, laboring mostly for the profits of the biggest corporations in Orange County, was charmed by the tough-but-fair honesty of patrolwoman Sierra Bravo, spent a few days in court, bear-baiting local prosecutors and judges who were clearly in over their heads, and not only won his case, but filed another one the next day against the councilman for false accusation. The case was settled out of court, the council member resigned and moved to another state, and Sierra received a healthy wad of change, even after deducting Lawyer Fornadel's share of the settlement.

They'd been friends ever since. Not great friends, exactly, because Chris spent most of his free time on the golf course or tennis courts, two sports in which Sierra Bravo had no interest whatsoever. But they occasionally had long liquid lunches at the Dolphin Lounge, a nice place in which to get quietly drunk—higher class than the many shot-and-a-beer joints that peppered other oceanfront suburbs.

Whenever Sierra needed advice, all it took was a phone call, and if Chris wasn't overwhelmed with gazillion-dollar deals for Fortune 500 CEOs, he was glad to supply her with whatever information she asked for.

On this day's phone call, she explained in a few sentences what goaded her on.

"What makes you think I know anything about little girls in men's restrooms?" Chris barked. "I'm no defense attorney, Sierra. I don't work for perverts."

"You know people who know people."

"I know everybody—but that and a buck will get you a cup of McDonald's coffee."

"McDonald's coffee is more expensive than a dollar. Parents sometimes pimp out their own children," Sierra said, "but I never heard of that happening in Sundown Beach."

"Nothing bad ever happens in Sundown Beach," Chris said. "A perfect, clean, safe place to live—as long as you pull in more than ten mil a year."

"We do have poor people living here, Chris."

"Yeah, with a roof over their heads, a bed to sleep in, and enough cash to purchase generic macaroni and cheese. You don't see many poverty cases sleeping in Sundown Beach doorways after the lights go out."

"That's why I took the chief job here, and not in Hoboken, New Jersey."

"Bad mistake. Frank Sinatra was from Hoboken." Chris glanced out the window at the endless sprawl of the ocean—his penthouse was tall enough to overlook the rest of the city. A kicked-up wind made the water dance a bit, the sun flashing on foam-topped waves. "Have you talked to any other cops on this subject?"

"The head of Anaheim Vice, who said it was none of my business."

"Sounds right to me. You're beating a dead horse. You run a nice, quiet town. No murders, rapes, or an armed robbery at a 7-Eleven. Some guy you never heard of spins out a tale that upsets you, though you're not even sure it really happened. He could make up this story for attention or to gin up some excitement. Or maybe he's one of those loony-tunes people who still think Communists or outer-space aliens control their thoughts and actions through silver filings in their teeth."

Sierra didn't respond.

"But let's say the guy actually saw what he described. If child and man were related, no crime was committed. If the little girl was backwards—not sharp enough to stay out in the lobby while the guy drained his lily—that doesn't sound like a crime, either."

"So?"

"So," Chris said, "you didn't see it yourself, you have no idea who these people are, and you don't know whether they live in town or in Tucumcari, New Mexico. So why waste your time and energy." For a moment, all she heard was his breathing. Then, "You never had kids, did you?"

"You don't have to be a mother to care about what happens to children."

"Care so much that you've got to do this?"

"I'm a big girl, Chris—but my father was a big guy, too—an

unhappy everyday drunk. He took out his unhappiness, disappointment and lack of success as a human being, on me—and my mother, too, but he saved his special rages for his one and only daughter. Up until I was thirteen, any week ending with less than three beatings was a good week."

He flushed, glad nobody could see him. "You don't need to tell me all this."

"It's not Breaking News on MSNBC—but I know you well enough to mention it."

Chris said, "If a child disappears—especially a teen or pre-teen—it's hard to talk any cop into believing it was kidnapping. They figure the kid got tired of all the shit they have to swallow at home every day and took a powder."

"They think my little girl in the men's room just upped and ran away?"

"*Your* little girl?"

Bravo didn't answer, wondering what had made her say "*my.*"

"Okay," Chris said. "I have a name for you. I've worked with him before, and if anyone in this area knows anything about missing child business, this is your guy." He cleared his throat. "You probably aren't going to like this, Sierra."

Sierra clicked open a ballpoint pen. "Why do I wish I'd never called you?"

"His name is Leonard Beckman."

"That rings a distant bell," Sierra said, doodling on the yellow legal pad in front of her. "Third-string nose tackle for the Arizona Cardinals? Ambulance-chasing lawyer? Or some weirdo who hangs around on the street and knows everything about everything?"

"Try *Special Agent in Charge* Leonard Beckman at the Los Angeles Federal Bureau of Investigation."

The point of Sierra Bravo's ballpoint pen nearly ripped through the paper. "Give me a break. The FBI has no use for cops, even from a big city. They'd rather chat with a homeless old lady sleeping on a heating vent. Since 9/11, they only care about terrorists. What would they know about missing children?"

"You'd be surprised. Beckman and I get along okay. He's arrogant—the Bureau trains them to be that way. But he has other things to do besides chasing down ISIS guys wanting to blow up Dodger Stadium. It won't hurt talking to him."

"He'll go out of his way to make me feel like a schmuck."

Chris Fornadel's staccato chuckle sounded louder over the phone. "You don't need any help doing that to yourself."

"Will you call him first, explain who I am and why I'm contacting him?"

"Call him yourself. You have a job and an impressive title."

"Why? Have you got a hangnail on your number-pointing finger."

Chris laughed. "I get three hundred fifty bucks an hour. So how much will it cost you for me to dial you a number?"

"I'll buy you a drink at the Dolphin some night when you aren't busy with your family or your girlfriend or making more money for your Fortune 500 clients."

"Sounds like a deal to me, Sierra—and for you, too."

"Why?"

"Because you're pretty," Chris said, "which means Beckman might even listen to you before he tells you to go fuck yourself."

Griffin Parrish sat across the desk from Sierra Bravo, sharing an early-morning moment with her as they both drank coffee. He had his own personal mug, too, emblazoned with the San Diego Chargers helmet logo, even though the Chargers moved to Los Angeles.

"I dealt with the Fibbies when I policed in L.A.," he said. "They won't cater to you; they think their own shit doesn't stink, with an imperious, better-than-you, don't-bother-me attitude. If a case interests them, they'll move in and steal it out from under your nose, waving their badges and telling you they're federal and they have the final say."

"I don't *have* a case, Griffin—as you damn well know."

"Why does Beckman bother seeing you at all, then?"

"Chris Fornadel," Sierra answered.

"Ah—the exalted city manager."

"He called Beckman and asked him to see me for ten minutes."

Griff warned, "You actually have ten minutes with such a big shot? Be still, my heart."

"I'm lucky to get ten minutes. Do you know him personally?"

Griffin Parrish shook his head. "Only by reputation. According to my lieutenant back in the day, Beckman's lordly conviction pops out all over his forehead."

"I'm not looking for a friend—just good information."

He nodded. "True. But you'd be better off getting that info on your own time."

"I'm the Chief of Police," she said. "I don't have any time to myself. Twenty-four/seven, I'm on the job."

"You think vice cops, middle school principals and the FBI will meet you at eleven o'clock at night?"

"Hardly."

"Then think about something else, too." Griff leaned closer to her. "You were out of the office yesterday—at our local school and then in Anaheim with the Vice head. In the evening you were at the Lyons house and got kicked out on your ass. This morning you're with me, looking for answers. Today, you huddle in Los Angeles with the FBI. None of it is about an actual crime. Forget Fornadel—you still have to answer to the city council."

"When did you turn into my grandmother?" Sierra demanded.

"A month after you started here," Parrish said. "You're tough, competent, and to a point, political. You relate to the people who live here. A damn good cop."

"Thanks—I guess."

"But you're too independent—and you'll wind up pissing on your own foot. Danielle Tokes is up your butt whining and complaining to you. All she can go on about is you're not being where you're supposed to be. And since she doesn't like you anyway—"

"Fuck her! But not the horse she rode in on."

Griffin Parrish leaned forward and put his arms on the edge of her desk. "Chief," he said gently, "what is there about this men's room thing that's digging into your gut?"

Sierra Bravo paused, her mouth dry. She swiveled her chair halfway around as if she were looking out the window. "Some things just do," she said quietly.

"Okay, I get it," Griff said. "But don't let it turn you into someone you're not."

She drove onto the US5 freeway toward Los Angeles, with Special Agent in Charge Leonard Beckman waiting for her. Clenching her teeth, she gripped her steering wheel too tightly and passed her own condo without even noticing it.

Griff Parrish had asked why the thought of that little girl was bugging her so badly. No, she thought, not exactly—although she would never answer Parrish about this.

It was more like digging into her soul.

The Los Angeles FBI Headquarters looks like a U.S. Embassy in a foreign country, with an impossible-to-scale wrought-iron fence surrounding it. Armed guards made sure no uninvited vehicles get anywhere near the building. As she drove up to the gate and waited for the guard to learn who she was and why he should allow her entry, the estate reminded her of a prison.

Once inside, she was given detailed instructions by a clean-cut young man at the front desk—probably a rookie, as his clothes were not as sedate or expensive as veteran Fibbies wore. As she proceeded down a long hallway, she was glad she chose flat black shoes. Her endless hike to Leonard Beckman's office would have called up a bunion if she'd trotted around in high heels.

Beckman had a secretary of his own in his outer office— young, attractive, and she *was* wearing a skirt and heels. Nothing provocative, of course, as her skirt covered her knees and her heels were no more than an inch high. She unsmilingly led Sierra through the double-thick door into Beckman's inner sanctum.

It was a large room, the desk mounted on a platform about two inches high to make Special Agent in Charge Beckman seem much more important, and gave him the edge of looking down on whoever sat across from him. Sierra remembered reading something like this about MGM movies chairman and dictator Louis B. Mayer in the thirties and forties, having a similar set-up in his office.

Beckman virtually inhabited a gray suit without a single wrinkle, fitting him well, as he'd had it constructed from scratch. His dark shoes were the color of dried blood, polished to mirror brightness. Dark gray socks to match the suit—matching *socks*, she thought—with a designer tie, louder and more aggressive than the rest of his FBI costume. Sierra wondered if he actually slept in a suit and tie.

He made a show of standing up to greet her, although his ass was never more than two inches off his chair.

Beckman said, "I only agreed to see you because Chris Fornadel asked me to. As far as I can tell, nothing happened in your town for the Bureau to get all upset about."

"I'm not sure anything bad happened," Sierra said, her gold-braided uniform cap in her lap. "I just have a gut feeling about it, and I'm trying to follow up."

"A gut feeling?" Beckman folded his hands on his stomach like a department store Santa Claus. "The Bureau doesn't have gut feelings." He spoke as if "bureau" began with a capital letter. "I've been in Los Angeles for seven years, and I never had a gut feeling, nor have I heard of a sex-trafficking organization in Sundown Beach, California, Ms. Bravo."

"That's *Chief* Bravo, Special Agent in Charge Beckman," she said coldly. "I'm not aware of an organization that's trafficking children in Sundown Beach, either—but you probably know better than anyone else around here where this might be happening."

"If it's not happening in Sundown Beach, *Chief* Bravo, why would you care?"

"Because I care about children."

"Enough to stick your nose somewhere it doesn't belong? I can't imagine why."

"You can't? Really? Do you think I have twenty or so kidnapped children locked up in my basement and am looking to sell them?"

Leonard Beckman said heavily, "You're biting off more than you can chew. You want to save this child from a life of degradation, and you don't even know who she is."

"I don't know if she even needs saving. But many children out there live the most terrible lives imaginable—and are often killed off when they're no longer useful. So that's why I'm here, Special Agent in Charge. Sorry I'm wasting your time."

She pushed her chair away from the desk and stood up, but before she got to the door—it was a pretty long walk in such a large office—Beckman asked her to wait.

"Don't go off half-cocked. Sit down—and tell me what you want from me."

Sierra stood there a lengthy moment, staring him down. Behind that arrogant, pompous conceit, was there a hint of a human being? She returned to the chair opposite Beckman, this time perching on the edge of it in case she wanted to leave quickly. "What's going on in child sex trafficking in Southern California?"

"Just name a crime. We've got loads of them. Every so often we hear about a family too poor to buy beer or crack or cigarettes, so they pimp out their own children. It's a rare occurrence, though."

"That's what you hear?" Sierra tried keeping disgust from showing on her face. "What *I* hear is the FBI is so busy chasing terrorists, they have no time for anything else."

Beckman protested, "If we don't track down and stop terrorists, we'll all be praying to Allah or speaking Russian five times every day, which makes it more important than sex trafficking."

"Most American Muslims don't *want* you praying to Allah. Terror-busting is the highly publicized hobbyhorse of your federal obsession," she said. "Famous bank robbers in the 1930s were John Dillinger, Bonnie and Clyde, and Baby Face Nelson—back when no one knew what *terrorist* meant. There were plenty of Nazi spies in the 1940s. Commies in the fifties, who did little harm—Senator Joe McCarthy was full of shit. Then there were hippie draft dodgers in the sixties, dopers in the seventies—"

"Lighten up, Chief," he said angrily. "Right now, we're in a war on terrorism—"

"For twenty years and counting."

"But we're aware of slavery prostitution, especially when it victimizes children. Shit happens—but some places in California that are busier than anywhere else in this country when it comes to what you're asking about." Beckman's hand wandered to his face, and he gently pinched his bottom lip with his third finger and his thumb as he squirmed uneasily in his chair. "A place generally regarded as the fourth most popular sex slave trafficking city in the country."

"Los Angeles?"

"Not even close," he said.

"Are you going to tell me which city, Special Agent?" Sierra said. "Or is this the FBI's version of cock-teasing?"

Beckman inhaled deeply the electronically clean air of FBI headquarters, sat back in his throne-like chair, and laced his fingers on his belly again. "Cock-teasing isn't a very nice expression."

Sierra Bravo, who never felt much like a chief of *anything* when she wasn't on duty, wasn't aware of hunger at seven-thirty that evening. She was too rattled to eat. Wandering out to some local restaurant to consume badly prepared food by herself would have been worse. Eventually she compromised, spreading six Ritz crackers with a semi-soft cheese she'd bought at the local

Trader Joe's, and taking a chilled bottle of Chardonnay out on her patio to watch the sun set. Looking out at the sky over the Pacific Ocean at the end of day was a magical time at least three hundred twenty days per year, and when she was able, Sierra endeavored to experience the silken moments, usually by herself.

Special Agent in Charge Leonard Beckman hadn't intimidated her in the least. His raised desk, bay windows, and suit without a wrinkle were obvious attempts to make her feel small and insignificant. They failed. All federal badge-wearers—FBI, CIA, Homeland Security, ICE, the Secret Service, ATF, and, as far as she knew, the Department of the Interior taking care of public lands—do the same thing. They love snatching authority from police departments to take credit for solving crimes and problems themselves, as if the local cops were elderly ladies who only volunteer to help little children cross the street.

She had to admit federal bullies did good things, too, sometimes—and hooray for them, else there would be complete anarchy in the USA. It was the attitude that got to her. A lot of men had "attitudes," whether or not they wore badges, and she had met her share of them. Her father, the miserable son of a bitch, had the worst attitude of all.

Even though the evening was warm and balmy, she suppressed a shudder thinking about her abusive dad and her spineless mother who knew all too well how to look in the other direction. She slugged down half a glass of Chardonnay in hopes the quivering would go away—but Sierra knew it would never completely disappear, whether she'd swallowed most of the wine or not.

That's why she decided to become a police officer—as far away from Ohio as she could get. That brought her to a Georgia college, but after four years of heat, sweat, and chiggers buzzing around her eyelids—in Georgia they refer to insect chiggers as the state bird and rarely call it by its true name, *Trombicilidae*—she was ready to leave and head west. Besides, the local Georgia drawl was hard to decipher. Her law enforcement degree helped her land policing a small California town that was mostly medium-sized industry and the rest of it family agriculture. She'd become a good cop there—a very good cop.

Chris Fornadel arrived to defend his corporate client, and she was on the other side, fighting for the workers injured in an explosion and fire at their manufacturing job that no one in the front office had bothered to fix. Her side lost, of course—Chris was a dazzling tap dancer in a courtroom. But he showed interest in a female police officer who stood up for the little people for whom she worked, and after a few dinners, though they never took the logical next step—taking each other to bed—their flirty but platonic relations turned into a friendship. A year later, Sierra ran into trouble again with another corporation, this time a business Fornadel did not represent, and he bailed her out of a lawsuit. He might have been lawyer to the one percent most of the time, but in his heart, he was on the side of the blue-collars— and of the pretty Sierra. When he told her a chief's job had opened up in his hometown of Sundown Beach, she applied for it with little chance of success. Thanks to pushing and shoving by Chris Fornadel—besides lawyering, he was also city manager— she received a big surprise! The job was hers.

Mostly decent people worked and lived within this medium-upscale town, Sierra thought. A few, like Danielle Tokes were impossible to like, and the rich, non-working moms in the area looked down their surgically improved noses and clacked their smoothed Botoxed lips at the working class, but her former police job taught Sierra to be as tough as she needed to be.

From the start, there was enough oceanside crime to keep her busy, even though Sundown Beach crooks were white collar and drove Mercedes, BMWs and Land Rovers, as opposed to villains in her previous small town who drove twenty-year-old pickup trucks, dressed in mom-jeans, shoes with the soles worn out, and the few teeth they still had in their mouths stained brown from chewing tobacco.

There was a definite lack of straight single men in Sundown

Beach—a rather married community. Sliding quietly into early middle age, Sierra had relinquished the idea of white picket fences and adorable houses that needed repainting every three years, two-point-five children, a dog, and memberships in the PTA and the Garden Club. She really didn't look good in the police uniform, but at her job, one wears the required costume. Imagine pro football players showing up for the game wearing suits and ties!

But this men's room shocker at the Sunset Beach movie theater was making her crazy, causing her to neglect her duties, though it took no agonizing or rending of garments to realize she couldn't do a damn thing about it. The big problem was not in Sundown Beach, or even in San Diego. It apparently centered in a neighboring metropolis right up the road.

Sweat City. That's what Leonard Beckman had called Hemlock Hills, which was a silly thing to call a city, for hemlock is the poison with which Plato killed himself. Sierra knew it was a lower-middle-class working community. She'd been there before, once for a police memorial event, after which she and a friend went to a well-known restaurant for a casual dinner, thanks to the hometown bragging of some minor TV actor who was a native of Hemlock Hills. Otherwise, her trips to the eastern edge of Orange County had been sparse.

Maybe, she thought, her entire adult life had been sparse. With non-violent and mostly non-criminal problems like Dylan Zack's reckless driving and pot possession she had to face each day grinding her down, and the irritation she felt since her visit with the otherwise ordinary Walter Lyons, the stars on her collar didn't mean much—not even as stimulating as being foreman at a small-time industrial plant manufacturing widgets.

The sun had disappeared, leaving orange streaks in the western sky, and only a quarter of the Chardonnay was left in the bottle. She sometimes drank too much, and she knew it. Most cops, though, drink off-duty to help them navigate the scum and slime they slogged through every day. She hauled herself out of the chair and wandered over to the edge of the balcony, hanging onto the railing so she wouldn't tip over. She deeply inhaled fresh air, hoping it would clear her head a bit.

It didn't.

What was she thinking when she chose to wear a badge? Too many TV shows like *Policewoman* or *Cagney and Lacey?* After nearly a century of being "allowed" to vote, American women were finally being given positions of authority, and when she completed her college education, police work looked appealing to her. But those TV women wore fake badges and even faker eyelashes, and carried guns with the firing pin removed to clean up big cities one hour each week, while Sierra wound up in a California beach town. Accepting the offer of chief of police was a big step up for her, and she'd looked forward to it, not realizing Sundown Beach was virtually nothing like New York or Los Angeles.

Good job. Nobody took a shot at her. For the most part, Sundowners were fairly nice, though mostly super-rich and stuck up. She could spend forever coasting along on those silver stars and the ability to go anywhere and do anything in the State of California by flashing her badge.

But then there was that little girl in the men's room...

CHAPTER FOUR

The morning was colder than usual. Pewter-gray skies threatened a rain-soak later that day. That's California—the weather is always consistent, except when it isn't. By the time one sees sunshine out the window and dresses accordingly, clouds have blanketed the sun and the Santa Ana wind from the eastern deserts lower the temperature by ten degrees.

Gliding into her parking spot, Sierra Bravo wasn't hung over but out-of-sorts, off-balance, and exhausted from lack of sleep, hoping for an easy shift. When Officer Nancy Flower approached her with a worried frown, she knew, without even checking her Libra horoscope, that this would be a difficult day.

"If I were you, Chief, I'd have some coffee now, before you go into your office."

"Why?"

"You have a visitor."

"When I was a kid," Sierra said, "I worried there were monsters hiding under the bed at night. Are they hanging out in my office now, at eight o'clock in the morning?"

"You want three guesses?"

"I don't need three, Nancy." Sierra started down the corridor, trying hard to stand up straight and look confident.

"Good morning, Danielle," she said, striding into her office with a proprietary attitude. "Have my staff offered you a wake-up coffee yet?"

Danielle Tokes, her short haircut so slathered with styling gel that it resembled a miniature football helmet, barely shifted around in her chair, not bothering to look up at the Chief of Police. "I wondered if you'd even show up today," she said, each word an ice cube. "You were out of the office almost all day yesterday."

"I'll have some myself, then." Sitting her desk, Sierra punched out two numbers on her phone. "May I have my coffee now, Nancy?"

On the other end, Nancy Flower said, "You always get your own coffee, so this must be an extra-shitty start. Coffee coming right up—and you've been warned."

Hanging up, Sierra said, "It's on its way. Well, I'm here now, Danielle. How can I help you before I get down to real police business?"

"You know damn well why I'm here!" Tokes' upper lip sneered, exposing her teeth and wrinkling her medically rebuilt nose. Once relatively attractive, she was currently north of forty-five—a trophy wife in her day but now divorced, overdressed, over-paid, over-suntanned and over-obnoxious. "Dylan Zack has to appear in court."

"We already talked about this, didn't we?"

"Yes, and you haven't done a goddamn thing about it."

"My job is to enforce the law. The next step is up to the court."

"Bullshit!"

"I don't think so," Chief Bravo said. "Dylan was driving recklessly. He could have killed someone, which is why he got stopped. He also had illegal substances in his car—too much of it, and that could be a felony. I won't get into a pissing contest about marijuana, because I don't care. But it's illegal—and the law is what I'm hired to impose—hired, if you recall, by *you*, along with the other council members and the city manager."

"You can get fired, too."

"Not simply on your say-so. Also—you don't get to cherry-pick which laws I enforce or who gets to break them. Not your job."

Nancy Flower came in with Sierra's mug of steaming coffee. "Sorry to interrupt, Chief."

"Thanks so much, Officer Flower." Nancy backed out, giving Danielle Tokes a quick once-over, her eyes rolling toward the ceiling.

"*My* job," Tokes growled, "is to keep this department and this city running smoothly. We vote for your budget and we make sure you're the best police around. One would think when we do you favors, you could do us favors, too."

"Favors for the police department? Really? If you did no *favors* like funding us, this city'd be in chaos, and then we'd really hear you bitch and complain." This was not the best morning to get a police chief ticked off. Sierra aggressively leaned forward, her own teeth bared, and Danielle Tokes feared she might be bitten. "Policing is no day at the beach. We make traffic stops, and when we get a report of something bad going on—drug sales, domestic violence, gangs, robbery—we make arrests, twenty-four seven. I'm on call for every one of those hours. So quit whining that a friend of yours did something wrong and we should just forget about it."

Now Tokes grew desperate. "I'm asking for a *favor*. Dylan's just a kid."

"Then let him go to court—maybe the judge will do you a favor."

"That's a shitty thing to say."

"Or maybe talk Ken Zack into asking for his own favor."

That was the final artillery blast. Danielle Tokes leaped to her feet, snatching her purse from the chief's desk. "You cunt!" she snarled, and blasted out of Sierra's office, slamming the door hard behind her.

Sierra sat there, thinking about it. As a street cop, she'd been cursed many times—also been spat on, kicked, punched by low-level bad guys in the town she'd patrolled for many years—but she'd never been called that name by a middle-aged, salon-tanned woman wearing a casual early morning outfit that cost more than a Sundown Beach cop's weekly salary.

Could Tokes be arrested for calling the police chief a cunt? Not in California, though religious fanatics in Idaho or Texas or Alabama were desperate to make cursing, especially by women, a felony offense.

Men cursing in those states, Sierra guessed, was fine.

Nancy Flower knocked on the open door. "Just think," she said, "it's only eight-thirty and you've already been called a cunt. What's the rest of your day look like?"

"You heard her say that?"

"They heard it in Fresno," Nancy said.

"Why is she making such a fuss over somebody else's son? Why doesn't Ken Zack call himself?"

"You haven't been around here long enough. You don't know all the secrets." Nancy Flower slid into the chair. "Kenneth Zack is one of the richest people in Sundown Beach—and in Sundown Beach, that's *saying* something. As for Tokes, she drives a top-of-the-line Mercedes she replaces every two years, she goes to New York every four months to shop for designer clothes, goes to Europe every year for a month. She gets a hair-do and manicure every seven days, and I have no doubt she's banging somebody on the side."

"Or maybe a lot of somebodies."

"As long as they don't live in Sundown Beach."

Sierra said, "That still doesn't explain why Ken Zack won't back up his own son."

"He doesn't give a damn. I don't think he's done a father-son thing since Dylan's pre-kindergarten days," Flower said, "so he sends Danielle to bitch at us without putting himself on the line—nor his country-club memberships, his gazillion-bucks company and all its outshoots, golf outings, and his million-and-a-half dollar Newport Beach yacht."

"If he doesn't care about Dylan, why bother at all?"

"Rich bitches bellow about everything. Tokes is on City Council, so she gets in your face when she feels like it." She tapped

Sierra's empty mug. "More coffee?"

"Not right now. She was nasty to me even before I got hired. Why is that?"

"Because you're younger than she is, and you're much prettier."

"Horse shit!"

"No, it's true. You don't paint yourself up like a Vegas hooker the way she does, but you're a knockout."

"*You're* pretty."

Nancy blushed, lowering her head. "I'm okay-looking—for a fading blossom. But Tokes is scared to death Ken Zack might get interested in *you*, so from your first day wearing that badge, she was trying to figure out how to throw you under the bus."

"I don't think I've met Ken Zack more than twice. He's not one of my late-night sex fantasies. Geeky-looking." She laughed. "Besides, I'm not on the mistress market."

"You're not seeing anyone?"

A pause. "Not at the moment." She riffled through a few papers on her desk. "If you find Sergeant Parrish anywhere, tell him I need to talk to him."

"Will do." Nancy stood up. "I still think you should have a boyfriend."

"Maybe tomorrow," Sierra Bravo told her.

She sat alone for a while, thinking—and Tokes did not intrude on her musings. She figured Griffin Parrish was involved in something else and would come by as soon as he could, so her thoughts were elsewhere. Finally, she flipped open her MacBook Pro, spent about five minutes searching the Internet, and then made a telephone call.

They were at the Dolphin for lunch. For a change, nobody brought an infant to cry during the meal, and there was no reunion of fortyish women who hadn't seen each other since college talking loud and giggling like teenage Justin Bieber fans. Sierra was deep in thought about other things, and Griffin

Parrish was disturbed and frowning.

"If I were you," Parrish finally said, "I wouldn't blow off Danielle Tokes."

"Why not?"

"She's one of three people who can dump your ass from your job—and all she needs is one of those other two votes to do so."

Sierra took a bite of her well-sauced scallops. "They'd fire me over Dylan Zack?"

"Not necessarily. One of the other two might ask you for a totally different favor, though, and if you tell them to go fly a kite, you might be in trouble."

"No one asked me for anything before. Besides, Tokes wanted my head on a stake from the moment she met me."

"The higher-up you go—in any business—the more people resent your success. You're the chief, so it happens." He sipped his tea. "Now you want a few days off, too?"

Sierra nodded.

"You took your two weeks' vacation between Thanksgiving and Christmas," Griffin said. "You'll have to wait for six months before another vacation."

"Then I'll rack up some sick days."

"You're not sick."

She smiled. "You're no doctor."

"Are you in pain?"

"Does a pain in the ass count as sickness?"

"What happens if you get ill when you have no more sick days?"

"Then," Sierra said, "I'll come in to work anyway and cough all over you."

"Funny. But that girl in the men's room—" Parrish lowered his voice. "You haven't thought of anything else since Walter Lyons came in Monday morning."

"So?

"That kid could be far away by now—maybe shipped off to work sixteen hours a day in a Chinese factory sewing buttons on cheap shirts—or to Saudi Arabia as a child whore for the sons of sheiks."

"Gross, Griffin—even for you."

"The chances of seeing her at the Sundown Beach Library or a public swimming pool are slim to none."

Sierra put down her fork. "It's not about that particular little girl anymore. There's a sex-trafficking business going on right under our noses."

"Not in Sundown Beach."

"How do we know that?" She shifted to a near-whisper. "Anyone in this restaurant might be part of a vast criminal racket that preys on children."

"We can't arrest everybody who looks suspicious, like the Red Hat Ladies?" Griffin motioned with his chin at three elderly women sitting at a table across from them. They were not wearing red hats, but otherwise they fit the description.

"I'm not arresting anyone."

"Then why do you need a few days off?"

"I'm going to Hemlock Hills. At a meeting with FBI Special Agent Beckman, he said Hemlock Hills is the fourth most-active smaller American city for sex trafficking."

"Being chief in Sundown Beach doesn't buy a damn thing in Hemlock Hills."

Sierra said, "It bought me a meeting with the head of vice in the Anaheim P.D."

"And what if you find a child sex slavery ring in Hemlock Hills?"

Sierra pushed her lunch away from her, not even half-eaten, and took a large gulp of her coffee. "I haven't the vaguest idea," she said.

She fretted on this problem through the rest of the week while handling things chiefs of police should handle—including several nasty phone calls from Danielle Tokes. Now it was a Saturday, a day off—and it still gave her a headache.

Tracking down that little girl from a crowded men's room wasn't her job, it wasn't her town, it wasn't her business—and yet it was, whether she wanted it to be or not. She felt it in her head, and coruscating inside her chest. It was hard for her to concentrate on even the smallest things.

She wasn't hung up on children. They were okay if they belonged to someone else. Her body clock never started ticking; she'd never felt longing for a child of her own. She wouldn't be good at raising one; her own family had taught her *that*—and more.

But an abused child? That was another story altogether for Sierra Bravo.

Was the little girl in the movie bathroom being molested, or was it a story fueled by Walter Lyons' over-active imagination?

His own adopted child, Olivia, had been sexually abused when she was an infant, and Walter was as sensitive about it as a fair-skinned redhead's reaction to a bad sunburn. At lunchtime, she headed to the public square; a scheduled concert showcasing some musicians from the local high and middle schools was about to commence. While she didn't enjoy kid orchestras playing Beethoven in the warm Saturday sunlight, she thought it was something to do with herself besides brooding. She'd forgotten to bring a folding chair, as many attendees did, and didn't feel like the four-minute drive home to get one. It would take longer than that to find a new parking space, anyway.

Parents were filling the seating area, and the young musicians filed in to where their chairs and music stands had been set up. Sierra wondered what possessed a teenager to choose a French horn, a standing bass or a long, skinny bassoon. These days, she supposed, kid musicians preferred guitars or drums.

The concert was ten minutes late getting started, and by that time her feet hurt and her back ached. She was about ready to quietly go home when someone appeared next to her and said, "Hey, Chief Bravo! I almost didn't recognize you without the uniform."

She didn't know her new visitor right away, either. The only time she had seen him before, he'd worn a short-sleeved dress shirt and a boring tie. On this Saturday he was more casual— polo shirt, designer jeans, sunglasses, and a creamy tan she hadn't noticed before. Not a bad-looking guy, considering.

She struggled for a moment to remember his name. Then: "Principal Quigley. I didn't think school executives worked on weekends."

"I didn't think police chiefs did, either." He took off his glasses, revealing hazel eyes. "This is more than a pleasant surprise. Music lover?"

"Not really. Just trying to keep myself from worrying about things."

"Like that little girl you asked about when you came to see me?"

She frowned. "You have a good memory."

"Especially when a woman like you has big blue eyes. It gets to me every time. So—have you learned anything about the missing child since last week?"

"Almost impossible. It's pretty much a dead end, Mr. Quigley."

"We're out here in the hot sun waiting for these kids to massacre music, so you can call me Chet." He grinned. "If you want to, that is."

"Chet it is, then."

He waited ten seconds before saying, "And I guess I can call you Chief Bravo?"

She laughed. "Only when there are silver stars on my collar. My name is Sierra."

"Exotic."

"Not really—at least not to me. Let's just listen to the music, shall we?"

"Okay—but I looked something up for you."

"You did?"

Chet Quigley blushed. "Well, not for you, exactly. What you

were asking about got me to wondering, too—so I dug into a few school records."

"And what did you find?"

"You remember I told you about Caitlin Haggerty? The girl from our school who went missing about seven years ago?"

Sierra nodded.

"I found her records in our files. Her mother—I mentioned she'd left town and was living in Arkansas? My mistake. She's in Kentucky. She left a forwarding address in case anyone heard anything about her daughter."

"But she hasn't been contacted since?"

He shook his head. "For all I know, Caitlin disappeared off the face of the earth."

Sierra's deep weight on her chest returned with a suddenness that surprised her. "What's her mother's first name?"

Chet Quigley took a few seconds to think about it. "Nicole. Her last known address was in Lexington."

The band leader stepped to the front of the ensemble and tapped her baton on the edge of her music stand, and the musicians all grew quiet, sat up straighter, and held their instruments high, ready to play. Then the downbeat—and out came "Tomorrow," which is the corniest song in Broadway musical history.

But Sierra wasn't listening. "I have to go," she said. "Something I need to do."

Startled, Quigley protested. "Go? You can't go! The music is just starting!"

"Another time." She turned and hurried toward where she'd parked her car.

"But I hoped we could go back to my place after the concert and open a bottle of wine," he called after her.

"Dream on," she said over her shoulder, and picked up her pace.

It took Sierra less than five minutes to reach the police station. She said hello to the weekend sergeant-in-charge, then scurried back to her office computer. Police departments have different sites and apps than civilians do, and it took only moments to pull up some names and phone numbers in Lexington, Kentucky.

Three listings for N. Haggerty—no first name. Most people whose phone listings only use an initial are female. Back in the day, women got more obscene phone calls than now, as most telephones display the identity of the caller. That way, women, and everyone else, can decide whether or not they want to answer the phone.

There was one listing each for N.C. Haggerty, Nicola Haggerty, and Nicole Haggerty. Sierra tried Nicole first. No answer, but the receiving message was delivered in a pronounced Kentucky accent. Sierra put a question mark next to that name, unsure if the Nicole she was looking for had southern roots. Then she dialed Nicola Haggerty.

This time, a human being picked up the phone and said hello.

"Is this Nicola Haggerty?"

"Yes."

"My name is Sierra Bravo. I'm the chief of police in Sundown Beach, California."

"Are you fucking kidding me?" The voice was young, sassy, and very annoyed. "Sundown Beach, California? That's a new one. You scammers usually reach me by email to tell me you're from Nigeria, you're an elderly widowed lady with terminal cancer, and you're going to send me eight million dollars."

Sierra was glad she couldn't see her smile. "No, I'm not from Nigeria. You can have my badge number if you'd like. I'm just wondering if you ever lived in Sundown Beach, or if you had a daughter named Caitlin."

"I've never been anywhere near Sundown Beach. I'm single, never been pregnant. I'm twenty-six, and an assistant professor of social studies at the University of Kentucky."

"One more question: have you ever been called Nikki?"

"Everybody named Nicola is called Nikki," the woman said.

"You're right," Sierra said. "Well, sorry I bothered you."

"I'm in my backyard in a bikini, soaking up sunshine and drinking beer with my boyfriend, so you didn't bother me—yet."

Sierra thought about that after she hung up. It was Saturday. She had no bikini, nor a backyard, wasn't a beer drinker, and there was no boyfriend.

What kind of life did she have, anyway? A cop life. A lonely life. Cops, as far as she knew, only got along with other cops. Their butts were on the line every day of their lives—and while relatively few officers died while on duty, they couldn't help considering any non-cop as someone suspicious, with something to hide.

She took a few seconds more to consider Chet Quigley. He was sort of cute, in a nerdy way. Aroused by her, obviously—but those mini-seconds were all she had to spare. Something more important drummed away at the back of her skull.

Once more on the phone, and this time the call was answered.

"Yes," N.C. Haggerty said nervously, "I used to live in Sundown Beach. I moved away about five years ago. Why?"

The conversation took Sierra to places she didn't expect, and N.C. Haggerty was surprisingly open about the most painful subject imaginable. When their daughter faded into the ether without explanation, Nicole Haggerty and her husband spent every cent they had on a private investigator, but after a year they'd discovered nothing and had run out of money. Whatever they'd enjoyed in their marriage turned to bitterness, silence, unspoken regret on both sides, and eventually an affair between Mr. Haggerty and the hostess at the Dolphin Club. Divorce followed, and then both moved out of town to hopefully begin again. But the torment, the ghost of their child who might have already *been* a ghost, lived with each of them every moment of their lives.

After Sierra ended the call, she battled dark thoughts. Children were kidnapped and murdered far too often—and sometimes their bodies were discovered, even on the west coast, where little corpses washed up onto some of the most sought-after beaches in the United States.

But a decade earlier, Caitlin Haggerty had disappeared without a trace, which meant it was possible she had been sucked into the multi-billion-dollar sex-traffic business, perhaps somewhere far away, and was never heard from again. The chances were good that if she'd wound up in a backwards third-world country, she'd never been treated to a public movie.

She'd probably never been "treated" to anything.

The man drove east on a part-residential, part-rural street. He was careful to go no faster than five miles over the posted speed limit. The late afternoon sun glared, making him regret not bringing his Ray-Ban sunglasses. He'd been far too busy making software deals with some big California corporations, which would eventually net him not quite half a million dollars. It's not as much as he'd hoped for, but if you don't own a corporation in the Fortune 500, you get screwed, always, one way or another.

A few years earlier, he'd discovered *investing* rather than buying was a good way to make extra money. He had a full-time job, too. Not exactly an executive—and he knew in his heart he wasn't nearly smart enough to do that. But his job was security chief—which really meant washing the boss's car twice a week, doing his errands, picking up his dry cleaning, and most importantly these days, taking care of his employer's "ward."

He glanced over at the child curled up asleep in the passenger seat, her mouth open a bit, snoring quietly. Not all that pretty, really—but she was young. In a few years, her body would fill out, her breasts would bloom, she'd be wearing makeup and sexy clothes, and that might make all the difference.

It bothered him she barely spoke English. He couldn't converse with her for more than a few words because he knew no Romanian.

Ilinca—that was a first name he'd never heard before. It had an ugly sound to it, but eventually someone would re-christen her with a name everyone could pronounce, like Anne or Amy.

He lived at his farm, a sixty-acre spread he'd inherited from his grandfather, the house and barn nearly a quarter mile off the back road and nowhere near any other home or business. Nothing grew on the farm, nor did he rais any animals, but it never bothered him. He liked being squirreled away from people when he was not doing his job.

Ilinca was allowed to use most of the house, but when he had to go into town to work instead of tinkering with his software inventions down in his basement, he'd lock her in her bedroom upstairs. The only window in there was boarded up—and it didn't face the road anyway, but the thick stand of forest in the rear. He left snacks for her, bottled water or canned Coke, a large bucket in case she needed it, and a crappy old TV with rabbit ears he'd had in the attic for decades.

When he'd had to be in San Diego for a week, he'd found an out-of-the-way motel—an almost ancient establishment that back in the 1940s was called an "auto court." He had no choice but to bring Ilinca with him. When he attended business meetings, he'd lock her in the motel bathroom, handcuffed to the pipes behind the toilet and a strip of duct tape across her mouth so she couldn't make any noise. It was hard on her, he realized, so he spread the motel's coverlet and a pillow on the floor so she wouldn't be too uncomfortable—but the trip was an absolute necessity for him, and he couldn't just leave her alone in the farmhouse.

Before Ilinca came into his life, he'd owned another young girl all by himself—a few years older and much prettier. She spoke English, having been born and raised in Istanbul, where many were bilingual. She was a bargain for him because she'd not been a virgin.

Her name was Jale, but he decided to call her Jane. An early teen, she was difficult to deal with at the best of times. Whenever he'd want sex, which sometimes was twice daily, she'd balk and refuse, and he'd have to beat her to subdue her temper before using her body for his own pleasure. Punishing the child often turned him off, so after eight months, he sold her back to the syndicate who'd found her for him in the first place—and he lost money on the deal. God knows where she wound up after that—perhaps in Dubai or some other brothel in the Middle East.

A better solution occurred to him before he negotiated the purchase of Ilinca. Her life was a bit easier for her. He didn't have to physically punish her. Whenever she wanted anything—an extra blanket, ice cream (a rare treat, because he didn't want her getting fat), or new clothing to replace the old ones she wore when kidnapped from Romania, she had to suck his dick first. If it were in the evening, he'd strip her, too, and play with her body to his heart's content. But that was all. It was a rule. No vaginal or anal penetration—that was the property of the man for whom he worked. He was well paid for that rule.

He actually enjoyed doing nice things for her as long as he reaped his own rewards, and he'd thought it special to take her to a movie, an animated Pixar feature with very little dialogue she could understand, anyway. He allowed her candy, popcorn, and a Diet Pepsi and purchased a large Pepsi for himself, too, hoping the film, which held no interest for him, would be over quickly.

The Pepsi, however, resulted in pressure on his bladder—and when the film was over, he needed a pit stop before getting back into the car. That left him no choice but to bring Ilinca into the men's room with him. He couldn't leave her alone in the lobby— she might throw a fit to get the attention of a policeman, and then where would he be? He was aware of the startled stares of the other men in the john, but they all looked at her and not at him, so he didn't worry about being recognized.

Now he drove toward rural quiet, with only chirping birds to invade his privacy—back home in case his boss needed both of them to be there. It wasn't an easy job. He was not part of the biggest sex-traffic organizations, only a middleman. He had neither guts nor street cred to inflict pain or make huge decisions, like slave owners.

He was just an agent for the boss he'd toiled under for twelve years. He delivered the money to the trafficker in Hemlock Hills—even though with his employer's twenty grand cash in hand, he considered taking off for Central America to live like a king for the rest of his days. They paid him handsomely, though, for being head of security for a major corporation, and for dirtying his hands if anything illegal arose—like delivering a pre-teen whore bought for the use of his boss.

The side benefits, he thought, glancing over at Ilinca next to him on the front seat, weren't bad. Deep within his heart, which was almost human, he was happy Ilinca smiled as she watched the childish antics on the screen, even laughing several times. For him, though, sitting through a child's animated film bored him to distraction.

It had been a most unusual moment—because before the movie treat, he couldn't think of a single other time he'd seen Ilinca smile.

CHAPTER FIVE

"I don't get it, Sierra."

Chris Fornadel came to Sierra Bravo's condo for an early Monday morning breakfast. She'd made pancakes and eggs and whipped up a pitcher of Bloody Marys. Chris wore one of his pricey gray suits; she sported khaki slacks and a blue silk blouse that almost matched the color of her eyes. They were seated at a table out on her patio. The rising sun cast its warmth on them but also brought tension. They'd been friends long enough to ascertain a certain amount of agitation was as much a part of breakfast as coffee.

"I figured you wouldn't get it," Sierra said, "but since you're the one who hired me in the first place, I want to let you know what I'm up to."

"Up to no good," he said, "but I can't talk you out of it." He salted the scrambled eggs. "You're a good cook. Do you realize this is the first time you ever cooked for me?"

Sierra smiled. "I rarely cook for anybody. This isn't a big visitor's hangout."

"Your coffee is exceptional. Want to come work for my law firm? Whoever makes our coffee in the morning is, I think, doing it for revenge."

"Sure. I'll give up my job as police chief to make a pot of coffee every morning for some upper-middle-aged white guys with big bellies who charge their clients five hundred bucks an hour for the time they take to drink it. I'll give that some serious consideration."

He compressed his lips. "I don't want a fight with you on a pleasant morning, but I'm surprised you're taking a few days off to stagger around blindfolded. A silly treasure hunt—and everyone else in Sundown Beach will think so, too. You're the top cop around here," he pointed out, pouring more coffee, "yet you keep disappearing."

"When was the last time terrible things happened in Sundown Beach?" she asked, making quotation marks in the air with both hands around *terrible things*. "If there's a problem, Parrish is in charge. He's been a cop here forever and can handle anything. If he needs me, he has my cell number—and so do you. And by the way—Hemlock Hills has not yet disappeared into thin air. It's less than two hours away by freeway.

"Glad to know that," Chris said. "I never hear anything about Hemlock Hills, one way or the other. What's the big deal dragging you there?"

She tried not to grit her teeth. "Child sex trafficking. Hemlock Hills is one of the worst small American cities for that kind of operation."

His brows lifted in surprise. "I never heard anything like that."

"It doesn't make headlines—but it's inland, far enough away from the Pacific and from Anaheim that nobody pays much attention. It's not *that* far from Mexico, which means there's lots of human traffic. A good place for smugglers—of human beings."

"So you're off to storm the battlefield and let loose the dogs of war."

She raised an eyebrow. "You quote Shakespeare at eight o'clock in the morning?"

"He's quotable twenty-four/seven. So—you're going to a shit little city where people never see the ocean anyway, and tear down the walls with your bare hands like The Hulk?"

"It's not easy being green."

"This nameless, faceless little girl is now in Hemlock Hills?" He speared another pancake from the serving dish. "You don't know that. She could've been shipped off halfway around the world to some brothel. Give it up. She might not be a kidnapped sex slave at all—and even if she is, you'll never find her again."

"I can't explain it."

"If you can't explain it, how do I explain it to council members?" Chris queried. "Danielle Tokes despises you, but the other two council members like you—*now*. I don't know how they'll feel if you take off out of town to chase a will-o'-the-wisp."

Sierra said, "Is that a threat?"

"I don't threaten. We've known each other forever," Chris told her. "We're good friends—unless you slipped cyanide into the Bloody Mary."

"You can't arrest me for thinking it," she said, words accompanied by a half-smile.

"Then I won't have to say goodbye yet." He sipped his Bloody Mary to prove it. "It won't fly with the council if you leave town for no reason."

"There is a reason!"

"To save some little girl from a fate worse than death?" He shook his head sadly. "You don't even know who she is."

"No, I don't." Sierra clenched her hands clenched into fists, then stood and relaxed them to clear her own plate and glass from the table. "But maybe," she called over her shoulder as she walked inside, "I might save some other child from a fate worse than death, which would make my trip more than worthwhile."

After Chris left, she put all the dirty breakfast dishes into the dishwasher. Her suitcase contained four changes of clothing, her iPad, and one of those awkward makeup kits traveling women always take with them. No police officer goes anywhere, on duty or off, without a weapon, and she owned a city-supplied Glock she wore holstered at her waist and a personal derringer strapped to her right ankle. In her left sock, inserted so it would be easy to get to in times of trouble, was a thin metallic nail file she'd bought from a beauty supply house while still in college in

Georgia and had sharpened to a deadly point—in case any of her male contacts on campus tried to push things too far. Her silver badge and ID were in the left pocket of her lightweight jacket, just long enough to cover the Glock.

Walking into the police station, she felt overly observed. Only a few in her department had ever seen her in civilian clothes.

"You look good, Chief," Nancy Flower said as she wandered into Sierra's office. "Sexy. Cute guys will be all over you."

"I can hardly wait." Sierra's tone was dusty as she thumbed through the files on her desk. "Is there anything I have to sign before I leave?"

"It'll keep." Flower chewed on her lower lip. "Danielle Tokes already called for you—at exactly 9:03 a.m."

"I'm not calling her back."

"What do I tell her," Nancy Flower said, "if you're gone for several days?"

"That I was carried off and eaten by a giant California condor."

Griffin Parrish poked his head through the door. "We didn't have time to throw a goodbye party for you, Chief."

"I'm not going to Mars."

He nodded. "You know if you need help—or back-up—I'm one phone call and two hours away."

"Me, too," Nancy Flower said.

Sierra said, "As far as I know, there's no danger on the horizon."

"Just over that horizon is what you've got to be careful of," Griffin warned.

Within five minutes, Sierra Bravo was heading east, rolling down the rear windows to get some fresh air circulating in the car without messing up her hair. She didn't turn the radio on while she drove. She was never hooked into music, even as a teen. To her it was background, like boring Muzak in an elevator. She knew stores and businesses researched and knew what kind of tunes made people buy more, but she personally didn't care.

Christmas music was something else, although she paid little attention to religious carols. "Deck the Halls" and "Winter Wonderland" seemed joyous, and she really looked forward to hearing "I Want a Hippopotamus for Christmas" whenever it kicked in on the radio. Not really in warm weather, though.

Her direct route didn't take her anywhere near the ocean. California had a long coast, but inland there wasn't much water to enjoy.

It took her about two hours from her office to Hemlock Hills, and another fifteen minutes wandering around town looking for the police department. Strange, Sierra thought—she was familiar with every inch of Sundown Beach, but in a strange city, she was just another lost and confused tourist.

She finally found the building and parked a block away to enjoy the warm sunshine on her short walk. In Hemlock Hills, they have more rain in spring and summer than they do in more inclement seasons, so she was glad she'd hit one of the good days.

The Vice Squad center was in a cramped office on the sixth floor, and the vista out the two large windows was not pictorial—a downtown city street, crowded at lunchtime. The head of the Vice unit was a redheaded woman, Sergeant Hermine Berenson, about the same age as Sierra, but three inches taller. How she moved across the room, the strength of her handshake, the low voice that could be mistaken for masculine over the phone indicated she'd once been military, probably a field officer, easing herself into law enforcement to learn even more about being no-nonsense tough.

"Welcome to Hemlock Hills, Chief," the sergeant said. "Is this your first visit?"

"There hasn't been much reason for me to come here before. This trip is serious."

"I gathered that from your phone call." She pulled a file closer to her and flipped it open. Sierra noticed there was only one sheet of paper inside—notes Berenson had taken during their phone call. "A female child you saw in a men's room in Sundown

Beach was kidnapped from Hemlock Hills? Have I got that right?"

"I don't hang out in men's rooms. I got this story from a witness." Sierra rubbed her tired eyes as she told her the story. She'd repeated it so often that it was becoming a memorized recitation.

When she was done, Sergeant Berenson took a thoughtful pause, almost a minute long. Then she said, "Chief—you've got nothing. This guy with a story didn't know a damn thing except what he saw with his own eyes—which wasn't much. His description could characterize ten million other people. For all you know, there might not be a crime at all.

"There might be no child abuse, kidnapping, or sex trafficking. You're guessing. And—this is important, Chief—it doesn't have the slightest thing to do with Hemlock Hills."

Sierra protested. "Hemlock Hills is a big sex-trafficking headquarters."

"True," Berenson said, "we have a shitty reputation for that, most of it deserved, which is why I run this unit. Houston has one. Atlanta. Miami. Tulsa. Toledo. A bunch of other places." She rotated her head around and Sierra could hear her neck bones pop. "We also have drug mobs, fraud, money-laundering and hookers. But they're *our* hookers."

"Nevertheless, it's a logical place to start."

"Start what? If that same little girl walked in here right this minute and bit you on the ass, you wouldn't recognize her. And she probably can't speak English, either."

"I understand that, Sergeant. Maybe I can't help that one child—"

"Assuming she even *needs* help."

"Then I can help somebody else. I've seen the FBI, which did me no good."

"Did you contact the resident agency in Anaheim?"

Sierra laughed. "Is that what the Fibs call their satellite office here?"

Berenson nodded. "Don't bother. Anything the FBI says past

'good morning' is in a different language. They'll bounce you right back to me. They have bigger things on their minds." She sighed deeply. "You're jousting with windmills, Chief—and one of them will pick you up by the seat of your pants and fling you all the way back to Sundown Beach."

Sierra's eyes slitted. "A child used as a prostitute? Is that a small problem?"

Berenson shook her head. "No, it's a big problem. It's just not *your* problem."

Sierra Bravo leaned forward in her chair. "I'm not getting help anywhere. Is it that I'm female? This isn't some Arab country where I should be veiled from head-to-toe, but I get doors shut in my face whether I wear my badge or not!" She took her badge from her pocket and slammed it on the edge of the desk. "I drove for two hours to talk to you—and I'm damned if you'll run me out of here like some little kid who walked on your lawn!"

Berenson was quiet, looking at the badge more than she did Sierra Bravo. Finally, she said, "Okay—you outrank me. But look where I sit. We have our problems. Gangs get shot on drive-bys—and every so often a toddler under five is killed in a crossfire. Gangs mean drugs. There's plenty of that going around, and those who have no money to buy drugs hold up gas stations or mug people on the street. There's domestic violence. More cops get shot or knifed checking on a man beating his wife than damn near anything else."

She stood up, wandered over to the window, and looked out. "When we were kids," she said quietly, "no armed police officers prowled the halls of our schools in case there's a mass shooting by some crazy shitbag with an arsenal of weapons in his base-ment. Things change. We have burglaries up the kazoo. There's plenty of traffic officers not just to nail speeders or drivers who change lanes without signaling or teenagers texting while trying to steer their cars. Sometimes drunks, out of their minds behind the wheel, or hopped up with God knows what, drive up on crowded sidewalks like fucking maniacs and run over anyone who gets in his way. Yet now we have to have armed cops in schools every day of the year."

Berenson turned and walked back behind the desk, but didn't sit down. "For this division, there's male, female, and tranny hookers on the sidewalks. Illegal gambling, high school kids sending pictures of their naked crotch all over the Internet, Peeping Toms—there's even video cams set up inside toilets in women's restrooms, for crysakes! Live-in boyfriends of unmarried moms have sex with their small kids! Once in a while, some teacher fucks a high school student—usually a female teacher and a hunky sixteen-year-old. There's too damn many rapes every day we have to investigate and try to run down—and to follow up with the victims so they get rape tests, and hope they identify the pond scums by looking at perp shots. We have plenty on our plates in this department." She leaned her hands against the back of her chair. "And when we go home at night to shake off all the shit we've seen, the last thing we want to do is watch one of those *SVU* shows about sex crimes. As for me—I gave my TV set away about two years ago."

"Jesus," Sierra Bravo said softly.

"Sex trafficking is interstate and international," Hermione Berenson said, "which means it's huge! No city cops, not even New York or L.A., can handle organized sex crime that spreads all over the world. That's why the FBI figures us bungling locals should stay the hell out of their way." She resumed her seat, pushing at the files and reports on her desk. "And that suits me fine."

No one spoke for nearly a minute. Sierra was mindlessly playing with a strand of her own hair—one of the bad habits she'd acquired whenever she's nervous or frustrated. "I appreciate what you do," she said at last, "and I understand why the FBI won't bother with me." She bowed her head. "But you're just about my last hope."

Berenson simply looked at Sierra for a long moment, then jotted something down on a notepad, ripped out the paper, and pushed it across the desk.

"There are places I can't go," she said. "and frankly, the FBI doesn't care if you're alive or dead. But here's someone who can give you background, maybe help with what you're trying to do. Good luck, Chief Bravo. I'm damn glad I'm not you."

Sierra felt almost at home in the bed-and-breakfast suite she'd rented in Hemlock Hills, in a neighborhood fairly dripping history—tacky postwar houses were cheek-by-jowl with antique stores and art galleries, stately homes a century old, and plenty of coffee houses. Since it was midweek when there are few tourists, she had the place pretty much to herself. The breakfast promised her for the next morning sounded scrumptious, too.

In her lap was the paper Sergeant Berenson had given her. Henrietta Silver was the name—Sierra had never known anyone named Henrietta—plus a phone number. Sierra feared few things, because cops don't get scared, but she was terrified to make this call. It could be a step toward the end of her personal mission—or it could be the re-awakening of nightmares.

Finally, after some deep breathing, she tapped out a number on her cellphone.

The woman who answered sounded middle-aged, with the faintest remnants of an accent telling Sierra that English was not her first language. She couldn't name it, but she thought it originated in Eastern Europe.

She introduced herself, but when she began to explain why she was calling, she realized that Hermine Berenson had been way ahead of her.

"The sergeant told me you'd call," Henrietta Silver said. "You're one person, not living here. You can't help us, which is a given, and we probably can't help you."

Sierra frowned. "Who is 'we,' Ms. Silver?"

"Didn't Hermine tell you? *'Extant.'* That's our name, or title, or whatever you want to call it. It means *surviving*—and *unde-*

stroyed."

"Can we get together? You pick the time. Is eleven o'clock tomorrow all right? Or make it a bit later and I'll take you to lunch," Sierra said.

Silver's answer was cool, almost chilling. "I don't eat lunch out, Chief Bravo."

Sierra shivered, but bounced back quickly. "Eleven, then. What's the address?"

The woman recited the street name and number, then said, "We're on the second floor. There's a buzzer downstairs. Ring the S.O.S code, if you're old enough to remember it. Long, short, long. Someone will ask your name and buzz you in."

"No name on the door?"

"Don't be an asshole." Henrietta said. "We don't want every pimp and pervert dropping by the office for a chat and a cup of coffee. Why would we put up a sign?"

After Sierra hung up, she stared out the window again. She'd hardly done anything yet, and she'd already stepped on the toes of everyone she's talked to.

Maybe she shouldn't have started this whole business. Maybe she should have blown Walter Lyons off as an over-imaginative kook. Now she'd risked losing a great job for a dubious hunt she figured that, at best, would not end well.

Which old cowboy movie actor said in one of those old Western shoot-em-ups, "A man's gotta do what a man's gotta do?" That was sixty years ago; now *women* gotta do what they gotta do, too—and floundering around far from her home, she was doing what was stuck inside her, scratching away on the inside trying to get out.

She was hungry. She'd served a big breakfast to Chris Fornadel, but skipped lunch. Now her stomach growled. A magazine on the desk recommended local eateries for tourists, and she found a Hungarian restaurant not far from where she was.

What the hell, she thought. Hungarian chicken paprika with a side of dumplings might make her feel better.

CHAPTER SIX

The address was in a Hemlock Hills rust belt section, small businesses broken off from larger firms who'd turned the city into what it was since the industrial revolution. On the first floor, a small company created glass art, having history with a giant of glass manufacturing that had closed down and moved to Mexico fifteen years earlier. Through the window Sierra Bravo could see a receptionist answer phones in a tiny office that had little going for it besides an eye-catching glass sculpture on the wall behind her head. A door on the other side of the room led to the factory.

Next to the entrance of the glass art shop was a heavy steel door, with a push-button doorbell and a discreet speaker system. Sierra followed Hermine Berenson's instructions, buzzed the S.O.S. code, and told the disembodied male voice her name and that she'd been invited, and waited twenty seconds for a return buzz. When she pushed open the door, she was shocked to find it so heavy. It would take a bulldozer to knock it down.

She climbed a flight of uncarpeted steps, bowed in the middle, and reached another unmarked door at the top. It wasn't steel like the one downstairs, but obviously thick and strong, not the kind of door a cop could kick in. A peephole could tell whoever was inside whether the visitor was friend or foe. She knocked, heard three police locks being opened, and then the door swung inward and she was face to face with a huge black man, six foot four and weighing at least three hundred pounds. Two hundred seventy of those pounds were muscle. His jeans, purchased at a Big and Tall shop, were faded and worn, and his unbuttoned dress shirt revealed a gray T-shirt with stylish sketches of tigers across the chest.

"You're Chief of Police Bravo?" he rumbled.

Sierra nodded. "I'm here to see Henrietta Silver."

"Got some ID?"

She showed him her badge.

"That doesn't mean anything. You could've stolen it."

Annoyed, she took out her wallet and flashed her driver's license with a photograph, which he examined carefully. "Follow me, please," he said politely, leading her down a long hallway, closed doors on either side. He stopped, rapped hard on one of them. "Chief Bravo is here for you, Hank."

A muffled response from inside, and he opened the door and stepped aside so Sierra could enter. A small, sparsely furnished office, a weathered desk and file cabinets, and a window looking out on the brick wall of the building next door. The female with short-cropped black hair rose, not smiling, and held out her hand for a shake. Wearing thick coke-bottle glasses, her eyes were watery blue and the rest of her face almost painfully thin. Her khaki pants were wrinkled to go with a plain white shirt, and what could have been a lab coat. Sierra studied her—it's what cops do—and decided she was in her mid-forties.

"Thanks, Tyler," Henrietta Silver said to the black man, who nodded, closing the door as he left. "Have a chair, Chief Bravo."

"I appreciate your seeing me, Ms. Silver."

"Hank. Everyone calls me Hank." She sat down. "After your phone call yesterday, I gave you a lot of thought. I relate to your concern—but I can't get my head around it. Your crime might not have been committed, but you drove halfway across the state on a hunch, and you show up in a city where you barely know how to find the freeway to get back home again. Why, for God's sake?"

"Because I need help."

"We're non-profit. We don't give handouts. We're damn lucky

we pay our electric bill every month."

"I'd never ask for financial help from you."

"I don't know who'd offer you a nickel, even if they had one. You're running up your own ass. This isn't some dumb schmuck sticking up a gas station. It's not a drug gang, or even what you'd call a criminal organization. It's so vast, stretching all over the world, that if you spend every minute of the rest of your life, you won't even scratch the surface." She laughed without mirth. "It's like trying to bail all the water out of the ocean with a little kid's sand pail."

"I can't ignore it."

"I don't ignore it," Hank said, "but when I leave for home at night, sex trafficking is a forgotten memory and everything is hunky-dory." She leaned back in her chair. "So I ask you again, Chief Bravo. Why?"

Sierra was quiet, her forehead wrinkled with a frown. Then: "I don't know. It's a hunch, and that's all I've got. In life, if your back itches, you either scratch it or you go batshit crazy. I'm guessing your back is itching, too, and that's why you're in this office every day."

Hank sat up straight, elbows on the desk, searching for what she might say next. "It's got nothing to do with itching." Her lips almost disappeared as she stared down at her own hands. The muscles at each corner of her jaw jumped. "You want to know why I work here? Okay. From twelve years old until I was twenty-three, I was a prostitute—and it wasn't my choice."

Sierra gasped. There was no reply, no comment to make. "I'm sorry" would have been downright insulting. So she said nothing.

"I'm originally from Budapest," Silver continued. "My mother died when I was born, and my father was a bum who could never get a job. He never had any money and often stole to get it. One morning when I was twelve, he sold me to a known criminal for about three hundred bucks American. My virginity lasted until four o'clock that afternoon. I was raped and beaten every day by three different men for about two weeks, and when every bone in my body ached—when I was broken and robbed of my spirit—I was shipped off to Estonia, sold again to another sex-trafficking outfit that put me to work in a seedy brothel. I worked twelve and sometimes sixteen hours a day, forced to have sex with at least ten men daily, and many more on Saturdays. But beatings got less frequent—only two or three times a week—so I was lucky. And there was another thing, too. They gave me an operation to keep me from getting pregnant—tubal ligation, they call it—so I wouldn't have a period that would force me to take off work every month."

She wasn't looking at her visitor, but staring off into a vast distance no one else could see. Her voice was flat, without feeling or emotion, like an adult reading a fairy tale to a four-year-old who'd heard it too many times before.

"I was sold several more times and always sent off to some other country, most in Eastern Europe, but eventually to Caracas, Venezuela. I was there almost three years—and that was where they got me strung out on crack. That way I could turn all those tricks and never really feel it anymore, not even think about it. Eventually they shipped me off again, this time to California—but I wasn't one of your Statue of Liberty's poor and wretched masses. I was an illegal alien and a working whore. Sacramento is where I wound up, a huge sex-trafficking center. I worked there four years, and I learned English pretty good. Sacramento is the state capital, so mostly I serviced people high up in the government—and those men hanging around the capital all the time who took or received bribes. I was often one of those bribes—vote like I want you to, and you can have a young hooker for the evening—so life was a little easier than in other countries. I was older then and knew how to stay out of trouble—so the beatings only occurred once or twice a month. Almost every weekend, I was sent to a party of some sort—fat men with cheap cigars, bad breath, hairy noses and tiny, mean eyes. They drank lousy booze and snorted too much blow, and this was the one opportunity they'd ever have in their lives to get sexually kinky."

Sierra wanted to say something soothing, to take Hank in her arms and hug her, but sensed she'd prefer not to be touched. Instead, she nodded solemnly.

"Eventually I ran away," Hank continued, "helped by this company I now work for. They couldn't let me stay in Sacramento, or I'd be discovered and killed horribly—even though several girls there needed help." She gritted her teeth. "Some from Eastern Europe, like me, or from Southeast Asia—even a few from Brazil." She suppressed a shudder. "I wanted to work for them—to save other children who've been sold, stolen or kidnapped. I don't have many skills, but I speak four different languages, and I learned everything there is to know about fucking, but that was it. Still, my rescuers paid my way here to Hemlock Hills where there's plenty of sex traffic, mostly kids. And there's *Extant*."

She sat back, took a few deep breaths. Sierra had a million questions she knew would not be answered. At length she asked, "Four languages?"

"Hungarian—I was born knowing that. Then Estonian, with some Russian thrown in, Spanish—and now English." She stopped for a moment, rubbing both eyes and then gently pinching the end of her nose, trying to get herself back together. "I've been here six years now. I'm what they call the day manager."

"Silver is a Hungarian name?"

"No. I changed my name because I didn't want to think about all the years I carried it. I chose Silver—because silver is shiny and pretty, but when it gets old it gets tarnished—like me."

Tarnished. Sierra had to say something. Something. "So you worked here into your forties?"

One corner of Henrietta Silver's lip curled upwards in a vinegar smile. "My forties? I escaped when I was twenty-three. I'm twenty-nine now."

Sierra squeezed tight to keep tears from falling. She had to; chiefs of police don't cry. "Oh—I'm so sorry. I mean—I didn't— oh, shit!" She bowed her head to hide her face.

"Don't knock yourself out," Hank said, her hands tightly inter-twined in her lap, her knuckles white. "Fucking three thousand different guys per year takes a toll on you. I know what I look like—including scars no one can see. I knew it the first time I looked in the mirror after I was sold and every day since."

Sierra had to push herself to a standing position, more shaken than she'd ever been in her life. "I'm so sorry—I had no idea. You'll never know how much respect I have for you, Hank—coming to work at a place like this after..." Her hands were flopping around, making her look silly, and she dropped them to her sides and held them there. "I promise I won't bother you anymore."

"Sit down," Hank said, making it sound more like a command than a suggestion.

"But..."

"I'm not through with you yet. Sit!"

Sierra sat.

"I can't give you much help, but maybe I can open your eyes a little." She crossed her arms over her breasts. "First," she continued, shifting around on her old-fashioned wooden desk chair, "almost every woman who works for organizations as such as this one is like me—a former victim." She gave a staccato chuckle. "Good-hearted rich ladies who want to save the world, and donate money to big-time charities who skim off eighty cents on every donated dollar to raise more money—women who have a manicure and pedicure every week, who spend months organizing a charity banquet to help the people who make a great living off those charities—don't even know that thousands of kids are kidnapped or sold every single day, all over the world. Most wind up peddling their bodies until they're too old or worn out and nobody wants them anymore. Then they're re-sold as work slaves where they make three bucks a day cooking, cleaning and ironing, get Sunday mornings off to go to church, and have to sleep in somebody's cellar or broom closet. Affluent Europe or Middle East countries are into this, but there are a lot of them in upscale American neighborhoods like here in California. Other kids work in factories that deduct their food and lodgings from their pay, so they end up with nothing. And then there are kids—probably not children anymore, who are no use to anyone—and they somehow disappear, never to be seen again. The only ones who know about that shit have been there, done it, got the T-shirt. You get what I'm saying?"

"I—do. Sure. But how can you stop it?"

"How can you stop illegal drugs?" Hank said. "Busting some punk with his pants down around his hips, showing his bikini underpants and peddling crack on the street in downtown Dallas? You can't, because there are drug lords and drug armies sending mules all over the world on airplanes with two pounds of heroin shoved up their ass. That's why you can't stop sex trafficking, either."

"Why not?"

"Royalty—bazillionaires. The top-level politicians—all make big bucks by selling or renting kids to perverts, and their overhead cost is next to nothing." She took a deep breath, and her shrug was massive. "If a cop nails some street filth for stealing a kid is a dandy idea—but it won't even ripple the water."

"Isn't that what you do, Hank? Try to save kidnapped children?"

Hank nodded. "It's *all* we do. We can't arrest anyone for doing it if it happened right under our noses. There are laws. Police follow them because they have to."

"I'm not following any law," Sierra said. "I'm here as a private citizen."

"Then why show your badge and identify your position when you came to see me?"

"Because you wouldn't have met with me otherwise."

Hank processed that. "True," she said. Sierra pushed her hair away from one ear, flushing as she realized it was a habit she'd never knew she had. "Why don't local police get involved? Why doesn't the FBI?"

Hank's fingernails tapped out "Kitten on the Keys" silently on her desktop. Then she stood up, opened the door and called, "Tyler? I need you."

Momentarily, the hefty black man who'd greeted Sierra appeared, looking quickly from one woman to the other. "What do you need, Hank?"

"Our guest wonders why the FBI aren't as interested as we are. Oh, you haven't been formally introduced. Sierra Bravo, Chief of Police in Sundown Beach, California—meet recently retired Hemlock Hills police detective sergeant, Tyler Calhoun."

Calhoun nodded, his facial expression more puzzled than annoyed. "Chief," he said.

"You can explain this better than I could, Tyler," Silver said.

Calhoun consulted his wristwatch. "I could," he said, "but I have an appointment in about an hour, so I'm just running out for lunch."

"May I join you, then?" Sierra suggested. "Lunch is on me."

The big man frowned. "You can come if you want, but we go Dutch around here at lunch. Otherwise, no dice."

They walked down the stairs, turned right, and sauntered for about a block and a half to a small coffee shop—not a "chain restaurant," but a mom-and-pop joint with aged red booths and red-and-white tablecloths that had seen yeoman service for many years.

The waitress, in her sixties and wearing a uniform that went out of style during the Lyndon B. Johnson administration, came over with menus and a big smile.

"Hey, Ty," she said, "I missed you. You haven't been in here for a couple of days." She turned to Sierra. "Welcome to Don's Diner," she said.

"I think," Tyler Calhoun rumbled, "the lady needs to study the menu."

"Take your time," Gladys said, "I've got all day," and bounced away.

"Everything's good," Tyler said. "But it's not the Four Seasons."

"From what I get paid," Sierra told him, "I can only afford the first two Seasons—and that's on a good day. Why aren't you a cop anymore?"

"Order first," he said.

When Gladys finally served them their lunches, he decided to talk.

"I don't know how much this means to you, but on the job, six years ago, three little girls in town disappeared within six months. We had no idea if they'd run away, were alive or dead, or maybe kidnapped. We didn't know if there was a serial pedophile walking around—and we did run an investigation. A year before, we'd arrested a family pimping out their underage little girl. That was local, in a lousy neighborhood where the parents were desperate for crack money. Otherwise, there wasn't a single lead."

He took a sip of his coffee. "We knew there was international sex trafficking, even back then. We're a relatively small depart-ment, though we're bigger than yours. There's no way to put on a high-press search for criminal empires importing stolen children through Hemlock Hills. The police don't have the personnel—the numbers."

Sierra poked at her salad, not planning to eat it. "The FBI is different," she said. "I lucked out getting a meeting with them—but they didn't seem that interested, either."

Tyler nodded. "Doesn't surprise me. Here's the thing. The FBI has a unit chasing sex-trafficking outfits with feelers all over the world, even in places you never heard of. What they don't have is the time, money or interest finding one little girl. Fibs are totally involved with terrorism, which scares the crap out Americans. Every law enforcement shop worries about terrorists." He took a bite of his sandwich. "When you get on a plane, you have to take off your shoes at the airport, open your carry-on luggage, and go through an X-ray machine holding your hands up like a criminal who got caught in the act, and if you're not one of the lucky ones, you get pulled out of line and groped. They don't suspect you as a pedo or a scam artist, Chief. They're looking for a stick of dynamite up your ass or a box-cutter in your pocket. So if you had a bead on an international sex-trafficking mob and you want to share it, the FBI will be your best friend. If you think maybe, just maybe, one child *might* be peddling her ass and hating every minute of it, they'll tell you goodbye—and they won't call back, either."

Sierra pushed her salad plate away from her. "But Extant, and the other non-profit rescue outfits—what are you doing, then? You say you're here to help kids..."

"People of all ages."

"How do you do that? They don't come walking in the door, do they?"

"Tips," Tyler said quietly. "Street informants."

"You mean you pay them like the regular police do?"

He shook his head. "We do sometimes—when we have the money. Mostly, we notice when kids disappear."

"And you know where to look for them?"

"We've been at it a long time," he snapped, obviously irritated. "We didn't just fall off the turnip truck."

"Then tell *me* where to look, and I'll take care of it on my own."

He laughed aloud. "You'd last about seven minutes before someone blew you away."

"I can take care of myself!"

"Great to hear. Got an AR-15 or a bazooka? Otherwise, you're in trouble. I know you're good—but read the manual! Police officers don't put themselves in extreme danger without a back-up."

"You can't be my back-up, Tyler?"

"I'm not a law officer anymore."

She leaned against the booth, the leatherette seats making the backs of her thighs stick to her slacks. "Why did you turn in your badge?"

"Same reason I'm telling you. Innocents forced into sex slavery—and other kinds of slavery, too—and not enough done about it by the local cops."

"So what do I do? Go back to Sundown Beach and forget about it."

Tyler nodded. "That'd be my first suggestion."

"What if I can't forget?"

"Then you're fucked."

A gasp would have felt terrific to Sierra, but instead she merely hiccupped. Finally, Tyler caught the eye of the waitress, who brought two checks. He studied them, then passed one across the table to Sierra. "You want a doggie bag for that salad?"

"Put salad in a bag and drive all the way back to Sundown Beach? Don't think so." She took twelve dollars from her purse and set it atop her check. "Tyler, if you can't stand with me, if you can't watch my back—I understand. I get that. Do me one thing, though."

"Which is?"

"Put me together with some of your squealers."

"What?" His single loud, boisterous word boomed across the diner, and a few heads turned to look at him. Then he whispered, "Squealers get paid for what they do, or they squeal to save their own asses from a long prison stint. Squealers? That's a shitty thing to call people rescuing stolen and kidnapped children from sex slavery!"

"I didn't mean it like that," she professed. "I'll be cautious. I promise."

"You can get yourself killed that way. You could get *them* killed, too."

"Just get me a meeting, that's all I ask."

Tyler clasped his hands on the edge of the table in front of him like a six-year-old in grammar school and stared at them. "It's not that easy. If I tell them you're a cop, they might not want anything to do with you."

"I have no jurisdiction in Hemlock Hills."

"Still." He sighed, then fished his cellphone from his pocket and pushed it toward her on the table. "Put your cell number on my phone so I can get in touch with you twenty-four/seven."

Sierra took out her own phone. "When do you think you'll call me?"

Tyler's voice was cutting, cold. "You think I browbeat informers every day to talk to police chiefs? I'll call you when I call you."

"I'm hoping," Sierra replied, her tone also frosty, "you'll contact me before I have to go back to Sundown Beach."

Tyler stood, tossing some money onto his side of the table. "Just take a deep breath, then," he suggested, "and hold it till you hear from me."

CHAPTER SEVEN

At ten o'clock that night there was a chill snap to the breeze, swooping down from Western Canada. Usually, the frigid Canadian air mass would head east to the plains and the Great Lakes. Only there they call them Alberta Clippers. Sierra Bravo, strolling through the darkness, illuminated only by the moon and by the lights beyond in the city, wondered not for the first time what she was doing here by a river, the road beside it several steps down from the street. She was armed, but nobody would have spotted her as a cop.

A bright red Ford Focus drove by slowly, gleaming and shiny as though it had been washed that day. It stopped. The passenger-side front window rolled down, and the driver leaned over, his jowly face filling the space, red nose glowing with the announcement to the world that he drank too much. Middle-aged, he sported a San Francisco 49ers jacket and a cap to match. "Hey, cupcake," he called out to Sierra. "Need a ride?"

Sierra's glare of contempt would have chased away most people, but it didn't scare the Focus guy one bit. She kept walking, and the car moved ahead with her. "Come on, baby girl, I got that seven-year itch. And I'll make you happy, too. Trust me." He chuckled, leaning closer to the window. "I'm hung like a horse."

"Then go find another horse to fuck."

"Hmm. Tough broad, huh? That's okay, I like playing rough."

"Fuck off, creep."

His tone turned aggressive. "Don't give me any shit. Nobody wants a bitch."

Sierra felt her breath coming faster as she thought about grabbing his head, pulling it out through the window so he couldn't move, then beating his face in. She could do it. Almost every police officer, male or female, is tough to fight—because they all know how *not* to fight fair.

"I'll make it worth your while, sweet cheeks," the driver said. "I got fifty bucks burning a hole in my pocket."

Sierra gritted her teeth. He wasn't just an asshole—he was a *cheap* asshole! "Want to see what's burning a hole in *my* pocket?" she snapped, and took her police badge out from under her jacket and flashed it at him, watching his eyes widen in fear. "Take a hike, buddy. Go home to your wife. If I see you cruising again, soliciting women on the sidewalk, by the time you get out of jail, you'll be too *old* to fuck. Move!"

He almost leaped away from the window, as if he'd touched something hideous and decayed, and grasped the steering wheel as the Focus roared off, turning on two tires at the first corner. Sierra jammed her badge back into her pocket. The john had either been too far away to recognize that she was no young street girl, or too dumb to know her out-of-town badge didn't carry much weight in Hemlock Hills. Not much.

Her jacket reached below her hips to hide the weapon she wore—alone, in a downtown neighborhood in the middle of the night. At least she no longer lived in movie days of the Old West when the one who drew and fired his gun the fastest was always the winner. Whoever she might meet on this chilly night wouldn't be The Fastest Gun in the West either.

Turning a corner, she wondered why anyone would be in this industrial neighborhood after dark. She tried not looking over her shoulder for what might appear out of the shadows. She'd never felt in peril while doing her job. Small municipalities were relatively safe—but Hemlock Hills was big enough to look scary.

There were local citizens, she knew, who could kill her as easily as looking at her.

Seeing movement out of the corner of one eye, she turned as a man approached her from the street, slowly, hands in pockets, the gray hoodie nearly covering his face. He was much past half a century old, with a lined, haggard mien and tired shoulders. His scuffed work boots made too much noise on the sidewalk.

Five paces from her he stopped, studying her from head to toe—but it wasn't the sexist approach too many men had—that faux-entitled power attitude like he owned the situation just because he had a few bucks to spare. This man's back was rigid, his knees slightly bent as if he might break and run at the smallest provocation. Another prospective perv? Or the man she'd been told would contact her?

Finally, he said, "I'm Stefan."

"Bravo," she answered. "Sierra Bravo." Neither of them offered to shake hands.

His posture relaxed slightly. "Tyler said you want talk with me."

She nodded. "Why do we meet here? Why not in a coffee shop with people around?"

"*People*, like you call them, only come down here for bad shit—drugs, whores, guns. They don't bother us, we don't bother them. But we don't need police to see us together." He crinkled his nose as if he smelled something awful.

"Tyler said you might be able to help me."

"Maybe yes, maybe no."

Sierra tried not being irritated. "I'm looking for a little girl—ten or eleven years old."

"You don't know how old she is?" The accent hinted Eastern European.

"I don't even know her name. I never saw her."

Stefan snorted, turning away. "You imagine this shit? Drag me out at night and don't know what you talk about? You waste my time, woman."

"Wait, please! Let me explain."

He looked furious, but eventually, he nodded. "Okay—you got two minutes."

Then Sierra told him the story.

He didn't answer her for a while, his sad, angry glare sweeping the deserted street a few blocks from the downtown business district. Then he stared her hard in the eye. "Why you come here?"

"Hemlock Hills is busy with sex trafficking. I thought I might get some sort of hint."

"You a cop," Stefan said. "No little hints can help you a goddamn bit."

"I had to do something."

He looked out at the river. In Southern California, as opposed to many other states in the middle of the country, there's never much of a river, as most of them dry up during the summer and never have running water until February. "A week ago, this little girl goes to a movie. Today?" He shrugged. "She could be in Kiev by now, or someplace worse. You climb a mountain to nowhere, lady."

"Tyler told me you were the one to talk to," Sierra protested. "You help children who've been forced into slavery or prostitution."

Stefan barely nodded. "When I know about them. When I find them."

"Here in Hemlock Hills?"

"Mostly."

"What brought you here in the first place?"

He spun around to face her, rage twisting his mouth. "None of your fucking business!" he roared. "Too many questions!"

"Asking questions," Sierra said quietly, "is my job."

"Ask someplace else!" Stefan turned and stomped away, up the steps to the street. Then he stopped, one hand grasping the side of the industrial building, gulping air as he tried to get control of himself. Then he retraced his steps until he was in front of her again.

He took a deep breath. "I'm from Estonia. I do building. Construction."

"Yes?"

"I did that. Had a family. Went to church." Stefan closed his eyes. "My daughter—Anya—thirteen years old when she disappeared. Went to school that day and never come back no more. Nobody knew why. I went to cops, they tell me wait awhile and she come back home." He shook his head. "That was sixteen year ago."

"I'm so sorry," Sierra said.

"So I ask around. I find out kids—boys and girls both—they get kidnapped, nobody knows where they are, and they get taken out of country—how you say it? Snuggled?"

"Smuggled. With an M."

"They could be anywhere in world. I ask around—even to Interpol. They say big slavery ring in America. Houston, Miami, Atlanta—*Hemlock Hills,* for cry sakes!"

"So you came to Hemlock Hills?"

He nodded. "After four years waiting. Never found Anya, but I met people who—look for missing kids. They find and send back to family—when they can."

"What happens to people who had the kids and were trying to sell them?"

Stefan stared quietly at Sierra, eyes glittering like two obsidian stones. He didn't blink.

Sierra said, "I see."

"You see. Good."

"Can you put me together with these people, Stefan?"

"They not talk to you. They not talk to cop."

"I'm on their side."

"Their side?" Stefan rubbed his hand all over his face, obviously in frustration. "If they do things not on your side, you put in jail, yes?"

Sierra thoughtfully ground her teeth together for a moment before she said, "No, I won't."

***

It took her half an hour to pack. The return drive from Hemlock Hills to Sundown Beach spread out over several hours because Sierra had to leave the freeway three times to close her eyes for a few minutes and then get hot black coffee to keep her awake. She didn't arrive back at her condo until after three in the morning—but despite nodding off on the road, she couldn't fall asleep in her own bed. Her trip had been a frustrating waste, learning nothing to help her find the young girl from the movie cineplex men's room.

Haunted by Stefan's missing daughter, Anya, kidnapped as a young teen, Sierra did the math in her head. The child would be nearly thirty years old now. Was she forced into degrading prostitution or some other type of slavery? Was she somewhere in the United States? Was she still breathing? Her unknown fate had completely destroyed the life of her father; now Stefan patrols the shadows of nighttime, his eyes empty as a snake's.

Everyone had heart-rending secrets turning them into what they eventually became. Often police find out. Good people, bad people, sad, broken people. Heroes or villains—all with skeletons in the closet. Her secret—the one she never spoke about to anyone—was what made her become a cop.

She had trouble closing her eyes despite the late hour, and she switched on the TV to an old Joel McCrea Western, sheriffs and outlaws banging away at each other. Not fond of movie violence, there were few cowboy films she liked, and this wasn't one of them. Though she'd been a police officer most of her adult life, she'd never fired a gun at another human being.

Eventually she drifted off to sleep, the repetitious movie gunshots like a soothing lullaby.

The alarm woke her at 6:30, as usual, and she calculated she'd only slept for two and a half hours and would be in one hell of a mood when she arrived at work.

A cold shower didn't help, and a hot shower afterwards just

made her more jumpy.

She didn't feel like breakfast, but finally stopped at a Dunkin' Donuts, ordering an extra-large coffee to go, gulping it down, hot, during the three minutes it took her to get to police headquarters, where Nancy Flower welcomed her as if she'd been gone several years. All the other officers came by her office to say they were glad she was back.

She stared glumly at the pile of paperwork that had accumulated on her desktop while she was gone. Sergeant Parrish appeared in her doorway.

"The prodigal daughter returns," he said.

"Thanks for holding the fort down, Griff."

His shoulders lifted and fell as he pointed to her desk. "I stacked up all the crap you'll need to read. Makes me glad you're the chief here and not me."

"Anything on the top of the list?"

"Three domestic violence cases," he said. "One perp is a well-known local character in this town. It'll depress you, but it's all in a file on your desk, along with a medical report that his wife has a broken nose and two knocked-out front teeth."

"God," she said.

"We busted a burglary just off the beach—exciting because the neighbor across the street saw the guy trying to break into a garage, called us, and then marched in there with a shotgun to make sure the burglar didn't get away. There was usual traffic stuff, including two BMV lawbreakers staggering out of that sleazy saloon downtown—a well-to-do, well-dressed couple, both being married to other people, driving expensive cars. I won't repeat some of the obscene names the female called me."

Sierra grinned. "Why the fuck not?"

He said, "Most people we bust here don't live here. They're from somewhere else, but come to Sundown Beach to commit their crimes."

"I know. Why do they do that?"

"Because Sundowners have money. It'd be silly to rob someone who's poorer than you are." He lowered his voice, now grave. "Learn anything worthwhile in Hemlock Hills?"

The anvil that had pressed down on her returned to Sierra's shoulders, and she found it difficult to answer. Finally, she managed to say, "Stuff that'll haunt me for the rest of my life—but none of it directly about the little girl I'm looking for."

"Forget it. There's a big job to do here."

"I'll do the job," she said, "but I won't forget." She rotated her shoulders to get the kinks out, and pulled the stack of papers toward her. "What do I look at first?"

At lunchtime she went home, changed into her uniform, and ate a tablespoon of peanut butter before driving back to the station. By mid-afternoon, she was halfway through her files when Nancy Flower tapped on her open door. "You have company, Chief."

"How many guesses do I get, Nancy?" Sierra put her elbow on the desk, supporting her face with her hand. "Shit on a stick!"

"Didn't you hear her Cadillac just now, blasting into the parking lot?"

"If a Cadillac became illegal for real estate agents to drive," she mumbled, "the brand would go out of business like the Gremlin and the Ford Edsel. Can't you tell her I went to Hemlock Hills and won't ever come back?"

"I answer most of her four-times-daily phone calls and try to soothe her—all for you. So I either need two weeks off with pay to drink myself silly on Two-Buck Chuck wine and watch lousy daytime TV—or you can sit with her and work things out."

"Is there a back door so I can escape?"

"From her, maybe," Nancy Flower said. "Not from me."

Sierra rubbed her eyes. "All right, Nancy—send her in, and after ten minutes, you rush in to tell me the entire U.S. Congress has been assassinated."

"Just the Republicans."

Sierra laughed. "That'll get her out of here if nothing else will."

Counting to sixty, for the hell of it, she had to stop at forty-two seconds when Danielle Tokes barged into her office like a SWAT team leader with a warrant. "Where in hell have you *been?*" Tokes thundered.

"Is that what you asked your ex-husband when he was ten minutes late for dinner?"

"Don't you sass me!"

"Sass you? Really?"

"Say your piece," Tokes snarled, "but I demand Dylan Zack's citation torn up and thrown away before I leave this office—before he has to appear in court."

"Destroying a citation is against the law—and just so you know, demanding makes a police chief very testy. As for Dylan's court appearance, take it up with the judge. It's out of my hands."

"You know damn well police rip up citations if someone important asks them to."

"Once written, it's illegal to tear up a citation. I don't, nor does any other cop in Sundown Beach—not while I wear the chief's badge."

Danielle Tokes screwed up her mouth the way Shirley Temple did in those 1930s movies when she was angry. "Do you want to keep wearing that badge? I'm on the city council, which determines whether or not to keep you or terminate you."

"Ah," Sierra breathed. "Now that *is* interesting. Want to know why?"

Tokes squinted her eyes but said nothing.

"You're now threatening a police officer—a police chief—because she won't break a *law.* That's a hell of a lot more criminal than anything Dylan Zack might have done. So I can legally slam your ass into a cell this minute, and you'll sit there for a few days until your lawyer can scare up the bail and present it to a judge—and Ken Zack can phone me until his skin turns green, but he can't do a goddamn thing about it." Sierra stood, walked around the side of her desk and loomed over Danielle Tokes. "It's your choice. I can have three policemen escort you to jail and make you comfortable—they'll have to take your belt and your nylons so you don't hang yourself in a cell—or you can get your fucking ass out of my office!" She retreated a few steps. "I await your decision with bated breath."

Danielle's white knuckles clutched the arms of her chair as if she were going down for the last time on the Titanic, her eyes narrowed with hatred. She hauled herself to her feet. "We aren't done," she whispered.

"Be careful, kiddo," Sierra said, "that cell is empty and waiting for you."

"Don't call me kiddo!"

"I will until you call me Chief, or by my name, which you've obviously forgotten. Whatever I do or don't do, you will treat me with the respect according to my rank! Now either get the hell out of this precinct, or strip off your nylons and hand them to the cop who'll lock you up."

Danielle Tokes opened her mouth to speak.

"Not one more word!" the Chief of Police barked. "Not *one!*"

Danielle's face turned bleached white, and Sierra actually heard her teeth grinding together. When she stalked off in a boiling rage, Sierra ran the whole meeting over again in her mind, a smile tickling the corners of her lips. She even heard the Cadillac lay down rubber in the parking lot when it blasted away.

Tough. She knew she'd been tough—but that's what cops get paid to do. Now, she thought, she could just as easily get tough in Hemlock Hills when she made her next visit.

Sierra Bravo was surprised when Chris Fornadel knocked on her door at seven thirty the next morning. She'd been awake for two hours, was completely dressed for work, though shoeless, and no makeup, which in other situations might have been embarrassing. Chris had a pretty wife, a gorgeous girlfriend, and who knows how many other women on the side—so she didn't care if he saw her without makeup. Romance with married men seemed as impossible to her as swallowing live goldfish.

"Did we have another pancake breakfast scheduled?" she said while he was still in the doorway. "I haven't whipped up any champagne cocktails yet, either."

"No, Sierra. It's important."

She stepped aside so he could enter. "You mean my X-rays came back positive?"

"Don't joke! This is serious." Wearing one of his many gray pinstriped suits and a lawyerly necktie, he eased into the overstuffed chair Sierra usually sat in to watch TV, and cocked one leg over the other, his socks almost up to his knee. "What have you heard?"

"That I'm moments away from what Scrooge told Bob Cratchit—in danger of losing my situation."

"Danielle isn't kidding, Sierra. You rubbed her the wrong way once too often."

"She demands I do something against the law? *Demands*?" She took her gun and holster from the front closet and strapped it around her waist and her left shoulder.

"Are you going to shoot me?"

"Not right this minute. Maybe after lunch."

"You threatened to throw her in jail."

"I did, and was within the law to do so."

He looked around. "You have coffee?"

"No," Sierra said, "I had the entire Los Angeles football team in here for a gang-bang last night, and they drank it all up."

"No coffee? Then what am I doing here?"

"I was wondering that myself."

"Look, Sierra—I'm the city manager. I hired you—but I had to get approval from the city council before making it official."

"Two thirds of the council."

"That two-thirds could also fire your ass, and I won't have a damn thing to say about it."

Sierra perched on the arm of her sofa. "That's horseshit, Chris, and you know it."

"Maybe. But if it's two thirds of the council, it's a done deal."

He changed crossed legs. "It'd smooth things over if you called Tokes to apologize."

"Even if I tore up Dylan's ticket, my apology wouldn't be worth a silent fart. And while we're on the subject—what's the deal with Tokes? I'm a problem to her because I'm prettier than she is?"

"Amen to that!"

"But why a hissy fit over this Zack kid? He's not going to jail for speeding and being slightly stoned. Maybe, at worst, six months' restricted driving—which is up to the judge, not me. But why does she act like it's *her* kid and I've sentenced him to the guillotine?"

"She's close to Ken Zack," Chris explained.

"I wondered about that. Is she his mistress?"

"Mistress?" He laughed. "Who uses that expression anymore?"

"Okay," Sierra said, "his main squeeze. His 'old lady.' His friends-with-benefits fuck. Is that better?"

"Sadly, no. He's been a widower for several years, and I've never really seen him with another woman."

"Fine—but what does that have to do with Danielle Tokes?"

"She's a great help when he wants to buy or sell a property locally. She's fantastic at sales, and she gets him the price he's asking for. In return, if anyone around here is looking for a house—naturally his very rich friends—he sends them to Danielle."

"Figures."

"She's also big on benefit circles, like the Hunger Network, the Diabetes Association—things like that. But her main thing is making money for herself—in real estate." Chris Fornadel's smile was crooked. "Ken Zack introduced me to Danielle when I was looking for a new house—and she got me one, too."

"Does she give Ken a kickback for sending her customers?"

He laughed again. "He's super-rich. To him, a kickback is like you or me finding a five-dollar bill in the street."

"I'm wondering, though, why he doesn't call me himself and

plead for his son—not that it'd do any good. Why send Tokes to do his dirty work for him?"

"Zack keeps his own skirts completely clean. His reputation is important to him."

"Reputations are important to all of us," Sierra said.

Chris shrugged. "We Sundown Beach leaders are required to behave ourselves to keep that reputation pristine and saintly."

"And Ken Zack?"

"Zack's money is widely spent buying his reputation."

Sierra shook her head, but her loose hair wouldn't fall naturally the way she wanted it to. "There's not enough money in the world to get his kid's citation torn to pieces."

"An apology would take care of it."

Her eyes narrowed. "You mean my breaking the law would take care of it."

"It's not that big a deal. Dylan's just a kid—and kids make mistakes."

"For crysakes, Chris, he won't be sent to prison!"

"He won't even go to court, Sierra, if you get canned within the next few days and they put in an interim chief who looks at things their way and destroys that citation."

"It's that important? This is supposed to be a nice, neat, angelic little city—not the kind of place one can bribe the police department—or threaten it."

"As I said, I'll be in your corner if need be."

"If the word gets out that I canceled a citation, I'd never get another chief's job anywhere. Fuck them! As long as I wear this shield, Chris, this is *my* town!" Sierra stood up and straightened her slacks. "Time for me to get to work—but as always, talking to you is like a day at the beach."

Chris Fornadel rose, too, and moved toward the door, then stopped. "Hey—before you slap on your war paint, how did your Hemlock Hills trip go?"

That took Sierra aback. A multi-tasker, she'd put the Hemlock Hills adventure out of her mind while speaking to Chris about the

Dylan Zack situation. "It was okay. Hardly the information I was looking for."

"It's too bad—but you should've been here doing your job."

"If you think I'll stop and forget about this, you're out of your mind."

Chris groaned. "You're walking on eggshells already. Don't make it worse."

"I'll let you know." Sierra headed toward the bathroom. "Meanwhile, I can't be late for work." She didn't even stop moving as she said, "Just let yourself out."

CHAPTER EIGHT

Applying her makeup, Sierra Bravo tried convincing herself she wasn't angry, but failed. Her heart hammered, and she was breathing too heavily for an ordinary morning. Carelessly, she slashed on her lipstick, making her resemble a sated zombie. One look in the mirror made her bitter, so she wiped it off, then reapplied it more carefully. Fornadel had warned she'd be stabbed in the back.

Her reflection stared back at her as she blotted her lips for the second time—a look both defiant and overwrought. Was this what it was like to be a chief of police? If she put one toe over the line, if she refused ass-kissing city council members, if she followed a non-case that gnawed at her liver, would she be totally alone and vulnerable? Nervous tightness in her chest rumbled at her to quit and go somewhere else. Where, though, could she continue her present career? Follow a different path? Become a business executive? Boring. Sales manager? Obnoxious. Insurance? Ghastly, and probably crooked to begin with. Be a cop somewhere else? Unlikely, as trouble invariably found her.

There's always becoming a private investigator, she thought grimly, but she was too young to spend the rest of her life going through records in a city hall basement, or spying on someone's cheating spouse from a dark car parked halfway down the street.

Could she leave her two good friends in the police department, Griff Parrish and Nancy Flower, and the rest of her cops, who'd been quietly defiant when handed a female chief and eventually came around to like and respect her? Sierra shivered.

Anyone who'd escaped a dysfunctional family growing up couldn't have many good friends Betrayed by those closest to them during childhood, one would find it impossible to trust anyone, ever again—and trust, to Sierra, was a word in some foreign language.

Therefore, she couldn't believe the man who'd steered a little girl into a crowded men's room at a movie theater did so without malice aforethought.

She decided to comb out her hair, then twisted it into a more casual bun, moved a few steps back to get the full effect, then put on her shoes and headed out for her job.

A long work shift—endless, or it seemed so to Sierra. The most unusual request that day was a from the Chamber of Commerce to give a talk at their monthly luncheon, three weeks hence. Usually talks like that were planned months in advance, so someone else had been scheduled, then canceled, and she was the last-minute replacement choice—or maybe even the third or fourth choice. It irritated her. She enjoyed talking to a few people at a time; giving a formal speech to a suit-and-tie business group gave her the fantods.

"It comes with the territory, Chief," Griff told her. "You still don't get it you're a pretty important person in our town."

"Ken Zack and Danielle Tokes are Chamber of Commerce members, and will be there? Talk about awkward!"

"Shake it off! By that time, Dylan would have been to court, the judge will do what it is judges do, and it'll be over."

"Either way, Tokes won't forgive and forget."

"You don't know that," Griff said.

"I know women. Danielle's last dying thought would be that I burn at the stake. That love thy neighbor business ends when the annual income passes two hundred K."

"True. But you're this town's top cop. Gazillionaires, ship owners and waitresses at the Dolphin Lounge and guys who cut grass in the public square all summer look up to you like you're Wonder Woman. If Dylan Zack goes to court, fine—but you have to be nice to everyone else who's nice."

"Is that a police chief's job? To be nice all the time?"

"Not to lawbreakers," Griffin said. "Feel better about life. I know you're upset about this movie incident—"

"I'm putting it behind me. I have to. I have nowhere else to go." Sierra tried not looking sad. "Even the best people fall on their asses. This was one of my times."

She thought about the Chamber of Commerce for several minutes before calling them back to accept their invitation, and spent the rest of the afternoon mulling over what she'd say when she stood behind that lectern.

She didn't want to offend the businesspeople in Sundown Beach, though she often disagreed with them and their ways. Perhaps she should have stayed in a lower-middle class California town and its Saturday night fights, robberies and domestic problems she could deal with. She was more comfortable with down-and-outers.

More comfortable than hearing about guys taking pre-teen girls into a men's john.

Stop! she told herself. She was helpless—a word she despised—and there was no point going ballistic over what might not even be a crime at all.

She locked up the files she'd been poring over all day, straightened out the top of her desk—her efforts to be orderly and keep everything neat was not something she was good at— said goodnight to everyone, and headed out to the parking lot.

Chet Quigley was leaning against the fender of his car, wearing a corduroy jacket with suede elbow patches, Dockers, and a white shirt and tie. "I worked late today," he said. "I was just driving by and saw your car still here, so I stopped to say hello."

Sierra was too stunned to answer for a moment. Should she be angry? Stern? Warn him that, when all is said and done, this is a police station? Should she let her sarcasm boil over, like a pot being heated for cooking spaghetti.

She decided on a simple "Hello."

"Good seeing you again."

"I'm not sure where you live, Mr. Quigley," Sierra Bravo said, "but I'm guessing you normally don't pass by the police station."

Chet Quigley grinned. "I get lost sometimes. And you agreed to call me Chet."

"Chet," she said, pronouncing his first name carefully, "are you stalking me?"

"Stalkers hide in the dark—but here I am, in daylight. I waited for ten minutes, by the way—and two of your officers came out to get in their own cars and said hello to me. Nice cops."

"I only hire nice cops. What are you doing here?"

"Truthfully? I came by to ask if you'd like to have dinner with me tonight."

Sierra felt the blood rushing to her face, and she coughed into her hand, trying to hide it. Eventually she said, "I—don't date very much."

"We won't pick out furniture together. It's just dinner."

"Look, Mr.—uh—Chet, I have a lot to do tonight."

"I won't ask you to fix a parking ticket or arrest my next-door neighbor for using his leaf blower on a Sunday morning. You have to eat, don't you? I figured dinner at the Dolphin. I wasn't planning on flying you to Paris for a meal."

She laughed in spite of herself. "You picked the wrong profession, Chet. You should've been a lawyer."

"Does that mean I win my case?"

She pondered. He was nerdy-cute, with a sense of humor. He probably was attracted to her, too—well of *course* he was attracted to her, or he wouldn't be asking for a date—and he was indeed correct. She did have to eat.

"I'm not going out to dinner dressed like this," she said. "I'll go home and change."

"I'll come with you," he said, "and then we can drive there together."

"Come with me, my ass! I'll meet you at the Dolphin in—" she checked her watch. "Give me forty-five minutes."

"You're tough, Chief Bravo," he smiled.

"Being tough is my job, Mr. Assistant Principal."

It was even tougher for her to pick out an outfit for the evening—the first real date she'd had since coming to work in Sundown Beach. The little black dress—everyone had a little black dress—was relatively sexy but a bit too formal for a waterfront eatery like the Dolphin. She tried and discarded several other outfits, eventually settling for a long-sleeved blue blouse that matched the color of her eyes, and an upscale version of khaki Dockers.

She couldn't help noticing that every man in the Dolphin looked at her admiringly when she walked in. As for Chet Quigley, the arrow of lust had pierced his heart—as if he'd been lost in the Mojave desert for a month and she was a tall, cool drink of water.

Sierra sipped her wine as she studied the menu, though she could barely keep her eyes off the exquisite sunset over the Pacific.

"How come you were named Sierra?" Chet asked. "I think it's a Spanish word. It means mountain. Originally, it meant saw," and he mimed the teeth of a saw with his finger, "because when you look at a range of mountains, the pointed tops of the mountains make it resemble a saw. You don't look much like a mountain, though—or a saw, either."

"Sierra is Spanish. Bravo is Italian."

He put his hand over hers. "One more thing making you fascinating."

She tried not sounding annoyed. "What's so damn fascinating?"

"First of all, you're beautiful."

She moved her hand out from under his own, trying not to make him feel bad. "Give me a break, Chet, I'm forty-two years old. 'Beautiful' is a sunset, a five-year-old kid, an Arabian stallion, a flower. I'm just—okay-looking."

"Don't kid yourself," Chet said. "Black hair and blue eyes is always amazing. You're tall, graceful, slim, well-built—oh, damn, that was sexual harassment, wasn't it?"

"Yes, but I can't arrest you for it."

"Still, there's much more to you than your looks."

"You don't even know me," Sierra warned him.

"I'm impressed you're a police chief—not a broken-down art teacher like me."

"Vice principal," she reminded him. "And you don't look broken-down, either. How old are you, anyway?"

"Forty-five next month, but I'm no tough guy."

"I've got tough guys all over the place," she said, "in the jail cells and out of them." She tasted her wine again. "I'm not into relationships, Chet. Sorry, that's how it goes. And I'm sure as hell not into one-night stands, either."

"This is just dinner. I spent all day today interfacing with twelve-and thirteen-year- olds—and I had a yearning to talk to a grown-up for a while. Besides," he said, "you're prettier to look at."

"You can flatter better than that." Sierra cocked her head. "Ever been married?"

Chet nodded. "A long time past. It lasted exactly nineteen months and three days. That was eighteen years ago." He leaned forward slightly. "What about you?"

"Nope. I'm a middle-aged spinster." Her staccato laugh was loud. "I don't think I've heard that word in thirty years. Well, I am middle-aged, but hardly an old maid."

"Congratulations."

"Even the best relationships are—difficult. It's easier to skip them altogether. I have enough trouble being a cop."

"So you don't have children?" Chet asked.

"Single mother? Nowhere near."

"Never thought about having kids?"

"Every woman thinks about kids when the time clock ticks—

but years ago I stopped winding mine. I'd be better off as somebody's mother's best friend, or the neighbor next door who bakes cookies."

"Then I'm wondering," he said, "what's gotten you so worked up about this little girl someone saw in a crowded men's room?"

Sierra seemed frozen in the moment, not speaking or moving. Finally, she forced herself to swallow. "Is that why you invited me to dinner? To ask me that?"

"Not at all. I told you, I think you're hot. We met, though, when you were poking around asking questions about that. Being a schoolteacher, it interests me. We can talk about football if you prefer."

"I know nothing about football." She shook her head to dispel the nervousness. "You looked up all the information you had on the little girl who disappeared from your school several years ago. I found that strange. Do you have an itch when it comes to minor girls?"

"Male teachers don't even look at minor girls. It's safer that way. I invited *you* to dinner, not some teenybopper. I care about children—that's why I teach. I'm interested in your case because it involves a kid who might be in danger."

Sierra considered it. Chet didn't seem like a pervert, a pedo— just a nice guy concerned with the education and welfare of kids. "You know everything I know. Certain things hit certain people, that's all. Your neighbors walk their dogs and you don't give it much thought either way until you see that one particular dog and your heart begins to ache because you can't have him."

Chet Quigley studied her, noticing her voice quiver when she answered him. "I don't have a dog, Sierra," he said, "and dogs are not little girls you've never seen before."

Sierra took another quick wine sip. "I can't discuss police matters with civilians."

"Can you discuss civilian matters with civilians?" Chet asked. "Have I gone too far? Is this our first and last date, or am I going to see you again?"

Would she? She was looking past him at the rest of the dining room without seeing anything or anyone. Maybe he was coming on too strong—the handholding, the flattery. He *had* actually stalked her in the parking lot that afternoon, whether he admitted it or not. He was pushing her on a non-case having nothing to do with him, unless there was something more to him about pre-teen girls. Therefore, did she really want to continue this—*thing*—until it became a relationship? Did she really want to be in bed with him naked, sweating, thrashing around on the sheets and doing things she didn't think about much anymore?

"Earth to Sierra!" Chet interrupted her thoughts.

"Sorry," she said. "My mind was on—something else."

"You're supposed to be thinking about me, especially when I just asked if we could go out again sometime."

"I'm not looking for a hookup."

He smiled. "Where did that come from? Hookup. Who started calling it hookup?"

"Probably," she replied, "because 'getting laid' is so—last century."

"Have you come up with an answer, or must I wait for next week's episode?"

"Well, I guess—sure, we can see each other again—if you follow the rules."

"No relationship, no-hookup." He sighed. "I can live with that—for the time being, anyway. Let's order dinner."

The meal was pleasant enough, considering both ignored what had been said before. They discovered, between bites, that their tastes in music were completely opposite, their politics were one hundred eighty degrees from each other, and they both had no agreement whatsoever about what they watched on TV or at the movies. Sierra was agnostic, if not an atheist, and Chet was a non-church-going Methodist. He liked summertime, the hotter the better, while she preferred a brisk, leaf-glorious autumn, rare in a California beach town.

They agreed on pizza, except she insisted on anchovies and he wouldn't dream of eating one, and they each were fond of a different brand; he always ordered Pizza Hut, and she stuck to Marco's. Neither of them liked Papa John's.

The post-prandial talk over black coffee and Courvoisier relaxed them—enough that he felt emboldened to ask her, "What made you want to be a cop, anyway?"

"Law and order," she replied. "Enforcing laws—even ones I disagree with."

He nodded. "And how about the order part?"

She took an extra two seconds to answer. "In my family, there was no such thing as order. I longed for it—which is why I majored in law enforcement and pinned on a badge."

"There's not much disorder in Sundown Beach."

"You'd be surprised. Arguments between next-door neighbors get out of hand, even a rape once in a while—and there's as much domestic abuse around here as anywhere else. There are real criminal residents, too, and lots of them are white collar. We're one of the nicest smaller cities in California—but it's not Shangri-La."

"I know. I've lived here most of my life."

"And never had any local trouble?"

"Just the disappearance of Caitlin Haggerty—which wasn't my trouble, actually."

"Well," she said, "don't make this current little girl your trouble, either."

Chet shrugged. "That's one more thing we're not supposed to talk about together, like movies or music or football—or relationships."

"We'll have lots of things to talk about next time."

He perked up at that one—he lifted his head, his eyebrows climbed, and he raised his brandy glass. "Let's drink to next time," he said, grinning, clinked the glass against her coffee cup, and drank.

CHAPTER NINE

The house wasn't huge, but large enough to make anyone notice. Spacious and beautiful—white with green shutters, sprawling over three acres of closely mowed grass, the work of a landscaper who showed up twice a week. It was a pleasant morning, warm enough for an outdoor breakfast. Five people—the homeowner and four guests—sat on the patio with coffee, bagels, and pastries. All four men wore expensive suits and quietly muted ties; the woman who lived there was dressed for business in a soft mauve blouse and a skirt the color of Pepto-Bismol. Later, she had appointments to show a client some houses for sale in Sundown Beach.

She wasn't nervous, never skittish about showing a house, as her sales percentage was through the roof. She wasn't uncomfortable about this meeting, either, which she had hurriedly called the previous evening. Danielle Tokes, a member of the city council, had invited the other council members to her home to enjoy breakfast, along with the city manager, Chris Fornadel, and another good friend—Kenneth Zack, who was the richest man in Sundown Beach.

J. Richard Stubblefield, twice elected to the city council, was one of those people who had a small face in a large head, and a bad comb-over which no one is rich enough to fix. He owned a huge construction firm in Long Beach, and from his private office was the best possible view of the *Queen Mary*, the ship that forever lies at anchor offshore. He also owned an imposing factory near the Los Angeles harbor. He built industrial complexes and skyscrapers all over the country, which netted him almost as much money as Kenneth Zack, but unlike his wealthier friend, he eschewed bragging about it. Nobody seemed to really know what the "J" stood for, as everyone called him "Dick."

Eben Flood was a high-priced Los Angeles attorney, his name imprinted on a letterhead along with three other law partners. It seemed there were more lawyers in California than there were cockroaches. Enormous corporations and mega millionaires were Flood's specialty clients. He defended them from suits filed by mistreated or injured employees, or customers feeling they'd been cheated—and every so often a suit filed by a trophy wife who finally decided it just wasn't worth it. He'd been on City Council longer than Danielle Tokes, but Sundown Beach had little for them to do besides meeting once every two months and accomplishing very little.

Chris Fornadel was the Sundown Beach City Manager when not being a lawyer and got more done in a week than the council did in a year. He munched on a tasteless bagel, wishing Danielle had served pancakes. He knew why this meeting had been called, and tried not to be upset about it, though Sierra Bravo was his friend and an excellent police chief. Why Danielle truly loathed Sierra was beyond his comprehension.

The fifth man there was Kenneth Zack, with no official city function. But his almost obscene wealth and powerful position allowed him to bank approximately one hundred twenty million dollars each year in his various accounts. His home, south of downtown and halfway up the side of a hill, was nearly as big as the White House itself. He lived alone with his son Dylan, both taken care of daily by a female housekeeper, a cook, a chauffeur for his limousine and for keeping his other three cars squeaky clean and serviced, a full-time team of landscapers, and five armed guards who stood watch over him in shifts so that neither he nor his home was in any danger. However, none of his employees actually lived on premises except the guards—two retired cops, two professional mercenaries, and an ex-convict. They slept in a guesthouse, in shifts, about fifty yards from the main house.

Council members were scared to death of Ken Zack, as were most other people in town except Chris Fornadel, who didn't give a damn about him one way or another.

When all were settled, Danielle Tokes cleared her throat and said, "I'm glad you all could make it today. Eat hearty, there's more bagels. There's something we have to discuss, though, because Sundown Beach has a definite problem."

Stubblefield and Flood looked at each other nervously. They weren't used to dealing with council problems, usually shoveling them over to Chris in hopes that he'd take care of them. Zack looked only mildly annoyed. Chris, however, turned up his nose as if something had died and was decomposing.

"Our chief of police is not doing her job," Danielle continued. "She took several days off last week and simply disappeared. No one knew where she was going."

"I knew where she was," Fornadel said. "I have her cellphone number if anything needed her immediate attention."

"Why don't the rest of us have it, too?" Flood whined.

"It's her personal cellphone. She gives it out to people she wants to have it."

Stubblefield hacked a cough. "Are you and she that special, Chris?"

"Special enough to have each other's phone number. Any other questions on your mind that are personal, Dick, I'll take as an insult." He turned to Danielle. "All right, then, go ahead."

Danielle glared at him. "We hired Bravo," she said, "and expected her to do what we told her to."

Chris interrupted, "You didn't hire her, I did—and no one at this meeting tells her what to do, because none of us has the slightest idea what a police chief's job is. She's quite experienced in law enforcement. Let her do her job."

"When her job steps all over our toes?" Ken Zack asked. "Is that how it works?"

"That's how it's supposed to," Chris said. "I know your son earned a citation. I hardly think the officer who issued that ticket waited behind a tree so he could specially ambush Dylan and write him up. A young man—even one who's rich and privileged, Ken—has to obey laws, just like everybody else."

"So that'll stick on his record for the rest of his life? Over my dead body!"

"In today's strange society, Ken, that could be a real death wish."

"Are you threatening me?"

"No—just pointing out your unfortunate choice of words."

Danielle Tokes tapped on the side of her water glass with a spoon. "Come, gentlemen, save this bickering for the golf course. There's something else. Sierra Bravo was seen at eleven o'clock last night in the Dolphin Lounge parking lot with Chester Quigley, who is the middle school vice principal—and his tongue was halfway down her throat. I find that extremely disgusting."

Fornadel said, "Both of them are unmarried, Danielle. But you find it disgusting that anyone would do that—except you, of course."

Behind her eyes, a campfire flared as if someone had tossed on a log. "I am not the chief of police, nor a vice principal dealing with children all day long. Both of them should be aware of their positions in society—role models for kids, not sex-crazed maniacs."

"One kiss makes them sex-crazed maniacs?" Chris laughed as he shook his head. "What kind of books have you been reading, Danielle?"

Stubblefield said, "Chances are there were no children in the parking lot at that hour of the evening."

"Maybe not," Flood said, "but she should be spoken to."

"She should be?" Chris said. "Not him, of course, because boys will be boys—right? But women who do that sort of thing should be *spoken to*. Which of us will to do that? Not me. I've never chewed out anyone over thirteen about their romantic entanglements. So who's it going to be, then?"

"Not me, either," Dick Stubblefield said. "I'm damned if I'm going to brace the chief of police for being kissed. And I don't think we should all be sitting here first thing in the morning discussing someone else's sex life. I move we drop this."

"Motion?" Chris raised an eyebrow. "I didn't realize this was an official city council meeting, Dick—which is why we're able to discuss someone getting kissed on the mouth."

"All right!" Danielle Tokes rasped angrily. "I thought we should be aware of the kind of people—people in authority—whose public acts our citizens might not approve of."

"Drop it." Kenneth Zack's voice was sharp and cutting, and it momentarily shut everyone up. He waited, then said, "She seems decent, and we're all picking on her."

"Not all of us," Fornadel said.

Then Danielle Tokes took over again. "Just one more thing about her."

Dick Stubblefield rolled his eyes skyward like a teen grounded for sexting, and Zack frowned, shifting in his chair. "Now what?"

"Well." Danielle lowered her voice as if gossiping with other women at the beauty parlor on a Saturday afternoon, "this trip of hers—the word out there is her knickers are in a twist because she was told some man went into the men's room of the local theater with a ten- or eleven-year-old girl!"

Flood and Zack were startled and shocked, not having heard about this before. Stubblefield was still as a statue, lips an almost invisible slash across his face. Finally, he said, "Oh my god! Where did she hear all this?"

Fornadel said, "The word out there, Danielle? Where exactly did you hear this 'word?'"

"It's around," she said. "It's all over town."

"It's gossip!" he snapped. "Gossip should not be discussed by the city council."

Danielle protested, "It's just a breakfast get-together for friends."

"Then let's discuss the bagels, and *not* Police Chief Sierra Bravo."

"But we hired her."

"Bullshit, Danielle. *I* hired her."

"Then I can fire her!"

Chris rose. "You'll have to get through me first. I'm a trial lawyer. Nobody plays dirtier than I do."

Kenneth Zack scoffed, "We'll see about that."

"Will you send some of your armed house goons to come break my kneecaps?"

"Why?" Zack said in a near-whisper. "Are you afraid of me?"

"Not nearly as much as everyone else is here, Ken." He put down his napkin and stood up. "I'll see myself out." Chris started for the house, then turned back to Danielle. "Thanks for the breakfast, Danielle. But next time—if there'll be a next time— there are professional bagel shops all over the place—so please don't buy pre-packaged bagels from a supermarket anymore. They taste like shit."

After he marched back into the house and out the front door, there was silence for a while until J. Richard Stubblefield spoke quietly. "Well, the bagels *aren't* all that good."

Outside, the visitors' cars were parked on an oyster-shell crescent driveway—all pricey foreign cars, especially a Ferrari with Dick Stubblefield's initials in plaques on both doors. But only the Bentley had a uniformed chauffeur, who snapped off a casual salute at Chris Fornadel. There was no need to guess which council member owned the Bentley.

Chris found his own Mercedes, hung his suit jacket on a hanger in the back seat—he loathed being seen with wrinkled clothes—donned his top-of-the-line Bolle Vigilante sunglasses, and headed downtown to do battle for everyone in Southern California.

Sometimes he wondered why he'd studied law in the first

place. It was a stuffy job, unless you happened to be Clarence Darrow. Suits. Ties. Shoeshines two or three times per week. Being incredibly polite to a jag-off of a judge as if talking to the Queen of The United Kingdom. The money was nice—the big house, though he and his wife were barely civil to one another, like sharing one's home with a roommate with whom you have nothing in common. Of course, the Mercedes and the pretty mistress made up for it. Naturally, the city manager's job in Sundown Beach gave him a livable salary all its own, and a certain amount of control in a small city with no major sports teams, no museums, no symphony of its own. Just a white sand crescent beach that made the rest of it all worthwhile.

Now Sierra Bravo, a good friend who was always on Chris's side even though she never became a hookup, was under attack by everyone in town with push-and-shove strength and seemed out to get her, the blitz engendered by council member Danielle Tokes, who was hiding behind her uncrowned power broker, Kenneth Zack.

Fornadel waited until he got to his own office before calling Sierra to warn her the war against her had shifted into high gear, though in his heart he was unsure how to handle this, or even if he were able.

He was determined to find a way, though. *Any* way.

Sierra sat at her desk for most of the morning, glum and sour-faced, going through all the reports and paperwork she did each day, but her heart wasn't in it. The call from Chris Fornadel regarding the city council's bagel breakfast had sucked the wind out of her sails. The dislike Danielle Tokes and Ken Zack evinced from the beginning has spread to other members of the city council. Sooner rather than later, she thought, they'd fire her.

Most cops working for her lined up to watch her back, but they hadn't really grown to love her yet, except Griff Parrish and Nancy Flower, who would arm themselves with automatic weapons and bulletproof jackets if necessary and sit by the door to defend her, which would make their jobs just as shaky as hers. The last thing Sierra wanted was to put those friends in an untenable position.

So when Griff Parrish poked his head into her office and suggested they go to lunch together, she turned him down.

"I've got too much to do here," she said, "and I'm not really hungry."

"Chief—we all know what's going on," he said kindly, "and we're with you. Come on, we'll break bread together, and you'll feel a whole lot better."

She shook her head. "Not today. I'm not up to it, okay? Please."

"Can I bring something back for you, then? A sandwich? Salad?"

"Nothing." It took her a moment to realize she hadn't added "Thank you," but by that time Griffin was gone.

What the hell would she do with her life when this was all over? She allowed it to bounce around inside her head until she wanted to scream. How would she support herself? Get a job at a department store for pennies beyond minimum wage? Try to get hired as an office assistant somewhere? Not in Sundown Beach, where her reputation would be shot to hell. She'd have to sell her condo and take an apartment somewhere else—another town, another state. She felt angry and disconcerted. Sundown Beach could get along without her—but could she get along without Sundown Beach?

Half an hour later, she downed two Tylenols. The pounding behind her eyes since she spoke to Fornadel had grown into a fearsome headache that threw her off balance. Everything in her wanted to quick-nap with her head on her desk—but police chiefs simply didn't do that. She did, however, turn off the overhead fluorescent lights in her office and functioned as best she could using only the desk lamp.

If she were canned, she'd be alone and adrift, relieved of all civic responsibilities but given freedom to follow her obsession about the nameless child. With no badge, gun, or job, she'd be like a suburban housewife declaring war on the *capo di tutti capi* of the Mafia.

It also might get her killed.

A few of the patrol officers dropped by her office and said something cheerful, or even asked a question. Griff, though, wisely decided whatever went on in the police station that day, he'd handle on his own and not bother Sierra.

Time dragged on. As one ages, time literally flies, or at least it was supposed to. This afternoon, though, Sierra's time moved with the rapidity of a glacier. The thumping in her head was like a jackhammer being used a block away to break through the street.

Her office door was open, but even if it were closed, everyone would hear her scream, so she discarded the urge. She knew the call from the Angel of Death carrying the scythe or one of the town council members telling her to pound sand—wouldn't come until morning or early afternoon of the following day. It made her feel like a terminal patient, lying in the hospital to watch the machine capture the beat of her heart, waiting for it to flatline.

Then, Nancy Flower was in her doorway—her face tight, tentative, as if she wasn't sure she should be there. She said, "Phone call for you—personal. He said his name was Tyler. I don't know if that's his first name or his last name. I asked him and he said, 'Just Tyler.' You want him, Chief, or should I blow him off?"

Sierra's skin tingled, as if invaded by five thousand ants, and all at once her mouth was dry. She licked her lips. "No, I'll take it, Nancy."

"On line five."

She nodded. "Close the door when you go out, please."

Nancy nodded and quietly disappeared from the doorway.

Sierra took a moment to get her wits about her. Then she lifted the receiver and said in her most professional voice,

"Tyler—can I help you?"

"No, but I can help you." Tyler's voice was a low, rumbly, half-whisper. "I stumbled onto some interesting information."

Now she was jumpy and alert. "What?"

"You really expect that over the phone, Chief Bravo?"

"No, of course not. I'm not sure I can get to Hemlock Hills. Can you come here? To Sundown Beach?"

"If you're fighting Middle East terrorists," Tyler said, "would you grab an assault rifle and head up to Finland to make war?"

"You found something solid?"

"Not solid enough. But it might interest you."

"What is it?"

Tyler sighed. "Over the phone again? Seriously?"

"I have a job here. I can't come again until Saturday."

"Saturday?" He sounded skeptical. "You're the chief of police. You can do any damn thing you want."

"I have some authority, Tyler, but I'm not the Empress of all the Russias. I could get fired. I've got to tiptoe, or I'll shoot myself in the foot."

"I guess it'll wait until Saturday," he said, sounding rueful.

"Where shall we get together?"

"At Extant. You'll meet with Hank in the morning. She'll bring you to where I am."

"Where would that be?"

"You'll find out Saturday."

"That sounds hush-hush."

"What the hell you think this is, a TV show?" Tyler demanded. "Of course we keep it quiet—or try to. In the past eighteen months, three different times, someone tried to kill me. They tried to kill Hank, too. This is dangerous shit we fuck with every day of the week—so if it scares you, forget it. We're on it. We do what we can—we always have, and we'll keep doing it whether you're in it with us or not."

"I'm with you, Tyler.

He paused for half a second before saying, "Good. I don't wear a badge, so I don't play the game by your rules."

Now she was the one who paused to take a deep breath. "I can't promise I can make it on Saturday, Tyler."

"Then don't," he said. A click, a dial tone, and Tyler was gone.

CHAPTER TEN

This was no time to hustle back to Hemlock Hills and get involved in a case that wasn't even a case, Sierra Bravo thought. This was a time to worry about her job, her next step (if there were to be one), and her future.

This was the first time in many years that she was alone—really alone. No family. No real friends. Nobody "had her back." Nobody to hold her and comfort her and tell her everything would be all right. If she looked up "lonely" in the dictionary, she'd find her own photograph illustrating the entry.

Chris Fornadel was a friend, of sorts—but how much power did he actually have going head-to-head with Danielle Tokes—who disliked Sierra with all the energy she could muster?

A return trip to Hemlock Hills might destroy her career—or perhaps even her life. A chill ran down her spine. Few cops are afraid of death—that's why they carry firearms—but it was never their first choice. Would anyone mourn or even care what happened to her? She'd made no plans for what would be done with her body post-mortem. In a knotty-pine casket interred in a forgotten, soon-to-be grassed-over plot in Potter's Field, wherever that might be? In some landfill overrun with hungry rats, decomposing food garbage, and discarded plastic pop bottles that would last for centuries? Or reduced to ashes and either stuck in a box to spend eternity on some shelf, or to be scattered to the four winds in the Pacific Ocean?

For the better part of an hour, she stared out the window. On this partially sunny day, the blue sky was dotted with fluffy gray-white clouds from horizon to horizon that could turn almost instantly into a crashing rainstorm. She hadn't watched the weather on the morning news, nor had she checked the report on her iPad before leaving the house that morning.

Eventually, Sierra pulled herself together and reached for her telephone. She held it in her hand for a long while, torn by things within her that were better left unexamined. She dialed a number, and the first ring sent her to shivering.

How many people had ever heard of anyone whose first name was Chester? There was an obscure U.S. President, Chester Alan Arthur, and an arcane actor of the 1930s and 40s named Chester Morris, whom Sierra had seen on a late-night TCM vintage movie about tough guy Boston Blackie. From her history classes, she vaguely recalled a World War II Admiral, Chester Nimitz, who commanded an entire fleet in the South Pacific.

The only other Chester she knew about was the city of Chester, Pennsylvania.

All of that ancient history flashed through her mind as she lay naked in bed next to the first Chester she'd ever met in person—the first Chester she'd ever screwed—Chester Quigley, the vice principal of the Sundown Beach Middle School.

Loneliness and a forsaken feeling had jump-started what turned out to be a wild night of fucking—an activity that had never crossed her mind that day as she struggled over her suddenly thorny relationship with Sundown Beach's antagonistic city council, and her investigation into what might be a pre-teen sex-trafficked slave.

Thrilled to hear from her, Chet Quigley offered her another dinner at a different restaurant, but she was less hungry and more horny, yearning for strong arms to hold her. She'd told him to be at her condo at nine o'clock that evening. By nine-thirty, their clothes were intermingled all over the floor of her bedroom, the bedspread was crumpled up in a corner, and they were shagging their brains out.

In not quite two hours, they'd screwed three times, taking only moments to recoup between sessions, desperately acting as if there were only minimal ticks left until the end of the world and they needed to squeeze in as many orgasms as possible. Now they lay quietly in the dark, side by side, thighs touching, thinking, studying the ceiling.

Sierra's carnal experiences were few and far between—unusual for an attractive fortyish woman who'd been approached often by many men, both politely and otherwise. She'd always shot down the romancer with cutting words of sarcasm, but couldn't decide if Chet Quigley was a great lay, or just okay in bed. She'd climaxed all three times, which she enjoyed more than she'd imagined, but it was still impossible for her to believe the earth moved, which only happened in breathtaking romance novels. Maybe she was out of practice—or was it Chet who was rusty and unwanted, and therefore as horny as she was?

She decided to find out. She rolled over onto her side and threw one arm across his chest. "All set to go again?" she whispered.

Chet closed his eyes, loving the parts of her body touching his skin, her tickling warm breath, the dizzying scent of her—part perfume, part perspiration, and part her own sexuality. "Really? Already?"

"Already." She put her tongue into his ear.

"Well—"

Her hand crept down between his legs under the covers. "Not interested anymore?" She began stroking him slowly and firmly, but didn't get the response she'd been expecting.

"Sure I'm interested," he said. "It's—I need some more time to recuperate. Unless," and he put his hand over hers as she massaged his penis, "you can help me out a little."

Bodies so close together that he was startled to feel every inch of her stiffen and her hand disappear as she moved away from him. "Help you out a little?" she said without a bit of warmth. "You want me to help you out?"

Now he was embarrassed. "Well—*you* know..."

"I think I do." Her voice crackled with frost. "You want me to go down on you."

His face flushed with embarrassment. "It'd get me hard quicker," he stammered.

"Well, *that's* not going to happen," she said, moving further away from him. Then she sat up and rolled out of bed, taking the blanket with her to cover herself.

"It's okay, Sierra," Chet Quigley said quickly and gently. "If you're not—into that, it's fine with me. It was just a—suggestion."

She sat down on a chair near the window, shivering, and wrapped the blanket around her as if it were January-cold. "A suggestion, huh?"

"I mean, you wouldn't have to—"

"No, I wouldn't have to. And I wouldn't want to." She turned her head away and wouldn't look at him. "You'd better go. I have to get to work in the morning. So do you."

"I didn't mean to offend you."

"But you did. Just—look, it was a fun evening and nothing else—but it's goodnight time, that's all." She sat quietly for more than a minute, her tongue teasing the inside of her cheek. Then she stood up. "Get dressed," she said. "We can't have a vice principal running around Sundown Beach with his ass hanging out." Then she went into the living room and closed the door behind her.

Chet Quigley lay there—chilled, as if drenched with a bucket of frigid water. It had been a great two hours, sweaty and athletic and loving and fun, the way first-time sex with someone new was supposed to be. He had no idea why the emotional cold front set in. He was more experienced than she, and knew most twenty-first century couples engaged in oral copulation during sex—

giving and receiving—but she didn't let him do that to her, either. His suggestion quickly and thoroughly turned her off.

He'd been attracted to Sierra from the moment she walked into his office, and even more so when he'd run into her on a Saturday in the town square. How had he fucked it all up in an instant, and how could he think of a way to fix it?

He stood up, not daring to turn on the light, fearing he'd offend her further. He groped around in the dark for his socks and underwear, feeling diminished, inadequate, as though he were only six inches tall—or even worse, invisible.

Finally dressed, he went into the living room. It was dark there, too, though Sierra had switched on the light over the stove and the illumination spilled to where she sat.

"Are you okay?" Chet asked.

"Just peachy keen." She still didn't look at him.

"Well—tonight was great, Sierra."

No answer.

He bent down to kiss her goodbye, but she turned her face away from him, and all his lips touched was her cheek.

"I'll call you," he said.

"I'll—be out of town for a while," she said.

"Oh."

"So don't call."

That was a hell of a way to say goodbye, Chet Quigley thought as he backed his car out of the visitor's spot and headed toward his own apartment, at least fifteen minutes away from the beach. He had no idea why.

As soon as Chet's car pulled away, Sierra returned to her bedroom and exchanged the blanket for a robe. Then she found her way to the kitchen and cranked open a bottle of white.

This so-called relationship—the first one in more than two years—had barely lasted the evening, and she knew damn well it was her fault—but she couldn't do anything about it. Now, the whole case that wasn't a case at all—a child who might or might not have been kidnapped and forced to whore—had distracted her once more.

She didn't have to imagine—only remember—a childhood that was far more than just difficult, and her adventurous escape into what had become her real world.

After working as a bag girl at the local supermarket for four years, baby-sitting for her neighbors and pocketing most of her money, Sierra Bravo graduated from high school at seventeen. The following Sunday, she stuffed everything important into a backpack and caught a Greyhound bus heading for Georgia and a two-year college, as far away from her parents as she could get.

She earned more money working hard at the college, in the school's cafeteria, and more importantly, for one of the professors who taught the basics of law enforcement, and her grade point was A-minus. That got her a scholarship for a smaller Georgia university, which eventually awarded her a degree in the same subject. Her own life had convinced her that the best work she could attain was to help other people whose lives were in danger, too.

She never looked back, never contacted her parents again. Her mother wrote her a few letters, but after a while, Sierra would burn them in her kitchen sink without reading them. She didn't know if her father was still alive, nor did she care. She'd stopped hating both of them—she didn't give a damn one way or the other.

She was not asexual, naturally, but a normal young woman. During her college years, there had been romances in her life— very different from what she'd learned too fast and too well before she even reached puberty. The liaisons were never serious, enjoyable enough for as long as they lasted. During her first college dalliance, she'd surrendered her actual innocence to a chunky, muscular law enforcement classmate with a sense of humor. She wound up dating him off and on for most of her senior year, and stayed friendly with him when it finally ended. After graduation, he chose to stay a cop for the foreseeable future, applying and being accepted as a cadet by the Atlanta

Police Ddepartment, and she'd said goodbye to him cheerfully. She liked him well enough, but she had no thought whatsoever of the word *love* and what that might entail.

There were other quasi-relationships in the small California town Sierra eventually chose for her first police job, too. They ended quietly and peacefully.

And that was it.

Even during stretches of sexual activity, she'd refused to perform oral sex on her partners. She had made some good gal pals during her college years, and they all did it, or at least talked about it and swore they had. But it was not for her. Even the thought was revolting, bringing back too many ghastly memories.

It was why Sierra had chased Chet Quigley out of her condo, and out of the picture as well, as she'd done to others before him.

After re-corking the wine and refrigerating it, she made up her mind to return to Hemlock Hills on Saturday, to Hank and Tyler, to prove once and for all if—and why—a middle-aged creep had shlepped a little girl into a crowded men's restroom.

If Sierra might not find and help that child, perhaps she could assist the Hemlock Hills people at the nearly invisible organization named Extant to save another one.

She kept telling herself Hemlock Hills wasn't a bad town, though not a magnet for tourists. In her few days there on this non-approved investigation of hers, she learned very little. She'd been there before, and after leaving, she stared out at the stretch of freeway ahead of her, which went on and on like an unwound ball of yarn as she made her way east—too damn early on a Saturday morning, as she was to meet with Henrietta at nine a.m. She'd stopped for coffee twice, buying two "nutritional bars" and pretzels on her second stop, as she knew she wouldn't be invited out to breakfast.

She wished Tyler had been more specific when he'd called her earlier in the week, but she understood why he'd been cryptic. Her phone at the police station wasn't bugged—as far as she knew, anyway—but perhaps Tyler's was.

A sobering thought. Human trafficking—those kids in the sprawling international sex trade—brought in billions of dollars exchanged for buying and selling people. If the perpetrators in Hemlock Hills knew of Tyler's indomitable courage, they must have a bug on his phone, his car, and even where he lived.

Where *does* he live? she wondered. Tyler was large and imposing, an invincible, proud, dark-skinned Thor. It's doubtful he could go anywhere without being recognized by someone.

She wore her medium-weight jacket that fell to mid-thigh, and carried the Glock on her hip. She also had a palm-sized derringer at one ankle, along with some aerosol pepper spray in her purse—but using any of these, she'd have to get pretty close to someone, as she would with the sharp nail file she kept in her shoe. As always, she hoped she wouldn't need any of them.

She'd tried to book her stay again at the bed-and-breakfast she'd used on her last trip, but they were crowded on weekends, so she'd made a reservation at an Econolodge—but she couldn't check in until 3 p.m. or she'd be charged for an extra day. Instead, she headed for the unmarked office of Extant.

Being a Saturday, Hank Silver had opted for casual dress—an unbuttoned man's shirt over a black T-shirt, work boots, and a pair of inexpensive jeans that drew attention to her wide hips. Her glasses were propped up near the top of her head. When Sierra Bravo walked through the door, Hank offered no smile, no "hello" or any other sort of greeting. Instead, she said, "Tyler was expecting you today."

"I wasn't sure I could come."

"He was sure. So was I. I'll call and tell him to meet us."

Sierra said. "Is it where he lives?"

"Hardly. But not far from here." Hank's eyes scanned Sierra's body up and down. "Carrying?"

"Yes. Are you?"

She shook her head. "I'm not a cop."

"Will Tyler be?"

"How would I know? Ask him."

"I will," Sierra said.

"This is no picnic, Chief," Hank said. "These are serious people dealing with serious money, and they don't like being fucked with. They could get nasty."

"Do they get nasty with you?" Sierra asked.

"They don't pay much attention to me. I don't go knocking on doors and stealing children away from the bastards who stole them in the first place."

"And Tyler does?"

She declined to answer. Then she checked her wristwatch. "Let's go." She opened her desk drawer and took out a typed list of instructions and handed it to Sierra. "This is where you'll meet Tyler. We have to be careful. We wouldn't want anyone knowing where he might be. So listen carefully—and then make sure you burn this piece of paper."

Sierra scanned the paper. "Okay, but I don't understand."

"Just do it!" It was not a suggestion. "Are you parked out front?"

"Sure."

"Pointing which way?"

"Uh—west, I think."

"Excellent. What kind of car?"

"A dark silver Honda Accord."

"New or old?"

"It's a 2018."

"Good." Hank rubbed her hands together in anticipation. "When you leave here—keep going west, the way you're pointed. You'll hit an intersection with traffic lights in about three blocks. Go one block past that to the next street, then turn right. Halfway down the block is a Walgreens drugstore. Pull into the lot. Keep your engine running. In about four minutes, I'll meet you there in my car—it's an eight-year-old blue Chevy Malibu—the old Malibu that looks like crap. When you see me, check your directions where to turn. It'll take about ten minutes to get to where Tyler is. I'll be following."

"You know where this place is," Sierra protested, "and I don't. Why can't I follow you?"

"I want to make sure no one else tails you—and I don't want them finding Tyler." Hank took a deep breath. "When you get within three blocks of there, I'll turn off, head for a Wendy's, and order a coffee. You keep on—where you're supposed to park, what door you go into, it's all on that paper."

"What if I *am* being followed?"

"Good question. Keep your eyes on my car. If there's trouble behind you, I'll call and tell you *'plans have changed.'* You got that, right? *'Plans have changed.'* Then get the hell away from here. Head to your hotel, go shopping downtown, go back to Sundown Beach. Just make sure nobody finds Tyler."

"What if someone does find Tyler?"

"Then," Silver said, "somebody is going to get killed."

CHAPTER ELEVEN

Sierra Bravo drove slowly until she spotted the Walgreen's and took over a parking spot near the driveway, waiting for Henrietta Silver—wondering what happened to her life all of a sudden.

She was relatively new to a nice cushy job, running a police department in a pretty, upscale town in which violent crimes rarely happen. The city council got pissed off at her for enforcing the law they'd hired her to enforce in the first place. A skimpy little guy she'd never heard of waltzes into her office with a story that he might have made up on the spur of the moment, which caused her to jump the rails and skitter off into the dark corners of her memories. She'd literally chased a man out of her bed and her life after two years of celibacy because he had innocently and politely suggested a blow job. Now, in a Walgreen's drugstore parking lot two hours from her home, she waited to march into a world of violent sex slavers who'd just as soon kill her as look at her.

Strange days.

Henrietta's car came creeping along, and Sierra headed into the street, keeping an eye on the Malibu behind her. The directions on her lap were followed explicitly until she saw Silver turn left and disappear down a dusty, half-empty street.

By the time she arrived at the building in question, a headache pulsated behind her eyes and slowed her down. She drove by a faded brick façade and then turned down an alley and parked where she'd been instructed, behind a clump of trees in a now-deserted backyard. She sat without moving for five minutes, watching the rearview mirror to see if anyone had followed, but there was no activity in the alley, and no traffic on the street she'd just left.

She leaned forward, took her Glock from its holster, and made sure it was loaded. Her derringer and a pepper spray can from her purse, she slipped into her pockets. Then, lighting a match, she burned the typed contents she'd been given, rolled down her window, and tossed the ashes into the breeze.

There was no identifying sign near the heavy steel door she'd been told to enter. It was, as promised, unlocked, and she made sure she re-locked it behind her as she stepped into a large, sprawling room that obviously had been vacant for years. It was a warehouse of some sort, dusty and abandoned. The only light came through the horizontal windows near the ceiling—two of them broken, probably by kids testing their skill throwing rocks.

At the far end of the room, a metallic staircase headed up to a landing on the second floor. Tyler loomed large at the top of the steps, motioning her to come up. He wore a thigh-length jacket over jeans and work boots. Standing above her, his formidable size reminded Sierra of an impossibly strong character from a superhero movie.

"Glad you decided to pay us another visit," Tyler grumbled. "Nobody followed you. Good. Hank prepared you well. Come with me." He led Sierra into a small, windowless room that had once been an office. The ceiling fluorescent light was turned off—if it even worked—but a small reading lamp on the desk provided enough illumination for her to see. The warehouse was alive with various stale odors—dust, sweat, aged urine, vintage farts, tiny disintegrating mouse corpses, and a lack of fresh air that kicked up Sierra's headache several notches.

She tried not to sniff. "Is this where you hang out, Tyler?"

"It's where I *hide* out," he answered. "When I need to. Nobody knows about this place except Hank and a few others."

"What is it you do here?"

"Things I wouldn't do at high noon in front of City Hall."

"Like?"

"Is this *Twenty Questions*?"

"I was brought here in secret," Sierra told him, "at your invitation. I had to wake up at four o'clock in the morning to get here. Either I get to ask questions because you refused to tell me on the phone why I should be here in the first place, or I'm gone."

"Gone with the wind," he said. "I'm guessing there's a slight southern accent in there somewhere. Am I right?"

"Are we trying to guess accents?" She was stunned he'd heard the faintest Georgia drawl in her speech, acquired during her college years. "Or are we talking about some old movie making southern slave owners out to be heroes?"

Inside her, an invisible moth fluttered, coming too close to the flame.

"I've discovered a child in trouble. Is it the girl you're looking for? Nobody knows. But it's a possibility, so I pass it along to you." Tyler indicated the dusty chair behind the desk. "Get comfortable."

"If I wanted to be comfortable, I would have stayed home. Come on, Tyler."

"Your call." He took a deep breath. "In the human trafficking business, especially with children, there are many players—at many different levels."

"So?"

"First of all—headhunters who buy children. They mostly operate in small countries where everyone is starving—but you'll find them in the poorest American sections, too. Approaching parents and offering to buy one of the children—but sometimes..."

"Yes?"

"The parents approach the headhunter. Hard to believe, isn't it? They'll sell their own kid for a few hundred bucks. There are kidnappings," Tyler said, "but in poverty-stricken countries, it's easier to buy them"

Sierra shook her head. It wasn't "breaking news." But from Tyler, who was in the business of saving children's lives, to actually hear it out loud almost blew her away.

"The next group, in this vast industry, are the movers. I guess you'd call them that. They oversee transportation—getting a kid as far away as possible from their family, and delivering them to someone who's studied the market and knows where the good deals are. Like shipping a kid off to someone who's bought and paid for her—or him."

Sierra couldn't help shuddering.

"By the way, wealthy johns are much more abusive to hookers than the guy you might run into at the tavern on the corner, having a beer and looking to get laid."

"Where did you hear that?" She leaned on the edge of the desk.

"I hear lots of things, Chief. It's my business to hear things. There are rich men who want a child—a real *child*—for their very own. For sex, naturally, because no forty-year-old guy would want to spend social time with a pre-teen."

"And what happens," Sierra asked, "when he gets tired of his sex slave—or that she gets too old to be a child anymore?"

"Usually he sells her again," Tyler said. "He's plugged in to child prostitution, which is how he got her in the first place. Even worse, he sells her back to the headhunter, who might install her in some really cheap brothel in a third-world country."

"Which means," Sierra finished, "that within two years she's either dead from AIDS or bad drugs, or some crazy person making even less money than she does kills her with a machete. All well and good, Tyler, but so far you haven't told me a damn thing about that little girl."

"Like I said, I don't know if it's the same girl, but someone that age recently got sold to a super-rich guy—from California."

The skin on the back of her neck tingled. "How do you know that?"

He cleared the frog from his throat. "Because the guy who moves children to where they've been bought was told by the man who took her away that he lives in California."

Sierra couldn't breathe for a moment, couldn't swallow, and she bent over from the waist and tried gasping air. Her mind raced, black spots flashing before her eyes. It took her a minute before she stood straight again. "Why would he tell you something like that?"

He moved away from her a bit, turning to the side so all she saw was his profile. "We just had an interesting conversation. Meeting of the minds."

"Where?"

"Uh—right downstairs."

Sierra stared at him. "Downstairs? How did you know this guy was a mover?"

"I've known him—or known about him—for years. I know lots of people like him. It's what I do."

"What's his name?"

"I was going to tell you that. Kurt Wimblehart."

She laughed. "What the hell kind of name is that?"

"A name," Tyler said, "belonging to a man who can sing louder than a canary if he's kicked in the balls several times." His inhale filled him up almost as big as the room itself. "Don't press me!" he bellowed, the words streaming out of him like a dam breaking and water rushing forward to destroy everything in its path. "You asked me to find something out, and I did!" He took several seconds to calm down. "When you see these people today, tell them Kurt Wimblehart sent you."

"What people?"

"You'll find out, Chief Bravo. But they won't be people you'll fall in love with."

"How bad did you hurt this Kurt guy, Tyler?"

"You mean on a one to ten scale?"

"I'm a sworn law enforcement officer. We don't do things like that."

"You *didn't* do anything like that, Chief Bravo. You're pure as the driven snow."

She cocked her head to one side. "Then don't tell me about it."

Tyler crossed his arms, rocking back and forth on his heels. "Here's what I know. The kid—and again, we don't know if this is the girl you're looking for—was a flat cash deal—twenty thousand bucks in fifties and hundreds."

"That's an awful lot of money for young sex."

"A piece of ass that's fresh, tight, virginal. She's too young to rebel—and they can really break their spirit down within two weeks—sooner if it's a prepubescent child."

"I know how easy it is to break a child's spirit," Sierra said, her voice shaky.

"So she's somewhere in California," Tyler said. "A pretty big state."

"Maybe," Sierra snapped, nerves at the breaking point, "but you could have told me all this over the phone—or sent me an email." She marched over to Tyler, her face very near his, and shouted, "What the fuck am I doing in Hemlock Hills, Tyler?"

"Do you kiss your mother with that mouth?"

"I'm waiting!"

"Then back away from me," he rumbled, "or I'll eat you for breakfast."

She waited for at least ten seconds more of a stare-down before reluctantly taking a few steps backward.

"That's better," Tyler said, and took a breath. "Are you armed?"

"Always, unless I'm in the shower. Why?"

"These people are dangerous as shit! If you shoot anybody, it'll look really lousy on your resume. If you aren't into that, go back home, no questions asked."

"If I'm not here," Sierra asked, concerned, "would you go by yourself?"

"It's your fault," he replied. "I do the best I can taking care of things around here—but you got me into this scenario, looking for some mythical child whore who might not exist—and now I can't back out. So come with me or don't, but I'm going myself."

"When?"

He opened his jacket like a flasher on a subway train, showing her a holstered pistol, a large knife and a blackjack, all dangling from the thick belt that held up his Levis. Sierra guessed he must have other weapons hidden all over him. That's the kind of guy Tyler was.

"Now," he said. "Right now."

"I wish I was as well-heeled as you are."

"Just for emergencies," he said. "I'll be as close as I can get—but for starters, you'll be on your own. In the meantime, don't walk in there armed. They'll frisk you, anyway, and take your weapons away from you."

"Jesus Christ." She checked her weapon once more to make sure it was loaded, then tucked it back into her holster. "I should have left this home."

Tyler said, "Don't worry, Chief. I've got your back."

"I wonder," Sierra Bravo said, "who's got my *front?*"

Another big, seemingly empty industrial building of fading red bricks, peeling paint on the doorways, and high windows looking as if they were last washed during the nineteenth century. Sierra Bravo knew there were classy modernist edifices all over Hemlock Hills, clean sparkling law offices, corporate headquarters, and financial institutions, and it chafed her she'd not been sent to some ornate building in which spiders rarely fall from the ceiling into her hair, or rats running over her feet instead of this tired old ancient wreck that had long ago outlived its time. A sharp, chill wind sent a wadded-up newspaper sheet bounding crazily down the street, hitting the brick wall, a fire hydrant, a high curb—like a feral dog in heat, ramming into everything to check whether or not it was mating time. Finally, the blast of air all the way from Canada chased the paper around the corner and out of sight.

Tyler told her to leave her weapons in the car and cautioned her not to carry her police badge. "If they find out you're a cop," he'd said, "you'll be crushed like a cockroach in their box of Crackerjack."

Sierra agreed, but she did retain her one method of defense—her can of pepper spray. She put it inside her underpants, relatively certain they wouldn't frisk her *there*. But damn! It was uncomfortable.

She had no idea where Tyler was—the guy with the deadly weapons—but she knew he'd be there if she needed him. She hoped not. Bullets flying, blood spattering everywhere, death or dying, was not her cup of tea. Most honest cops went through twenty or thirty years of serving and protecting, and never fired their weapon at another human being, and she'd always hoped she would be one of them.

She was supposed to ask for a Marvin Dreskler. Kurt Wimblehart had given Tyler that name after Tyler kicked his testicles up into his throat. Under those circumstances, Wimblehart would've squealed on Mother Teresa if that would get him relief.

She made a furtive readjustment of her panties and then rang the buzzer at the doorway nearest the corner. She waited more than a minute, growing more and more nervous, and was ready to leave when the door opened.

"Yeah?"

The man's appearance took her aback. Skinny as a pool cue, the Stetson knock-off on his head and the bandana he wore around his neck combined with a slightly cocked eye gave him the appearance of some long-gone character actor who played bank robbers in old westerns. The gun bulging beneath his jacket emphasized the similarities. However, old-time cowboys never chewed gum.

"Hi," she said, "I'm here to see Mr. Dreskler."

The cocked eye twitched. "Who's Mr. Dreskler?"

"Kurt Wimblehart suggested I see him."

"Oh, yeah? And who might you be?"

He certainly didn't sound like a cowboy, as his accent was pure Midwestern plains. She showed her driver's license, not identifying her job or title. If anyone there decided to Google her, they might discover who she was—and then she'd really be in trouble.

"Sierra Bravo?" the man said, pronouncing it "Bray-vo" and examining her license as if it were an ancient find in a dig at an Egyptian pharaoh's tomb.

"Brah-vo." She said her own name carefully.

"Why you wanna see Dreskler?"

"Are you his personal secretary?" Sierra snapped, her tone real and deliberate. She didn't want to appear a shrinking violet. "My business is with him," she continued. "Not with you. Unless you *are* Mr. Dreskler."

"What if I am?"

"Then," she said, "you show me *your* driver's license."

The cowboy's "Oh shit" came out like a sigh. He said, "Wait here," and started to close the door in her face until she put out a strong arm to stop it.

"I'm damned if I'm going to stand out here in the street like some beggar. I'm here to do business. The least you can do is invite me inside."

As if deciding whether to invite a leper to share his toothbrush, he finally stepped aside so she could enter the building.

She was momentarily startled. While the abandoned warehouse in which Tyler frequently hid from trouble looked as pitiful and worn inside as it did outside, here the walls were painted a cheery light yellow, there was high-grade carpeting on the floor, the entire first level occupied by six men behind new-looking desks and office chairs spread widely apart so no one could hear what anyone else said over the phone. They were huge men like NFL rejects, but they all had HP laptops instead of weapons, and they knew how to use them, despite the musty, decaying smell of vintage buildings that had been uninhabited for decades.

"Wait here," the cowboy grunted, shuffling off into another room without inviting Sierra to have a seat. There were no empty chairs in sight, so she stood there, hands fisted in her jacket pockets, meeting the cold gawks of all six men with a chilly stare of her own. Few women ever walked in here—at least of their own accord. This was a place in which men *bought* women from other men, ergo the quizzical looks from the low-end workers.

In her mind, she'd constructed a story she hoped would sound legitimate to Marvin Dreskler. If it didn't fly, she might exit this premises under her own power, or be carried out wrapped up in a rug—unarmed except for the pepper spray can rubbing against her crotch whenever she moved.

Time crawled.

The cowboy reappeared, looking even more irritated than before. He came no nearer to her than fifteen feet and made a small come-here gesture with his hand.

She moved toward him, aware that every other man in the place stared at her. She knew from experience that strange men often ogled her ass—but these were not admiring or lustful looks. Suspicion hung in the air like a stale food stink.

The cowboy told her to extend her arms out to her sides and frisked her for weapons or recording devices, spending a few seconds too long at her breasts. When he squatted down and ran his hand up between her legs, she tightened her knees and said, "If you go one inch higher, I'll kick you so fucking hard, you'll be singing soprano for the Mormon Tabernacle Choir."

"What makes you think I give a damn about your cunt, lady?" he mumbled. Then he stood up and jerked his head toward the door he'd just come out of. "Let's go."

Sierra followed him into a smaller, more modern-looking room where a man was seated at a large desk, with three telephones and a large-screen desktop computer taking up a lot of space. He appeared to be about ten years her senior, with thinning hair and rimless glasses. His dark blue sweater was lightweight cashmere, and his gold wristwatch was expensive.

"Have a seat," he said, not bothering to stand. Opposite him was a metallic folding chair. Apparently, he had few visitors who didn't worry about comfort. She slid into it.

"Who are you?" the man said.

"Your butler checked my driver's license. Didn't he tell you who I was?"

"Don't be a smart-ass."

"I'm more of a bad-ass, in case you're interested. My name is Sierra Bravo."

"Is that supposed to ring a bell?"

"Why don't you tell me who you are," she said, "and then we'll be even. I asked to see Marvin Dreskler. If that's not you, I'll be on my way—and pissed off that I had to wait outside in the bullpen for nothing."

"And what happens when you get pissed off?"

"How bad do you want to find out?"

He sort of smiled, but there was no warmth behind it—just a scintilla of respect. "Okay," he said. "I'm him."

"I'm glad. Your posse out there was measuring me for a hangman's knot."

"They do what they're told," he said. "They're not going to pull out their guns and shoot down some guy delivering pizza."

"I didn't bring any pizza. I have a business proposal for you."

"We have many businesses here, lady. What did you have in mind?"

"I represent my employer," she said.

"What's his name?"

"It's not important. You're dealing with me anyway—no other names involved."

Dreskler raised his brows and closed his eyes momentarily. "He wants something from me, and he sends a broad to negotiate? Peculiar..."

"Calling me a broad is peculiar. My employer is rich and powerful. But he's older—and since his wife died, he's very lonely."

She cleared her throat noisily. "If you get my drift."

"You want me to go over there and hold his hand?"

"Thoughtful of you, but unfortunately, you're the wrong gender—and the wrong age."

"Wrong age, huh?"

"He—enjoys the company of children. Prepubescent, if you know what I mean."

Dreskler ran his tongue over his front teeth, a gesture usually associated with men much older. "So Kurt Wimbelhart told you to get in touch with me, huh?"

Sierra nodded.

"When was this he told you?"

"He told my employer on the phone. Then my employer told me."

"Is that right?"

"That's right."

"Interesting," Dreskler said. "Because when you showed up here a few minutes ago and announced yourself to my assistant—"

"The cowboy."

Dreskler didn't laugh. "When he told me you were here, I called Wimblehart to check up on you—and he didn't answer his phone."

"Maybe," Sierra said, "he was busy."

"At ten o'clock in the morning? The only reason he wouldn't answer the phone is getting a blow job—and that usually doesn't happen at ten o'clock in the morning." He quietly slipped open his right-hand desk drawer and drew out a pistol, which he cocked and pointed at her face. "Enough bullshit, Sierra Bravo. You've got ten seconds to tell me exactly who you are and where did you get my name."

Sierra glared him down. She'd been through cadet school and could fight better than most male cops. She'd learned tae kwon do from a Korean trainer in Los Angeles, and she knew she could take that weapon away from Marvin Dreskler and shove it up his ass faster than the ten seconds he was allowing her. However, there were six other guys in the adjoining room, and they might be armed, too. She said, "You know damn well who I am. Your dog-robber checked my license before he let me in the door, and then told you all about it. You think I ran out and paid two grand for a forged driver's license for the chance to spend a few special moments in your exalted presence? Get real."

"I am real, bitch!" He stood up, but the muzzle of the gun didn't jiggle. "Now before I blow a big fat hole in your pretty face—where did you get Wimblehart's name in the first place?"

Outwardly she showed no sign of being frightened, but her mouth went dry. "My employer told me who I should contact," she said. "Where he got Wimblehart's name, I have no idea. I didn't ask. I'm paid too much not to ask."

Dreskler looked her up and down. She was dressed casually well. Not big money dressed up—but she dolled up to purchase a virgin child from a pedosex supermarket? "Goodie for you! So what exactly do you want from me?"

She tried not looking flustered and did a pretty good job of it. "What I want from you," she said levelly, "is a slim, pretty girl, about ten or eleven years old—and a virgin. That last point is not negotiable. We prefer she's quiet—and obedient. If she does what she's told, her life will be lovely. If she's a rebel in any way, we're not interested. She doesn't have to speak English, necessarily—in fact, that's preferable in case her hysterical family is comes looking for her clear across the ocean. *You* won't be looking for her, either, which is why I'm being careful. These are my employer's specifications, not mine." She took a deep breath. "Anything else you want to know?"

"What's your employer's name?"

"Cash," she said.

"That's it?" His voice rose to an angry tenor. "Like Johnny Cash?"

"His first name," Sierra replied, pronouncing every syllable carefully, "is Twenty-five Thousand Dollars. Twenty-five Thousand

Dollars Cash."

Deskler's eyes widened. "Are you fucking kidding me?"

"Small bills," she assured him. "Twenties and fifties—serial numbers random."

"You have it with you?"

"Sure—want to guess where it is? Jesus Christ!" She shook her head in disgust. "You're a lot dumber than I thought you'd be. You think I'd walk in here with that kind of money? You'd take it away from me—and shoot me dead afterwards."

"Where do you have it, then?"

"Where do you have the girl?"

Dreskler waved his free hand around at the setting. "You think we keep children locked up in a place like this?"

"I wouldn't put anything past you."

"That sounds like you disapprove of what we do."

"What I approve or disapprove," Sierra Bravo said, "is none of your business. I'm doing one of many jobs I'm assigned, My boss asks me to do some things I—disapprove of. That's why I get the big bucks."

He slowly lowered the gun, but didn't put it back in the drawer, either. "You're a tough broad, Miss—uh..." He looked at a paper the cowboy had left with him. "Miss Bravo. Or is it Missus?"

"What do you care?"

"Like I said, tough broad. Were you at one time a Marine, by any chance?"

"You want my life story—like the name of my third-grade teacher? The first time I kissed a boy and gave tongue? What did I major in college?"

"Like I give a shit."

"Fine. Then cut the small talk. You want money, I want the girl. End of story."

"And when is that supposed to happen?"

Sierra stopped to think. She hadn't worked out all this in her head, and she had to make quick decisions. "Two days from now."

"Time?"

"Eleven o'clock in the morning. How's that?"

He replaced the gun in the drawer and locked it. "It could be done. We'll see."

"I want a picture of the child—now."

"What for?"

Sierra scoffed. "You ever think about buying a car or a house or expensive furniture without even knowing what it looks like?"

"So you want to see her picture, huh? You think I carry one in my wallet?"

"I think you have it somewhere." She looked over at the rows of file cabinets. "Right here in this room, if I'm not mistaken."

That took Dreskler aback. "You don't miss much, do you?"

She jerked a thumb toward the filing cabinets. "Let's take a look at it," she said. "If she's ugly, the deal's off."

"Ugly," he commented as he stood and moved to the files, "is a matter of opinion."

Using a key, he unlocked the top drawer and slid it out noisily. It sounded as if it could use a shot of 3-In-One oil. From where she sat, Sierra could see the drawer was full of files in different colors. He pawed through the first file, then taking it from the drawer and pulling out two photographs. "We have two girls with us today, around the age you're looking for. Take your pick."

He tossed the photographs onto the desk in front of her. One of the girls was dark-skinned, possibly from the India-Pakistani region. The other was lighter-skinned, Asian—and both were pretty, though they wore flowered dresses the rest of the world had stopped seeing in the 1950s. The first girl looked terrified. The other looked scared, too—but her eyes radiated fury.

Dreskler pointed at the first photo, Sierra noticing he bit his fingernails. "This one's from Bhutan," he said. "The other one—" and he moved his finger to the second picture, "is from Cambodia, and already a bitch, which is why I wouldn't recommend her. She's pissed off that she's not still home, that her father sold her, and really rebellious. She needs some training first—to calm her down and make her easier to handle." He took his hand away and chuckled. "They aren't like cars, you know—there's no return policy once she walks out of here. No refunds, no exchanges."

Sierra tried not to shudder. *Needs some training first.* What would that training be like? Bullhooks and whips on baby elephants? Electric cattle prods on lion cubs? She said, "I don't know if my boss would be interested in someone from Bhutan—I doubt he even knows where that is. But tell me about this girl from Cambodia."

"Are you buying a home," Dreskler snapped, "or a child?"

"If I don't get the information I want," she said, "I'll leave here empty-handed, and you'll be fucked out of twenty-five K. It's up to you."

He glared at her for half a minute without speaking. Then: "You're a real pain in the ass."

"For this kind of money, you'll grin and bear it."

Sighing as if carrying the world on his shoulders, Dreskler opened the folder and took out three sheets of paper stapled together. "Okay," he said. "This one—her name's Lakela. She's ten and a half years old. Seems healthy enough, but she has a few cavities in her teeth. She doesn't speak a word of English, and she can't read—she comes from a dirt-poor family. She wasn't stolen or kidnapped or anything. Her father sold her, straight out, for three hundred and twenty dollars American." He grimaced. "That'll fill his family up for a month."

"How did she wind up in Hemlock Hills, California?"

"This is no travel agency. She's in Hemlock Hills because she's in Hemlock Hills."

"And she's going to get here, to this building, in forty-eight hours?"

Dreskler nodded. "If that's when you want her. You'll bring the money with you?"

"I said I would."

He put the paper and the photos back in the folder. "Where can I call you in case there's a glitch?"

"There'd better not be a glitch."

He nodded, frowning. "Where do I get in touch with Kurt Wimblehart, then?"

"He's your person, not mine."

"He didn't answer his phone this morning."

"Not my problem. You know what *is* my problem? That girl better be a virgin, or else it's no deal."

"We took her to a doctor last week. She was a virgin then."

"And now?"

He shook his head. "We're in business, for cry sakes. If anyone in our organization fucks her, she loses half her value."

Organization, she thought. This was bigger than she'd imagined, possibly huge. Butting heads with an international corporation worth hundreds of millions of dollars—unarmed and with no badge, she was two hours from home with nothing for protection but a can of pepper spray half-lodged in her vagina.

He picked up the phone, pushed a button, and barked, "Get in here." Momentarily, the cowboy appeared.

"Show the lady out," Dreskler said.

Sierra stood up. "Don't fuck with me. Forty-eight hours."

"I can count," he said.

The cowboy spoke little as he led her back through the other room where all six men looked up from their work and stared at her as she passed through. She wondered if they were checking out her ass again, or measuring her for a coffin.

When the cowboy finally got the steel door open for her, he simply said, "See ya," and slammed it behind her, leaving her standing on a deserted sidewalk. She walked around the corner to where she'd parked. Across the street she saw Tyler in his car. Their eyes met, and they nodded at each other, which made him sort of smile—the biggest smile of which he was capable. He pointed back in the direction from which they'd come.

She opened her car door and started to enter, but then stopped, bent over double from the waist, and violently threw up, narrowly missing her feet.

CHAPTER TWELVE

Tyler's hideaway in the warehouse seemed overcrowded. Sierra Bravo sat in the only chair in sight, Hank Silver was half-perched on one corner of the desk, and Tyler, who took up enough room for two, paced back and forth in front of them, his eyes brighter than Sierra never noticed before. He almost looked like an eight-year-old—a massive child who'd just been told he was going to Disney World.

"You've got hold of this by your teeth," Tyler said, "and you won't let go. But this is more than we can handle alone. We've got to call in major troops."

Hank said, "You can't make local cops move on a 'maybe.' And if we get through to the FBI somehow, it'll take them two weeks to start anything."

"Calling in the Marines?" Sierra asked bitterly. "By the time anything happens, that little Cambodian girl will be ruined for life—if she lives that long."

"You still haven't found anything about this other child in the movie theater where you live, though," Hank pointed out, "which is why you're here in the first place."

Sierra's throat began closing with tension, and she coughed it clear again. "There's more to it than that now. The Cambodian is in Hemlock Hills. They'd send her anywhere they can make a buck off her back. We've got to stop this. How do we do that?"

Tyler didn't stop to think. "Marshals," he said.

"Who?"

"United States Marshals."

"How can they help?"

"The U.S. Marshal's office has more police powers than anyone else," Hank said.

"Blow your nose," Tyler added, "or shoot someone's head off—it's all the same to them. There's an office here in town. I know a lot of them personally. I'll call."

Sierra was troubled. "Can you get enough of them together in less than two days?"

"In two days," Tyler told her, "We could conquer Russia."

That evening, a meeting took place in Sierra's motel room. It wasn't a big room, as motels go. Sierra was on the bed, Henrietta Silver was in an easy chair, and Tyler and the new arrival were standing. United States Federal Marshal Cass Garfield was a large man, but not in the way Tyler was. Well over six feet tall, his body bespoke working out in a gym five days per week, biceps bulging under a black polo shirt, an automatic pistol resting comfortably holstered on his right hip. Thirty-six years old, intense, ruggedly handsome, with a receding hairline and a scar on his left cheek, he seemed to look right through everyone he met, studying their insides, their brains. This time, while listening to Tyler, he was looking at Sierra Bravo.

"I've heard of Dreskler, sure," Garfield said when Tyler finished talking. "We couldn't nail him for anything. He's pretty smart when it comes to law enforcement." He turned to Sierra. "You're sure he doesn't know who you are?"

"He knows my name, and that's all."

"Garfield's got enough power for all of us," Tyler said.

Silver said, "Where's the rest of the marshals in your outfit? You think you and the chief here are going to take down this whole operation all by yourselves?"

Garfield said, "I'm a federal employee. We get assignments.

We're not supposed to hunt around and scare one up ourselves. I'm sticking my neck out just talking to you."

"We can't go in there like Delta Force," Tyler said. "We have to figure this out."

"Then what can we do?" Sierra said.

Garfield scratched his forehead, even though it wasn't itching. "Something that's not in the rule books."

She scoffed, "You're federal, I'm local. Different rule books, Marshal Garfield."

"Yes," he said, "but you're breaking your own rules right now, like I am—so let's settle down and figure out an approach."

Chagrined, Sierra shifted her weight on the bed. "That's why you're here, isn't it?"

"That's why we're all here," Tyler said. "And for the same reason—saving children from being sold as sex slaves."

Garfield swiped buttons on his smartphone. "Here we go," he said, and read Marvin Dreskler's home address aloud. "Unmarried, no servants, and as far as I know, one bodyguard."

"He has plenty of them at his warehouse," Tyler said.

"Not really." Sierra shook her head. "He's got one—a cowboy type. The other ones who work there are on the phone all day, or on their laptops. They're tough-looking guys, but I think they're clerks. I didn't see any of them packing heat, either."

"You couldn't tell if they were all at their desks."

"I'm just guessing, Tyler," she said.

"We're all guessing." Garfield hiked his foot up on the stand at the foot of the bed people used for unpacking their suitcases. "It comes with the job. But we'd be better off to waylay Dreskler at his home."

"Waylay?" Sierra said. "That's a nineteenth century word. What happens once Dreskler is waylaid?"

Garfield shrugged. His was a poker face; one never could tell what went on inside. "You don't get answers," he said, "if you don't ask questions."

"The Cambodian girl will be brought to the warehouse tomorrow, eleven o'clock. If we bag Dreskler now, what will become of her?"

"There are a hundred thousand children all over the world forced into slavery and prostitution every day," Garfield said. "If we can stop this local outfit cold, we'll be saving a lot more than one Cambodian kid whose name we don't know. But you're right on the money, and I spoke without thinking. We have to be at the warehouse, not his house. We don't grab Dreskler tonight. The day after tomorrow is soon enough."

"True," Sierra said, "but we *do* know her name. It's Lakela."

Sierra had plenty of questions as she spent the following day in her motel room. She realized she was in over her head, despite the assistance of Extant and the U.S. Marshal's office. Burning inside her the most was that the little girl from the Sundown Beach movie theater wasn't going to be saved by the local police chief chasing shadows in a city clear across the state. Despite her shiny gold badge and silver stars, she couldn't make an arrest in any other city than her own unless she was an eyewitness to a crime. Otherwise, it would be illegal.

A good regulation, when she thought about it. Police officers in one city can't drive all over the place, making arrests in a town they just visited. So cuffing Marvin Dreskler wouldn't have meant a damn thing unless she actually saw him doing what he does. It's a far cry from armed robbery, assault, rape, or even murder. Those are hands-on crimes; what Dreskler does is more complicated.

Yet she'd hung on in this non-case so far, and had no intention of running back to her home precinct. She'd called Griff Parrish to tell him she was staying in Hemlock Hills for a few more days. He didn't sound happy, begged her to come back where she belonged, warned that her pay would probably be docked, and reminded her that at least two thirds of the city council would come after her ass with both barrels blazing if she stayed away, but she no longer cared.

She had a childhood to live down.

Sometimes she had to step back and take a good look over her shoulder at herself. So many children subjected to physical and sexual abuse when barely more than toddlers grow up to be a pathetic mess, turning to drinks, drugs and promiscuity before they could consider what kind of person they were supposed to be. Most who actually had money to spend dribbled it away on mental therapy, which took years to make any headway.

Sierra was different.

Her final contact with her drunken father when she was thirteen was a violent attack she'd launched against him. The fact that they never spoke a word to each other again until she left the house for good made her teen years at home a bit more pleasant—even though in the best of times her father was a slurring asshole. At eighteen she went off to do whatever she chose, without a single sad look backwards. Her hatred of child abusers sent her to law enforcement, satisfied she'd have the power if she ever needed to use it.

Now she needed it.

In her previous gig in southern California, she'd dealt on more than one occasion with alcoholic, quick-to-punch locals tumbling into a tavern parking lot on a Saturday night, but they presented no problems to her. When it was too hard to slip handcuffs on roaring drunks, one arm twist and one hard karate chop to the throat usually took care of them. Physical training in the police academy on hand-to-hand combat taught her to be a no-nonsense cop, and she kept in shape working out at her local fitness center.

That was back in the day when she was a patrol officer in a small town. Now, being a chief in an elite oceanfront suburb meant more pay, more public persona, stars on her shirt collar, and less punch-outs in taverns. Sierra still hadn't come to terms with that.

She went to a firing range twice a month, comfortable shooting at paper targets, but she'd never discharged a weapon at a human being, nor unholstered her gun to point it at anyone.

Now facing a situation in which she, Tyler and Cass Garfield would be armed to the teeth with no authorization, taking on child-sellers at what could lead to the exposure of a multibillion-dollar criminal organization, it gave her pause to wonder what the rest of her life would be like if she actually did kill someone. Could she ever again close her eyes in sleep? Could she ever, for one moment, forget the look in her victim's eyes the moment she pulled the trigger?

She ached for a good, stiff drink, but couldn't take the edge off when her mission was set for the following morning. She disregarded one of her own addictions, having only one cup of coffee before ten. She couldn't be in the forefront of an armed raid which might involve shooting, arresting and handcuffing, and realize she had to pee.

Her motel had cable TV, and she spent most of her time watching ancient films on the Turner Classic Movie Network. This day was a salute to a long-dead character actor. Awakened from a restless nap at six-thirty in the evening by a sharp rap on the door, she was instantly alert, Glock in hand. She crossed the room, worried some bad guy would stamp on her bare toes. "Yes?"

"Tyler," came the reply.

She released the door chain—one of the more useless ways of protecting oneself from intruders, as a ten-year-old kid could blast the door open with one good kick—and tripped open the double lock. Tyler held an extra-large pizza box on which he'd balanced another tray with two large Cokes and two boxes containing something else.

"Tell me," he said, "you're one of those few insane people in the world who doesn't like pizza. Then I can eat all this stuff by myself."

She let him in and turned off the television to blissful silence as he opened boxes on the desktop. "I didn't know what toppings you like, so I got some of everything," he said. "But no anchovies. Who in their right mind eats fish on pizza?"

"Who eats pineapple on pizza, either?"

"Push them over to the side, Chief. "He opened one box. "A dozen cheese sticks, too. The other box has desserts."

"I won't be able to fit out the door if I eat all this," Sierra said.

"Then you'll be stuck in Hemlock Hills forever. But eat hearty. You'll need your strength tomorrow."

He handed her a slice on a napkin. She said, "We're going to be in trouble, then?"

He nodded. "It's not New York or Chicago, but it *is* a city. Cities have problems—and sex traffickers have guns. You're damn right we'll be in trouble tomorrow."

"Will we have to shoot anybody?"

He passed her a Coke. "I don't like guns in the hands of ordinary citizens. You and Garfield aren't civilians, though, so blast away. Me, I'm a civilian now—but bad people in this town know who I am, and they'd shoot me on sight. So I have weapons, too—especially when I'm dealing with the worst kind of criminals."

"Are you carrying now?"

He raised one eyebrow at her. "Sure—to make up for the target on my back."

She took a bite of the pizza slice. "This stuff is good."

"It's not from an international franchise—just a nice Italian guy from Hemlock Hills who has his own recipe and bakes his own pizza every day. See, there's a lot of nice things about Hemlock Hills, too."

"I'll have to come back and take the tour," Sierra said. "Pass me one of those cheese sticks, will you?"

He did. "They expect you at eleven o'clock. You'll get them to unlock the door."

"Dreskler's bodyguard—the cowboy—frisked me before he let me see the boss. That means I'll have no firepower at all?"

"No." Tyler told her. "Today is a different day. I need you to have every weapon that they won't see when they open the door.

Guns, knives, mace, hand grenades, an AK-47 combat rifle—whatever."

"They don't have street cams, do they?"

"I cased the whole block and didn't see any. Were there TV monitors inside the building?"

"I didn't notice—but they might be hidden." She bit into a cheese stick and washed it down with soda. "Don't forget the child will be there. The last thing I want is for her to get hurt."

Tyler started on his second slice of pizza. "My life's work is trying to keep children from getting hurt. Finish your pizza."

When Tyler left and she finally lay down again and tried to sleep, the pizza felt to Sierra as though she'd swallowed a Frisbee, and she remained awake for most of the night, staring up at the unfamiliar ceiling of a motel room and thinking maybe—unlikely but *maybe*—this could be the last morning of her life.

An even more disturbing thought was that she might, for the first time ever, shoot and kill another human being. She'd have nightmares reliving that—and daymares, too—until the day she died. She'd never considered it when choosing a law enforcement career—and fortunately,, neither of the cities in which she'd plied her trade suffered crimes during which shots were fired. The real on-the-street John and Jane Law don't act at all like the endless variety of TV actors waving their guns around.

Actors aren't cops. Cops can't act, except maybe the late Dennis Farina.

Sierra tossed until morning.

All the participants involved—Sierra, Tyler, Henrietta Silver and Cass Garfield—met at Tyler's hideout the next day at nine o'clock—with one addition.

Marie Blazek was dishwater-blond, solidly built, five foot eight in her stocking feet, though she wore thick-soled work boots into which she'd tucked her faded blue jeans that made her look an inch taller. A long denim jacket over a checkered Wrangler shirt hid the awesome heat packed on both hips. She introduced herself as "Marshal Blazek."

Sierra shook her hand. "Garfield told me this wasn't an official federal operation."

"It's not," Blazek replied. "But I'm his—significant other—and work with him a lot. When I heard about this, it hit a nerve. So here I am."

"The more the merrier. Do you know everyone else here?"

Blazek nodded to Henrietta Silver and Tyler. "I live here. I get around."

Tyler said, "Who's running the show here? Who's the general?"

Cass Garfield glanced at Sierra. "You're the one who started this, Chief."

She said, "This is my first major raid, Marshal. Your experience is way ahead of mine. You take over."

"Everybody okay with that?"

There was an affirmative mumble.

"Okay, gather around the desk."

They all moved forward. Garfield said, "Everyone here have handcuffs? Two pair?"

Except for Henrietta Silver, they all nodded. She said, "I don't carry handcuffs—or guns, either. I don't have a badge."

"Neither do I," Tyler said, "but that won't stop me. I have cuffs—and weapons."

"The only ones who have the total right to discharge those weapons are Marshal Blazek and myself," Garfield said. "Chief Bravo, too, if you stretch it. Tyler can shoot if his life is in imminent danger. Not otherwise."

"Or if *your* life is in imminent danger, Marshal," Sierra offered.

Garfield cocked his head and looked at her. "Thanks for worrying about my ass." He cleared off the desk, making room for a black canvas bag. Unzipping it, he removed five smaller boxes and handed one to each of the others. "This is a twenty-first century version of a walkie-talkie," he said. "You need the earpiece plugged in and the receiver turned on, so we don't fall

all over ourselves. But when it's time to break in, take them off and leave them in the car. They belong to the United States government." Then he tilted the canvas bag sideways to show what else was inside. "Here's the twenty-five grand, in small bills on the outside. Inside it's just cut up newspaper, but with any luck they won't get a chance to count it." He looked at Sierra Bravo. "You'll carry it in. Use your left hand and keep your right hand free if you have to draw a weapon."

Sierra opened her small box. She'd never seen one of these thingamajigs before. Prior to this, all her communication with other fellow cops had been over police radio.

Blazek, standing next to her, quietly said, "I'll show you how to work it."

"We've each got a car," Cass went on. "We'll need all of them, because we're going to bust everyone there and haul them off to jail."

"What if we run out of handcuffs?" Tyler asked.

"Then we stuff the excess assholes into our car trunks. If any of you have crap in yours already, dump it to make room for them." He looked at Henrietta. "Not you. You're going to take the little girl to the Marshal's office. When we get everyone back there and sorted out, we'll call somebody who can take care of her."

"Unless," Marie Blazek said, "you and I get reamed out by the big boss and get our butts fired."

Cass Garfield took out one gun, checked again that it was loaded, then tucked it back into his hip holster. "He won't can us when he sees the child. He's a sucker for kids. As for us—we're downright lovable. Now—who'll be where when this attack goes down?"

The quintet moved out ten minutes later. Sierra Bravo in the lead, as she was the one who'd made the "deal" with Marvin Dreskler and the only one he could recognize. The satchel full of newspaper was on the seat beside her.

Then came Tyler—strong enough to bust in most doors, in

case they had to.

Third in line was the United States Marshal, driving a large black Ford Fairlane. There was a solid iron screen between the front and back seats. In the rear, welded into each side, were two sturdy metal bars, and another one crosswise across the front seats. On the floor next to him was a sawed-off shotgun. Following him was Marie Blazek—same make and model car, except hers was dark green, and the same set-up inside. Both cars had bulletproof windows.

Unarmed Hank Silver brought up the rear, but she had a pile of blankets, pillows, and snacks with her, as if she were going on a road trip with a child instead of rescuing one from a life of torment, torture and abuse.

Sierra, more nervous than since her pre-teen days with her drunken father, kept looking in the rearview mirror to make sure her tiny army was behind her. The troubles that had thrown her off-stride, like Danielle Micaela Tokes and Kenneth Zack taking aim on her job, and the awkward, embarrassing moment with Chet Quigley were now so far in the back of her mind that she wasn't aware of them anymore. She'd never dreamed of the truly dangerous sortie she was now undertaking.

The faceless child, created in Sierra's own imagination, tormented her. She might save the little girl in question—Lakela— this morning. But that other little girl, the one in the men's room who started the whole thing, thanks to Walter Lyons, would weigh heavily on her for the rest of her life.

Four of the posse parked their cars around the corner from Dreskler's hangout, but Tyler, who drove a somewhat ancient Toyota Camry, was down at the far end of the street, his car pointed away from the door of the warehouse. He was bent over, almost resting on his side so as not to be seen, his mirror adjusted so he could watch everything that went on. When everyone was in place, Garfield's voice crackled.

"Everyone where they're supposed to be? Good. Now we wait."

Wait, Sierra thought, grinding her teeth. Time waits for no man. Waiting rooms. Waiting in line. Waiting for the phone to ring. Everything comes to those who wait. Waiting for Godot. Waiting for Santa Claus—and though never in the military, she was familiar with the saying: Hurry up and wait.

Waiting sucked—it was one of Sierra's least-favorite pastimes—and now she was stuck with it, accompanied by strangers in a strange town who were there to help her right a wrong—and maybe to save her butt in the bargain.

She scrunched in her car for more than an hour, uncomfortable because her two guns and the can of pepper spray in her underwear made it impossible for her to relax. Each minute seemed like an eternity, and she wished someone would give her a dollar every time she looked at her wristwatch. The time seemed to go even slower. Nothing to eat or drink except one coffee since she awoke. Now she might kill for another one.

What if no one showed up with the little girl? How long after eleven o'clock should they hang around there, jacked up and disquieted in their vehicles, and how stupid would all of them feel when they eventually had to leave empty-handed?

At ten minutes after eleven, when she was wishing she could turn back the clock to the morning she first heard about the little girl from Walter Lyons, there was a startling crackle in her earpiece, then Tyler's voice saying, low and intense, "We've got company," and she sat up straight, teeth gritted and the skin on the backs of her hands tingling as if they'd gone to sleep.

Around the corner, a short man built like a fireplug got out of a black GMC truck, his arm tightly gripping the elbow of a young and very frightened Asian girl. She wasn't crying or screaming, but she struggled a bit to loosen his grasp on her arm. Angrily, he shook her, which calmed her down. He banged on the warehouse door with a closed fist, waited a while, and then it opened and he and the child went inside.

Tyler's voice: "There's no one else in the truck. Give it five minutes. Then we *go!*"

Sierra carefully raised her head and looked around. Her other three partners had risen up, too, and were reconnoitering the situation. She inhaled almost all the air in the closed car, held it for about fifteen seconds before blowing it out noisily in a hiccup. She was the one who would knock on the door first. As she touched the weapons holstered on each side of her, to ensure they were still there, she studied her wristwatch to time the regular hiccups as the second hand ticked toward her destiny.

Then Tyler's voice cut through the silence. "Let's *move!*"

She quickly swung her legs out of her car, snatching up the black case, and began walking toward the corner. Tyler, Cass Garfield, Marie Blazek and Hank Silver followed, several lengths behind her.

They turned the corner, marching steadily toward the warehouse entrance, all but Sierra brushing against the wall so as not to be seen. Sierra finally stopped, waiting until the marshals moved to the left of her. Tyler and Silver posted themselves on her right. She made eye contact with each of them, then stepped forward and knocked on the door hard enough to make her knuckles ache.

Wait.

More wait.

Then she heard locks being unlocked. The door opened slightly more than a crack to reveal an eye of the cowboy once more.

"Yeah?"

"Remember me?" Sierra said. "From two days ago?"

"So?"

She lifted the case. "Look—I brought Marvin Dreskler a present. Let me in."

Shrugging, the cowboy opened the door a few inches more. "You gotta be patted down again—and don't complain about it this time, bitch!"

That's when Tyler threw his entire weight against the door, blasting it wide open as the cowboy was literally knocked off his feet. It took less than five seconds for Sierra, Tyler, Blazek,

Garfield and Silver to be inside. All had weapons out except Hank.

"United States Marshals," Garfield shouted. "Don't even blink!"

There were only two other men in the room this time, one possibly a paper pusher from two days earlier, seated at a desk working on a laptop. He leaped from his chair and reached for the holster on his hip, then froze as Marie Blazek pointed her weapon right at his face. "Don't even think about touching it, pal," she said. "You'll hate it if you do—for less than one second."

The other man, the square, squat one Tyler had watched delivering the young girl earlier, stared with his eyes were saucer-wide and terrified. He was evidently unarmed, because he stayed in his chair, clasped his hands on top of his head, and hoped nobody would shoot him.

When the cowboy got to his feet, Cass Garfield gripped him at the back of his neck after relieving him of his gun and tossed it across the room under an unoccupied desk.

"Where's Dreskler?" he demanded.

"How the fuck would I know?" the cowboy whined—approximately two seconds before Garfield smashed him across the bridge of the nose with his weapon. The noise of bone cracking was as loud as a detonated bomb. The cowboy screamed and raised his hands to his nose to stanch the blood that began pouring out. Garfield said, "The next one's going to be in your eye. Where's Marvin Dreskler?"

The cowboy groaned, and Garfield raised his gun again. "I think I forgot how to count to three."

"All right!" the cowboy said, his words difficult to understand. He finally pointed with one hand to the door leading to the next room.

"Is that little girl in there with him?"

Now all the cowboy could do was nod.

"Anyone else?"

The sound the cowboy made through his fingers trying to staunch the nosebleed sounded much like "Nuh-uh."

Garfield told the other man with his hands clasped on his head to lie down on the floor, and said to Marie Blazek, "I don't think our cowboy and his girlfriend there are going anywhere—so as soon as he stops clutching his broken nose, cuff both of them. If they give you any trouble, shoot 'em—and not where it would kill them. Tight. Empty your gun at their knees, and then at their balls before you put 'em away for good. Make sure they suffer big time before they die screaming."

The cowboy stopped groaning and shouted, "Police brutality!"

"Right," the marshal said. "Police brutality That was my major in college. Blow it out your ass."

Sierra Bravo said, "We have to get the little girl."

Garfield nodded. "You come with me, Chief—but be careful. Dreskler is probably armed." He turned to Henrietta. "You, too, Hank. It's your job to get her out to your car."

Silver's nod was short, jerky. "Got you, Marshal."

"Stand away from the door." Sierra nodded, looking stressed, thinking guns would be fired the moment the door opened. Then Garfield said, "Ready?"

"Never been more ready," Sierra told him, both weapons in her hands, and Garfield kicked the door open so they could storm in together.

Marvin Dreskler was standing in the far corner of the room, his left arm around the neck of the little girl, who was screaming in total terror, her teary eyes red and puffy. His right hand held a gun to her head. He'd heard the noise through the door, and threatening a child with a gun was the best idea he could come up with. His face was ivory white—but he still looked defiant.

"Drop your guns," he croaked, "or the kid gets it."

"Are you going to shoot her in the head?" Garfield said. "I'd be sad about that—and sad for you,too, Dreskler. You're more of a dumb shit than I thought you were."

"We'll see how sad you'll be when this fucking kid loses the whole side of her head."

"Don't you realize," Sierra said, "that if you pull that trigger, you'll be cut in half before she even hits the floor?"

"Give it up, Marvin," Garfield urged quietly. "You're fucked."

"Are you arresting me?" Dreskler's voice was shaky, but he still pressed the gun to the child's temple. "You got no proof."

"I'll think of something. Littering. Jaywalking. Farting in church—and whatever prison you wind up in, every inmate will know you're an international pimp of children—I'll make sure of that. You won't get through the first night—and if you do, they'll be able to drive a Mack truck up your ass without ever touching the sides. So let the little girl go, put your weapon on the floor, and relax."

Breathing heavily, Dreskler wavered for about five seconds before Sierra raised her right-hand gun higher, closed one eye, and aimed carefully for the point between his eyebrows. "My patience wears thin, Marvin."

"All right, all right!" he said, and gave up his grip on the little girl, Lakela. Hank stepped forward, arms outstretched, and Lakela ran into them, her sobs louder than Sierra Bravo had ever heard. This was a child's abject terror she'd never seen before.

Sighing, Dreskler put his weapon on the floor in front of him—gently. "Don't shoot," he said. "The gun is on the floor. Please don't shoot, okay?"

Hank Silver was cuddling the child, dabbing at her nose with tissue she'd stuffed in her pockets before she left. "Shh, sweetheart," she was murmuring, even though Lakela didn't know a word of English. She buried her face between Hank's bosoms and held on for dear life. "You're all right now, Lakela." She pronounced the little girl's name carefully. "You're safe."

CHAPTER THIRTEEN

The man who owned the old house on a farm site inside the limits of Sundown Beach drank a beer and watched the eleven-year-old child, Ilinca, eating her dinner. It was a decent meal—for her, anyway; a deli chicken sandwich on white bread with mayonnaise, lettuce and tomatoes, a generous handful of generic potato chips and a glass of root beer. He could have served her milk, but milk leaves some people with stale breath—and bad breath would not be tolerated on this particular evening. Milk or no milk, she looked more relaxed than usual because she hadn't been forced to service him sexually before she was allowed to eat.

The homeowner, of course, was not at all relaxed.

Edgar Pratt was his name. He'd spent more than sixteen years making his career profitable—security, negotiation, and many other personal responsibilities he provided his boss. Until the first time his job was to find a child sex slave for his employer, he'd never considered himself a pedophile. His fantasies had scared him to death, but he never dreamed to act on them until the man who paid his handsome salary shared with him his own Short-Eyes tendencies and made him the messenger, babysitter and watchdog the first time he'd bought a child.

Of course, the girl now had to live at Edgar's house, as she certainly couldn't be seen hanging around with the high level of affluence of the plutocrat from Sundown Beach who'd purchased her. The man was super-rich—he could afford virgins. Edgar wasn't nearly that wealthy.

Now he was Ilinca's caretaker, which meant a great deal in his business career. He made sure she didn't gain or lose weight, indulged in no abusive habits to her other than the fellatio he demanded at least twice daily, and he knew better than to actually fuck her. That, his boss told him, was forbidden—her anus and vagina were reserved for him alone.

He was jealous. He couldn't help it. His employer had enjoyed Ilinca's virginity more than Pratt could have imagined. He talked about it to Edgar for weeks afterwards. He'd used her body regularly, at least two evenings per week, but wouldn't allow Edgar to do so. Taking advantage would cost Edgar his job, benefits, everything he'd worked for—and possibly worse, since no one dared to defy a multimillionaire who signed paychecks. Ilinca wasn't worth it, he knew. Still, the jealousy ate away at him.

After she finished eating, he led her upstairs to her own room and forced her to put on a pretty dress he'd purchased for her, gut twisting and penis stiffening while he watched her stripping and then re-dressing. Afterwards, telling her to stay where she was, he went back down and washed the dishes. It wouldn't do if the child developed dishpan hands.

At a few minutes past eight, he heard the car engine, watched as the headlights found their way up the bumpy road to where he lived. On the rare occasions he had visitors—usually handymen to perform some repair or other—he'd wait for a knock and then open the door. Tonight, he didn't have to. He knew his employer had a key.

"Hey, boss," he said when the man walked into the living room.

"Where is she?"

Edgar needed to cough and clear the frog from his throat, but he only had a one-word answer, so he chose not to. "Upstairs."

His boss made an airy, dismissive wave toward him. "Take a hike, Edgar," he said.

Driving away down a road that hadn't been repaved in two decades, Edgar Pratt was keenly resentful, as he always was when his employer visited his home to see Ilinca and told him to leave. It's a damn good thing he was paid extra, off the books, besides his own generous salary and bennies at the office.

Maybe, he thought, turning into the parking lot of a saloon right on the ocean, if he played his cards right and invested much of that bonus cash in blue-chip stocks, someday soon he'd be able to walk away from his longtime job and his greedy, demanding boss, sell his Sundown Beach farm, settle in a city far away, and buy himself his own little girl again—a virgin child no one else could touch but him.

He went inside the tavern and swung onto a barstool. The crowd was considerably younger than he—loud, boisterous, and heavy beer drinkers. He'd begun loathing raucous young men when he turned forty, hating them for their good looks, youth, stamina, and better luck with women. He scanned the crowd for a pretty girl—found several. But no, he didn't really want them anymore. They were in their twenties, flirting non-virgins who probably knew more about sex than Edgar had ever learned. One of the women, already half-snockered, gave him a small, discreet smile, but he wasn't interested in that, either, nor did he return the look. Over the past few years, his sexual proclivities had changed, thanks to his employer. But she was indeed horny—and yes, she'd get laid that night by some hunky stud even drunker than she, and would tiptoe out of her place before she awoke.

Fuck them! He had no use for millennials. There was no point in being stupid, no matter how old they were.

He ordered the most expensive beer they had in the place—a Heineken, since the tavern was far from a top-shelf cocktail lounge—and slammed it down with three giant gulps. Then he ordered another, not seeing the TV screen behind the bar, as he had little interest in sports. Damn! Now, he thought, he couldn't return home for another two hours. He gnashed his teeth in quiet anger, had three more beers, and spoke to no one.

***

Finally, there were just the three of them in Dresker's office—Chief of Police Sierra Bravo, U.S. Marshal Cass Garfield, and Marvin Dreskler. No one spoke, but Garfield's glare at Dreskler cut right through to the bone. The silence was deafening.

At length, Dreskler said, "Aren't you going to arrest me?"

No one answered for a quarter of a minute, which made Dreskler squirm. Finally, Garfield said, "Oh, we'll arrest you, all right. It just depends."

"Depends on what?"

Sierra said, "On what charge and how much you'll tell us."

"About what?"

"You're not running this international child-smuggling ring, Marvin," Garfield said easily. "You're a twit. You're not even a *low-level* twit. So, who is it you work for, Marvin-boy? Names. I want names."

"I don't know any names," Marvin replied, obviously terrified. "When I get the money, I take ten percent off the top and send the rest to a Cayman Island account. I'm not—what you said. I'm a middleman. Whoever owns that account probably doesn't live in the United States."

"Are you bullshitting, Marvin?" Sierra demanded. "Two days ago, you wanted me to think you were the top-shit guy." She shook her head. "Now I see you're a liar as well as a pimp. I had no respect for you from the beginning—but after this, you're lower than whale shit to me."

"I'm telling the truth!" Dreskler said and took two steps forward. One step too many. Marshal Garfield smashed him across the face with his gun, sending him spinning off into the corner. Dreskler's hand was up, covering his face, blood spurting between his fingers.

"Get it into your head," Garfield rasped, "because this isn't an arrest yet. Not yet." He moved closer to Dreskler. "You don't move, you don't even *blink* unless I tell you to. I want answers," he said. "If I don't get them, I'm going to hurt you—worse than anyone ever hurt you before. The government doesn't allow agents and cops do that because it's against the law. So just ask me, Marvin, whether I give a fuck." He leaned forward to speak right into Marvin's ear. "The beauty part is—no blood, no bruises. Your busted nose won't count—that was for resisting arrest. You won't tell anybody how bad I'll hurt you, because nothing will show. Sure, you'll piss blood for a few months, but they won't blame that on me. You won't get a woody for the rest of your life, either. So, you'd better start talking. Names, Marvin, I want names—or I'll put your dick in that opened desk drawer and then slam it shut. Hard!" Marshal Garfield rotated his shoulders to get the kinks out, actually making a popping sound. "I'm not kidding."

Half an hour later, Marvin Dreskler was huddled up on the floor in one corner of the room in a nearly fetal position, rocking back and forth. The buttons on his shirt had been ripped off, his pants were down around his ankles, and his whitey-tighties announced to the world that he'd peed all over himself. The blood from his nose had stopped gushing, but it soaked his torn clothes, along with his own vomit. His eyes were tightly closed and his face flushed deep red. He whimpered softly.

Sierra Bravo didn't want to look at him. What she'd witnessed for the past half hour sickened her, and she'd fought successfully not to barf. Cass Garfield, his jacket slung over the back of Marvin's chair and two holstered pistols in full view, sat on the edge of the desk, wearing leather gloves and breathing hard. "I'm getting too old for this," he panted.

Sierra approached him. "Marshal—you think maybe he really doesn't know the name of the guy who's been giving the orders?"

Garfield considered it. "Probably not. He would've told me twenty minutes ago if he'd known."

"He gave you the Cayman Islands bank number, didn't he?"

"That bank wouldn't tell anyone the name of the President of the United States. We haven't learned a goddamn thing."

Sierra sucked in two lungs full of air and expelled them slowly. "Not yet, Marshal."

"Oh?"

"Wake him up again."

Garfield's eyebrows struggled upward toward his hairline. "Are you kidding? You almost yakked up your breakfast."

"I got over it."

"Why wake him up, then? You think I enjoyed hurting him?"

"I can't tell you how much I hate this. But I came here for a specific reason—and he's the only one who can give me an answer."

Garfield had to ponder that for a moment. "Well—it's your ballgame, anyway." He walked over, slapped Marvin's face and shook his shoulder until he opened his eyes, wide as saucers and bulging with fear, as he cringed, trapped in the corner.

"No more," he croaked. "Please! No more!"

"Talk to the Chief, Marvin—and we'll see about the 'no more' business."

Sierra eased herself between the two, squatted down, and looked Marvin directly in the eye. "You won't have any more worries if you tell me something, Marvin," she said. "You can tell me the easy way—that's my first choice. Or you can eventually tell him—and that's the hard way, as I'm sure you realize. But, easy or hard, you will tell me what I need to know."

His chin dropped to his chest, and his sigh turned into a shiver. "What do you want?" he asked, his voice soft and shaken.

She glanced up at the marshal, who nodded back at her. Then she said, "Someone sold a little girl to a man who lives in Sundown Beach or the surrounding area in the past year. I'm guessing. I'm also guessing you know."

"I don't know anything about that."

Sierra straightened up and moved out of the way so Cass Garfield could get closer to Dreskler.

"Okay, Marvin," he said. "Here's how it's going to work. First, I'll dislocate your right shoulder. You can't imagine how painful it will be. If that doesn't get your attention, I'll dislocate the left one, meaning that for the rest of your life, any time you feel the need to scratch your ass, you'll have to ask someone to do it for you." He grabbed Dreskler's right biceps with one hand and put his other one hard against Dreskler's shoulder.

"No, no, NO! Please!" Dreskler's voice rose to hysterical levels, and his body jerked and writhed like a marionette dangling from the strings of a puppeteer who'd suddenly gone insane. "I'll talk. I'll talk!"

Garfield looked triumphant as Sierra moved in front of their victim again. "Tell me all about it, Marvin. Take your time."

Dreskler put his hands in front of his crotch, though everyone had seen him lose control of his bladder. He croaked, "I did—provide a girl to somebody living in Sundown Beach. Maybe about three months ago."

"For how much?"

He closed his eyes. "It's hard for me to remember right now. I think about twenty grand. Twenty-five, I think it was."

"Write you a check, did he?"

"Cash," he said. "All cash all the time."

"And how much of that went into your pocket, Marvin?"

Sigh. "Ten percent."

"Cute. What do you do with the rest of it?"

"Send it to that account in the Cayman Islands."

"And you don't know whose account that is?"

Dreskler shook his head. "I don't know. Maybe a person—a big corporation. I don't even know where they are. My guess is it's not in America."

"So far, so good, Marvin. Now—the name of the guy in Sundown Beach."

He shook his head. "I don't remember his name. Honest to Jesus."

Garfield said, "Marvin—regarding the discussion of selling prepubescent children to be whores—I suggest you leave Jesus out of the conversation."

"You have no records on paper?" Sierra said. "You exchange thousands of dollars with people for baby sex slaves, and you don't write down their names?"

Dreskler swallowed loudly and licked his lips. "Can I have a drink of water?"

"No," Garfield snapped. "Where are your records? Your files?"

Marvin Dreskler glanced sideways at a set of double doors in the opposite wall.

"Get up off your ass, then. Walk over there and show me your files."

"And for cry sakes, Marvin," Sierra said, "pull your pants up."

Marvin got shakily to his feet, hiked his pants up around his hips and buttoned them, not bothering to secure his belt, and limped across the room to the double doors, hardly able to move after the damage inflicted on him by Case Garfêld to make him talk.

Behind the doors was a wall safe. Marvin's hand quivered as he attempted to twirl the dials. Sierra Bravo moved him along more quickly by jamming her pistol into his ribs.

"I'm going as fast as I can," he whimpered.

"Want to talk about how you can go faster?" Garfield stepped forward menacingly, which made Marvin moan. Finally, using one hand to steady himself against the wall, he managed to click all the correct numbers, and the safe swung open. Garfield shoved him aside and removed everything that was stored in there.

"Some money," he said to Sierra. "Not a hell of a lot, though." He riffled through a rubber-banded stack of bills. "Probably not much more than three grand. Marvin—this is a cheap-ass operation you run here."

"Not true, sir," Marvin whined. Cass Garfield tried not to smile at the "sir."

"Where do you keep it all, then?" Sierra demanded. "Under your mattress?"

"Like I said—I take my commission off the top and wire the rest of the money away."

"And you don't know who to?"

Marvin shook his head. "These people are no amateurs. They hide everything, even their own names. If you went to the Cayman Islands and hung around that bank waiting for someone to come and pick up their money, you'd still be wasting your time."

Sierra reached over and took the stack of files from the marshal. "Let's see how good you've been in hiding things, Marvin." She sat down behind the desk and began examining the records. "Hmm," she murmured, "some of them name names."

"Let's see those names, please," Garfêld said, and Garfield flipped through them. "A few names in California. One's in Bakersfield—and holy crap! One who's probably a tech genius—in Silicon Valley!" He looked quickly at the rest. "Everyone else is in Arizona or Nevada—and one in Portland."

"Why did they shop with Dreskler, then?"

Garfield shrugged. "If they lived in big cities, they'd have local markets there. But shopping for full-time child sex in your own hometown would be too dangerous—so they came to Hemlock Hills instead."

Sierra found a record that totally blew her mind, and she gasped.

"What?"

Catching her breath, she didn't answer for a moment. Then: "Here it is, Marshal," she said, staring at the paper. "It's dated about four months ago, like Marvin said. Twenty grand changed hands, and the child was from Romania. No names—but she was delivered to someone from Sundown Beach." She looked up, shattered. "*My* town."

"Damn," Garfield said.

"How are we going to find her?" Sierra bounced between tears and fury.

"The main thing is to find the guy first."

"How do we do that? We don't have a name, an address, *any-thing*!"

"True," Garfield said. "But we do have something. We have good old Marvin, here."

Dreskler flattened himself against the wall, his throat once more closing in panic. "All I know is what's in there."

"Maybe," said Sierra. "Maybe not." She stood up from her seat behind Marvin's desk and offered it to him. "Make yourself comfortable, Marvin. We have lots of things to talk about."

Three hours later, Sierra Bravo drove back to Sundown Beach. She felt almost good about herself.

Almost.

The Cambodia child, Lakela, was taken to the marshal's office in Hemlock Hills, fed, soothed by Hank Silver and given some ice cream, and then turned over to a nationally known group whose only mission was to place abused or kidnapped children with those who keep them safe and secure. Hank assured Sierra that she'd given Lakela to a Chinese-American foster family—the father was a California native, and the wife had been born and raised in Denver, Colorado, but both spoke a smattering of Mandarin Chinese. That had been a huge boulder lifted from Sierra's shoulders ever since she'd met up with Marvin in the first place, now that she'd actually taken part in saving a little girl from a 24/7 nightmare. She kept her car windows open, the breeze in her face. She felt free—and victorious.

The initial force that had thrown her into international slave trafficking in the first place had not yet been solved—but at least she had a direction in which to proceed.

Marvin Dreskler had sworn he never knew the buyer's name, even though he had demanded proof of Sierra's identity the first time she knocked on his door. He insisted that the man had come to him through a phone call from Kurt Wimblehart, one of his Hemlock Hills associates.

Sierra told Dreskler that Wimblehart had sent her, but Wimblehart had not reached him, probably because Tyler had beaten Marvin's name out of him, injuring him so badly that he'd evidently decided Hemlock Hills was no place for him anymore. He'd skedaddled to someplace where he hoped angry black men who were built like a middle-sized building wouldn't find him and torture him half to death.

Sierra was uncomfortable with that—sort of. Torture was horrific to her, even when used by the CIA to make would-be Islamic terrorists spill their guts. It was painful for her to be there when the U.S. Marshal inflicted the unspeakable on Marvin Dreskler for the better part of half an hour. It would be eons before she'd forget the dribbling saliva, the snot-streaming screams.

Worse still, small children were ripped from their homes and forced to be prostitutes. What little she'd learned from Dreskler clearly implied that her initial fears for a specific little girl she'd never seen had been correct—and had nibbled away at her guts ever since Walter Lyons squirmed into her office and told her the story.

Dreskler was in federal custody now, thanks to the Marshal's office, and Sierra would return to Hemlock Hills to testify against him. He might moan and whine that he was abused into giving testimony, but Cass Garfield had already told him that if he didn't keep his mouth shut, every inmate in the prison to which he'd be sent would be told about his revolting "business" selling children to child-fuckers, in which case Dreskler might last three nights in the slammer, but not much longer.

Unlike having little ability to make arrests unless she made them in Sundown Beach, Sierra could bust damn near anybody connected with Dreskler in her home base. She had no true inkling where she would begin her investigation—but she had a pretty good idea.

CHAPTER FOURTEEN

The day before Sierra Bravo returned from Hemlock Hills, Sergeant Griffin Parrish of the Sundown Beach Police Department got a surprise visit from Kenneth Zack. Griff's usual spot was up front at the desk, the first cop to see everyone arriving, with a clear view through the long windows and the thick glass doors of what went on in the parking lot or on Sassafras Street, which runs past the station. He was immediately aware of the Bentley moving softly into the lot, stopping right in front of the door in a No Parking spot. Zack got out, nodding once to his African American chauffer, straightened his cuffs beneath the sleeves of his two thousand-dollar suit, checked his reflection in the car window to make sure his gray hair wasn't mussed, and headed straight for Parrish. They had met several times, but the police sergeant was certain Zack didn't remember him, or if he did, he couldn't recall his name.

Before Griff could utter his usual "Good afternoon, sir, may I help you?" Kenneth Zack said brusquely, "Am I correct that Chief of Police Bravo is not here today?"

"That is correct," Griff said coldly. It wasn't that he was annoyed with the Bentley, nor irritated at how Zack had primped himself in the reflection of his car window. It was the attitude that got to him. Politicians had it—the narcissistic arrogance of obscene wealth hand in hand with power and elitism. Some sports stars had it, too, and almost all movie actors, although

Sundown Beach was a bit too far from Beverly Hills and Bel Air for film people to bother with.

The toxically wealthy people had it, too—just like Kenneth Zack.

"That's good, Sergeant—" Zack peered at Griff's metallic name badge. "Sergeant Paris."

Paris, Griffin Parrish thought. Zack hadn't forgotten his name, as he could read as well as anyone. The mispronunciation was on purpose—just to set the rules here as to who was big and rich and powerful and who was *just* a civil servant. He decided not to push it; life was too short.

Kenneth Zack looked around—not nervously, because money-crunchers never lost their nerve over anything, but only to see if anyone was listening. There were too many cops around to suit him, so he lowered his voice. "Is there a private place we can talk?"

Griff motioned for Zack to follow him down the hall to the chief's office. He stepped aside politely so Zack could enter. The obscenely wealthy Sundowner moved around to sit in the chief's chair behind the desk.

Wow! Griffin thought. Talk about entitlement!

"Sit down, why don't you?" Kenneth Zack said.

"I'm fine like this. What's on your mind?"

Zack leaned back comfortably in Sierra Bravo's chair. "I'm certain you're aware a traffic citation has been issued to my son, Dylan."

The response was a subtle nod.

"Dylan was stopped for speeding—and an unlawful examination of his car revealed that he was carrying a small amount of marijuana."

"That's what I hear," Griff said, "except for the unlawful part. The officer smelled marijuana in the car, which gave him the legal right to conduct a further investigation."

Zack tilted his head, speaking the way a pre-kindergarten teacher would explain to one of her students that pooping on the floor is unacceptable. "We're not talking about enough marijuana to sell, Sergeant, or about heroin or meth or crack cocaine. And the road Dylan was driving was pretty empty at that time of night."

"So?"

"I've been trying to get Chief Bravo to tear up that citation ever since it happened."

Griff said, "Strange, but I don't think I've ever seen you visit this station, Mr. Zack."

"I—sent someone in my place. I didn't want to personally intimidate the chief."

"I see. And how exactly do you personally intimidate the chief of police?"

Zack's smile became a smirk. "I'm afraid I intimidate most people—because I'm rich. Very *very* rich."

"I don't think you intimidate the chief one bit."

"No? How about you? Do I intimidate you, Sergeant?"

"You love that, don't you, Mr. Zack? You love to see people shaking in their boots because you think it makes you a really big man when you stand on your wallet."

"I can have you fired, Paris. I can fire the officer who issued that violation ticket—and I can have Chief Bravo out on her ass, too." He held up both hands, palms outward. "I don't want to do that. You're a good cop: I know that for a fact."

Griff nodded. "Make sure whoever told you what a good cop I am is generously thanked, though they probably told you to mispronounce my name. But I'm still waiting for the reason why you and your Bentley are here."

Kenneth Zack's face changed into a pose of elite arrogance, reminiscent of the World War II dictator of Italy, Benito Mussonoli. "Very well. Chief Bravo is absent, which leaves you as the highest-ranking officer. Since she can't quash that traffic violation for my son, you can."

"I can indeed."

"Good."

"But I won't."

Kenneth Zack frowned so broadly that his eyebrows almost met. "You're walking on thin ice, Paris."

Paris again. Griff spoke through clenched teeth. "I don't think so, Mr. Zack. First of all, that would be against the law—and I've spent my whole life upholding the law, so I'm not about to break it. Secondly, there's no ice to walk on at any Southern California beach, so you'd better make up a better threat. And thirdly, my name is Parrish—with an H on the end. I suggest you begin using it."

The phone on Sierra's desk rang once, and the Number Two button flashed, but both men ignored it. Ken Zack snarled, "You'll regret saying that. I'm not somebody you can fuck with."

"Actually, I can fuck with whoever I want," Griffin said. "I've got a badge and a gun. You can't make me do anything—and your girlfriend Danielle can't, either."

"She's not my girlfriend," Zack protested.

"I have no interest in your sex life one way or another. No regrets here, Mr. Zack—other than my letting you sit in Chief Bravo's chair. So if you'd kindly remove your ass from it and move your Bentley out of the No Parking Zone, I can get back to doing what I'm paid to do."

Zack pushed himself up from Sierra's executive chair and walked to the doorway. "You've been warned," he grumbled. "Remember that you've been warned."

"Good enough. But I warn you, too—if you fire me, and if you fire Chief Bravo, the rest of this department is going to say kiss my ass to you and resign, too. Then, unless you've already lined up an entire brand new department, professionally trained the way we've been, but told any illegal acts you and your kid have committed or might commit is off-limits to local and federal laws, you've got a city without a police force. Reckless driving and speeding here will go up. Crime will go up. So will violence. Sundown Beach will be a mecca for illegal substances—not just marijuana, but coke and meth and horse, too."

"That's bullshit!"

"I'm not finished. Fire us and the reason you did so will be all over the newspapers, clear down to San Diego and up to Los Angeles—the chief and I will make sure of that. I know you've got all the money in the goddamn world and the so-called power to go with it, but frankly, your reputation will stink to high heaven—and eventually you'll lose business because of having no police force."

Kenneth Zack turned to leave, but Sergeant Parrish stopped him. "I wouldn't be surprised if the entire fire department doesn't resign as well—because, unlike you, they back up the police. So, wish hard your hillside mansion doesn't go up in smoke, because the only way you'll be able to put the fire out is to piss on it!"

The bastard! Parrish thought after Zack had slammed all the doors on his way out. In large cities, the cops served at the pleasure of the mayor or the elected managers, and so much political crap goes on there that sometimes it was difficult for law enforcement to do its duty. But Sundown Beach, a resort area stretching from the inland foothills to the Pacific Ocean, doesn't allow its residents to use threats and bribery.

Maybe Kenneth Zack *could* get him fired, this close to his retirement and pension, and could get rid of Sierra Bravo, too, if he had a mind to. The other members on the city council were nearly as rich as he was. Eben Flood charged five hundred fifty bucks per hour for legal consultation and was managing partner in the law firm bearing his name. Long-divorced, he had no one on which to spend millions but himself. Dick Stubblefield didn't build as many staggeringly expensive places to live or work as did Donald Trump, but he was right up there, too, eager to remind everyone how silk-stocking opulent he was.

As for Danielle Tokes, she did make lots of money selling real estate, and was always on the side of Ken Zack, hell or high water, so she'd vote any way he ordered her to.

Of course, all Sierra and he had done to anger them was to

refuse destroying Dylan Zack's traffic ticket—so Griff figured that if it costs them their jobs, he'll contact a lawyer. The only lawyer in town who was on their side was the city manager, Chris Fornadel—at least he was on Sierra's side. Though also prosperous, he seemed a pretty decent human being. Maybe he would help.

Griff was concerned about Sierra. She hadn't answered his phone calls. He had no idea where she was, or why. He knew she was on a mission to locate the little girl Walter Lyons had seen, though why she went out of town to do so escaped him.

He wasn't psychic. He couldn't tell the future, to read the minds of other people, to spot a good guy from a bad guy by looking, even though many cops are able to do that. He was convinced that all psychics became TV mountebanks as an excellent way to get rich. But he had that gnawing 'feeling' that Sierra Bravo tiptoed too close to danger, and there was nothing he could do about it.

After about two minutes, Nancy Flower walked into the chief's office. "What the hell did you say to him, Sarge? He left here madder than a kicked-over wasp nest."

"How could you tell?"

"It's the first time I ever heard of someone in a Bentley laying down rubber pulling out of a parking lot."

Parrish laughed.

"I sent a call in here, but you didn't pick up."

"I was too busy thinking about selling stolen oranges on a turnpike exit ramp after he gets me fired. Was it important?"

"Well," Flower said, "it was Chief Bravo."

He stopped smiling and leaned forward in his chair. "Where is she?"

"On her way home. She'll be in first thing tomorrow."

"What did she say? Did she get that—little girl business tied up?"

Flower shook her head. "Didn't say anything about it—but she did suggest you and I spend tonight sharpening up our marksmanship at the shooting range—whatever that means."

Sergeant Parrish rose heavily from his chair. "You think she found out the bad guy is a paper target?"

"I wish," Nancy Flower said.

Sierra arrived back at her condo exhausted, relieved, but with mixed emotions and a pounding headache.

There was much good news. Marvin Dreskler and any hangers-on who were around that morning had been carted off to the Office of the U.S. Marshal, and the FBI had been called after it was too late for them to demand the credit. Dreskler would not resume his lucrative business in human trafficking. Lakela, the little Cambodian girl who had much spunk and courage during a horrible situation, had been taken in by one of the most active child-rescuing organizations in the country. Whether to return her to her original family in Cambodia was not the best idea in the world, as the family had already *sold* her.

Better still, Dreskler had volunteered information that opened a door Sierra hadn't thought of, and would allow her to investigate Walter Lyons' original report of possible child abuse.

That was the good stuff.

The bad stuff—and Sierra would be a long time falling asleep having to relive and shudder over every moment of it—is that Marshal Cass Garfield had brutalized Marvin Dreskler for half an hour until he spilled the beans about everything he was asked. Sierra had been forced to stand there and watch. It was truly one of the truly ghastly experiences of her life. She loathed torture; it violated everything in which she believed. However, the very existence of children was at stake, which made the astonishing cruelty she'd witness almost acceptable. She also realized she'd had access to Marvin Dreskler because her new friend and ally, Tyler, had beaten the crap out of someone named Kurt Wimblehart. It was illegal on Tyler's part, although Tyler was a civilian— but it was also illegal for Garfield, an employee of the federal government, to commit violence to learn important information, and illegal for her, a licensed police officer, to stand there and allow it. But she'd learned something that might save that little girl in the theater restroom from a horrible life, and that made it all worth it.

Or had it?

In the Middle East war during years 2003-2008, the President of the United States and *especially* the vice president, came out in favor of horrific torture to be administered in secret prisons somewhere in the world, usually under CIA supervision. Water-boarding was at the top of the list. That news drove Sierra into the arms of the opposing political party. She was too young to really remember, but she'd read much about Gestapo tortures and the Soviet Union methods of getting people to confess, and even the racist torture-lynch mobs all over the South in her own country until the middle of the twentieth century. It made her wonder how human beings got that way in the first place.

Yet, how could those like Marvin Dreskler and Kurt Wimble-hart and the rest of them so far into profits that they'd become immune to the abominable lifestyles of young children either kidnapped or family-sold to become sex slaves and unpaid whores?

She chose not think about it. Not bothering to unpack from her visit to Hemlock Hills, she kicked off her shoes, dropped her clothes in the middle of the bedroom floor, and took a shower almost too hot to stand. Afterwards, wrapped up in a terry-cloth robe over a T-shirt and shorts, and wearing ridiculous bunny slippers she'd never allow anyone else to see or else she'd have to kill them, she huddled in her reclining chair watching TV and drinking inexpensive white wine. It wasn't until she went into the kitchen to refill her glass that she realized she had three phone messages on her landline, as the red light on the voice mail machine was blinking.

She played them back. One was political, asking for money for a would-be senator from North Dakota of whom she'd never heard. The other two were from Chet Quigley.

"Hi, it's Chet. Just wondering if all is OK with you. Call when you can. I miss you."

Miss me? They hardly knew each other—and a one-night stand that didn't turn out well made it strange for him to call her. Had he phoned the station, too, while she was away? She'd have to check with Nancy Flower in the morning.

She listened to the second message.

"Hi, Sierra—Chet again. I'm wondering if you're still mad at me. I'm sincerely sorry. I wouldn't do anything to hurt you or upset you—and if I did without knowing it, I apologize a thousand times. I'd really like to see you again, so we can get to know each other better. I don't want to bug you, but I'd really appreciate it if you'd call me back. Okay, bye."

Sierra deleted both messages. Apologies aren't worth a damn. "I'm sorry" is for when you step on someone's foot by accident, or spill your drink in their lap, or when your shopping cart runs into their ankle in a busy supermarket aisle. It's *not* for when a relative stranger asks you to suck his dick.

She considered that after pouring herself another glass of wine, not knowing if it was her third of the evening or a number somewhat higher. She replayed that night of sex with Chet over in her mind. It was pretty good sex, actually—or perhaps it just seemed that way since she'd been celibate for several years before she took over her Chief of Police job in Sunset Beach. What he asked of her was not all that terrible, she thought. Lots of women did it—*most* women, and most men, too, if she allowed herself the truth. Only to her was it awful—because of memories she hadn't been able to shake off for almost three decades.

A childhood of abuse, and she's taking it out on poor old Chester—and he doesn't even know why.

He *is* nice, she thought, and was momentarily flattered by his obvious attention. Not bad-looking, and would be more so if he got rid of his awful Leave-it-to-Beaver wardrobe. He was a good conversationalist, making her smile and even laugh. Sierra Bravo had never been much of a laugher.

Did she want more out of Chet Quigley? She didn't know. She didn't love him. It takes more than two dates and a long night of shagging to fall in love. But she might fall in love with him—someday—if she let this relationship flourish.

Did he love her? Again, probably not; that old saw about love at first sight was a crock. He certainly lusted after her. He proved that—almost too well.

She chased him away—and now, after a daunting experience in Hemlock Hills and a clue that might lead her to the solution she'd been looking for in the first place, she was alone, hair tangled from her shower, slurping on room-temperature Cabernet Blanc she'd bought at Kroger's for nine dollars a bottle.

She shuffled into the bathroom to use her dryer, then combed her hair until it was halfway decent. The face looking back at her seemed ten years older, so she dabbed on dry, subtle lipstick, went back into the living room, and picked up the phone.

She held it in her hand for almost five minutes, her thumb hovering over the first digit of Chester Quigley's phone number. She sighed more than once, finally murmured, "Fuck it," and punched in the number.

After the hellos and small talk, she said, "I've been out of town for a couple of days."

"I know. One of your cops told me that when I called the station."

"Yes. Well, I'm back, now…"

"Welcome home," Chet Quigley said.

"Thanks."

Quiet.

"I guess I should apologize to you," he said.

"No need."

"I'm not even sure what I did wrong, but whatever it was…"

"It wasn't you, Chet. It was my fault. I should be the one apologizing."

"Great—but I don't know what you're apologizing for." He heard her sad sigh. He said, "You don't have to tell me."

"Thank you. Maybe I will—someday."

"Okay."

"For now—"

"Yes?"

"I need—" She stopped. She didn't want to crumple up completely, and "need" was a word hated using. It indicated weakness. "I'd like to see you tonight, if you're not busy."

"It's eight o'clock in the evening, Sierra," he said. "I'm not busy."

She looked down at herself, at the white terry-cloth robe, and ran her free hand up and down the collar. "Give me thirty minutes, can you?"

After she hung up, she dashed into her bedroom and checked her closet, worrying what she should wear. A bathrobe was out of the question.

She decided on a pair of jeans and a blue T-shirt, and stayed barefoot, embarrassed as she realized why she chose casual—it was easy to get out of those clothes on a moment's notice.

She looked at herself in the mirror for perhaps the twentieth time, aware of the frown lines that crept in when she wasn't thinking about them. She made faces at herself, trying to look adorable, sexy, seductive, relaxed—but that seemed like a lot of work. Maybe tomorrow she'd take the next step in the case she'd relentlessly pursued, which might be more dangerous for her than the trip to Hemlock Hill.

No sir, Sierra thought. This was no night to spend alone.

When she opened the door to admit Chet Quigley, he stood there nervously, Dockers and a long-sleeved polo shirt. His smile was genuine, but somewhat careful. "Hey," he said. "I would have brought you flowers, but it's past eight-thirty—all the flower shops are—"

He didn't get to finish his sentence because, like a force of nature, her mouth was all over his, her tongue, her hands, her grinding pelvis sending a message no one could refuse.

Or want to.

CHAPTER FIFTEEN

When Sierra returned to the police station the next morning, her officers stopped by to welcome her back, but it was only Griffin Parrish and Nancy Flower who made anything like a fuss over her. Nancy Flower had bought her an electric mug-warmer to sit on the desk at her left hand while she always drank multiple cups of coffee, and even plugged it in for her before she took her first sip of the day.

Being a longtime cop, Flower was quick to notice things. "You look like you've been somewhere romantic and exciting, Chief."

"Hardly."

Nancy Flower raised her eyebrows. "You have that certain 'glow' on you."

Sierra blushed even as she said, "Bullshit."

"I don't think it is. Us married women can tell."

Sierra thought, does it show? Do orgasms appear on your forehead like adolescent zits? Was she now wearing an imaginary sandwich sign announcing to the world, "I just got laid?"

She finally said, "I wasn't anyplace the least bit romantic or exotic, Officer Flower." She lowered her voice to a semi-whisper, trying to avoid the guilty grin she felt spreading all over her face. "Any 'glow' I have came from fifteen blocks from where we're sitting—and if you breathe a word of this to a single soul, I'll have to kill you."

Griffin Parrish wasn't sentimental. After Sierra finished her phone calls and written up her reports and signed off on anything she needed to, he came into her office, shut the door, and told her of the unpleasant visit of Kenneth Zack.

"If I jumped every time someone threatened me," she replied, "I'd quit my job and go work in an insurance company typing pool. But to hell with him. In Hemlock Hills, I got a huge clue that might lead me to the bad guy in this case I've been chewing on."

"Can you do anything about it?" Griffin said. "I don't want to quote laws to you, but you head the police in Sundown Beach. You can't make arrests anywhere else."

"I can make one right here, though," Sierra said.

"Then I'm with you."

She shook her head. "No, Griff, I won't put your retirement pay on the line. If you get sacked, that retirement income might disappear—depending on who gets mad at you."

"And depending on who gets arrested. You have to let me in on this."

"Not yet. I appreciate the offer."

"At least tell me where you're going."

"I'll tell you in the morning," she said.

Parrish's voice grew firm. "That's dumb. What if you don't show up tomorrow? What if you disappear, and nobody—I mean *nobody*—knew where you were? I don't give a shit about your precious secrecy. You are the Chief, and someone needs to know where you're going and who you're going to talk to." He frowned. "Your jaw is getting all jutting out and stiff, so don't get stubborn on me. If you don't trust me, you don't trust anybody!"

Sierra bowed her head. After finding a path that could lead to the end of her off-the-book investigation, after her glowing experience of the previous night, she once again felt beaten down and defeated, this time no one's fault but her own.

"Shit," she said. "You're right, Griff."

"Pin on that badge and you have a supportive family of fellow cops—even if they don't particularly like you." He smiled. "But I *do* like you. So give me a break and tell me where you're going tonight."

The house was built into the side of the mountain, about halfway up, shimmering white as though it was scrubbed and repainted every morning, although now, at twilight, it almost seemed subdued. Almost. The view from the second floor with carved balconies and floor-to-ceiling windows, overlooked Sundown Beach and out to the broad Pacific—a great place from which to watch the gray whales swim by, coming from the bone-freezing waters below the North Pole down to the Sea of Cortez on the west coast of Baja California, and six months later swim back north again. On one of the balconies, a table, a portable bar, and reclining chairs circled an expensive telescope with which anyone could peer into almost any window in town at will, or up to Mars and Jupiter. Teens and twenties who lived in town with their eye-catching bathing suits frolicked on the beach from April to October, so there was always something to look at, an undeniable perk of living in Southern California.

Sierra had never been to Kenneth Zack's home before, though when she first signed on for her job she'd driven by it slowly, just to see how the other half lived. That telescope could invade all the non-curtained windows in Sundown Beach, and the residents could gaze up at the magisterial mansion, reminding them each day that they didn't have a shot in hell of ever living there.

It was ugly, in a truly presumptuous way. It would look better hanging off the side of a glacier in the Arctic.

There was actually a tollbooth on the road leading to the home, and two armed guards manned it at all times. They stopped Sierra and demanded to see her identification, even though she wore her blue uniform with all the trimmings. As far as she could tell, they weren't former police officers, which made her uncomfortable to wonder where Ken Zack had found them.

Another tough-guy guard stood at the entrance, and again she had to identify herself, pissing her off these clowns couldn't take a chief of police's uniform for granted.

Sierra approached the front door, thinking there's no accounting for taste when one is this rich. She even donned her cap, gold braid and all, and straightened her collar on which she'd pinned her silver stars. She couldn't miss the tiny surveillance camera over the door, so she waved at it as if it were an old friend at a crowded cocktail party. Then she rang the doorbell; a classical theme sounded from inside, recorded with wind chimes, but she couldn't recognize it. Bach? Beethoven? She had always enjoyed classical compositions, but couldn't name any by heart, probably because to her, all music was background for her life.

After about thirty seconds, she rang again, and this time she heard footsteps from inside, coming closer. The door was thrown open by young Dylan Zack, wearing designer jeans and a sweater that probably cost more than half a police officer's weekly salary.

"Oh, shit," he said. "What did I do *this* time?"

"You tell me, Dylan," she said.

"I didn't do nothing! I hardly drive except to school since your cop gave me a ticket."

The son of a multimillionaire whose daddy could buy him into Stanford like anyone else could put down a dollar bill for a Snickers chocolate bar, but still said "*I didn't do nothing.*" She sighed. "I'm not here about you. Is your father home?"

"Yeah, I think so."

He thought so? The house was so large he didn't know whether or not his father was at home? She said, "Who else is here?"

"Nobody. The cook went home after dinner, and the housekeeper put everything in the dishwasher and left afterwards."

"No one else?"

"Just the—security outside."

"Does anyone sometimes spend the night here?"

"Some of my buddies do. Not very often."

"No girls?"

"No way. My old man is really strict about that."

She shouldered her way inside and shut the huge door behind her, finding herself in a vast front hallway with tile as white as Colgate teeth. She took off her cap and tucked it under one arm. The paintings on the wall, some eight or ten feet wide, should belong to a Museum of Modern Art. "Do any of your father's girlfriends stay overnight?" she asked.

Dylan rolled his eyes heavenward, and Sierra wondered where all teens learned how to do that. She'd never met one who didn't. It was probably genetic. "He doesn't have any girlfriends," he said with a soupçon of contempt. "He's too busy making money."

"If he's not making a lot of money now, I'd like to talk to him for a few minutes."

"He's watching a movie. He's got about three thousand DVDs, and he watches one just about every night."

"You ever watch them with him?"

Dylan shook his head. "Not unless it's a Dirty Harry." He pointed his index finger at her like a handgun and whispered *"Go ahead. Make my day."* Not a bad Clint Eastwood impression. Not a good one—but not bad.

"Will you tell him I'm here, Dylan?"

"I'll try—but I bet he's not any happier to see you than I am." He jerked his chin toward a metallic bench, also white, with bright red cushions. "Take a load off," he said. "I'll get him." He scampered up the winding stairway and disappeared into a room on the second floor.

This gave Sierra time to study the paintings hanging on every wall. They were mostly abstract. Colors, such as they were, almost faded into the off-white backgrounds. She didn't understand one single work, and though the home's owner had paid hundreds of thousands for them, her guess was that he didn't understand them either.

She waited for about five minutes until down the stairs came Ken Zack, wearing a white silk shirt, black pants and an ascot. An ascot, for God's sake, in his own home! It made her wonder if the ascot was supposed to impress her, or did he dress up like this all the time for the cook and the housekeeper?

"I'm surprised to see you here, Chief Bravo," he said, "but I hope you changed your mind about Dylan's traffic citation."

"I didn't come about Dylan at all, Mr. Zack. I have some questions to ask you."

He pursed his lips in annoyance, as if he were being forced to kiss his grandmother. "This couldn't wait until morning?"

"If it could, I wouldn't be here now."

"I see." He looked around, hoping for inspiration. "Come into the library."

The library, with windows overlooking the sea but at a different angle from the ones upstairs, was crammed with more books that anyone could read in a lifetime. It would have taken her fifteen minutes to look at all the titles on the bindings.

"Sit down." Zack offered her one of those overstuffed leather chairs most often found in private social clubs for elderly millionaires. "Would you like a drink?"

"Thanks, but I'm on duty."

"Do you mind if I have one?"

"Why should I mind? It's your home."

He moved to a rolling table with several kinds of hard liquor. Did he have one of those booze tables in every room in the house, including the bedrooms of the housekeeper and of his son? The ice bucket was full. He filled a short glass with cubes, poured expensive Laphroaig single malt Scotch over them and sat down opposite her.

"Cheers," he said, and sipped. "Now, what's all this about?"

"Just a few questions, Mr. Zack, mostly business. Does your company office here in town have an executive vice president?"

"We have several."

"Tell me about them, please."

"Why?"

"Just interested."

"Really? Are you looking for a job, Chief Bravo?"

"I have one, thanks. Now, about your vice presidents…"

"All right, you can poke your nose into my business—or businesses, actually, though I can't imagine why. I have no secrets. There are four exec VPs. One lives up near the Los Angeles harbor. He's married with six children—all boys."

"Six?"

Zack nodded. "A good solid Catholic. God help us all if his wife has any more."

"Okay," she said, "that's one."

"Number Two—he's in charge of Public Relations. He doesn't come into the office very often, because he's up there in Los Angeles on the phone all damn day. He does a great job, though."

"Married?"

"Uh-huh. Is this his third wife? No, check me on that. It's his fourth. One of them was a minor TV celebrity, I think—some sort of sitcom where she was the leading lady's best friend—but that didn't last more than a few years."

"Okay," Sierra said, "how about your sales VP?"

"She lives in Long Beach, but travels all over the country for us. She's been with us for about nine years. As a matter of fact, I hired most of my top people a long time ago—and they've stayed with me and been loyal." He took another sip, looking at her over the rim of the glass. "Loyalty is important to me."

"Is she married?"

"Yes—and her husband works for my company, too." Zack almost puffed out his chest like a bantam rooster.

"No kids?"

"Two girls. One of them is a sophomore at USC, and the other one is near Dylan's age, senior in high school."

"Okay. What about the fourth VP?"

"Actually, he's the CFO—chief financial officer. He lives in Redondo Beach. Man in his sixties, and an orthodox Jew—always wears that little cap on his head. What do they call those things? A Yom Kippur cap?" He frowned and shook his head, realizing he was incorrect. "Well, whatever. His wife—I think she's a few years older than he is—has pretty bad cancer, and he's shattered by that." He took a deep breath. "It won't be easy when she goes—but I don't think it will keep him from doing his work."

"He's religious, then?"

Kenneth Zack shook his head in annoyance. "Who would anybody be an orthodox Jew without being religious?"

"You've got me there."

"Well—not as ably as you've got me."

"I don't have you, Mr. Zack. I do have Dylan, though."

His face darkened. "I don't like that."

"I don't care. Now—you have a housekeeper, don't you? Is she here?"

"She usually is, but tonight I told her to go home early."

"I find it strange," Sierra said, "that a man of your wealth, a widower, has another woman in your house every single day and evening, and there's—nothing going on?"

Zack looked angry but couldn't help laughing. "My housekeeper is sixty-seven years old and was hired by my father almost forty years ago. She worked for him, and she stayed and worked for my late wife. She's still here. What the hell would she do at her age? Scurry around town looking for another job? No, Chief Bravo, there's nothing going on."

She said, "I'm sorry to get personal—but there's a reason for it." She cleared her throat. "A company your size must have someone in charge of security."

"Of course we do. He's an Army Ranger, a Desert Storm veteran. He oversees a staff of six, has his office in Los Angeles down the hall from the one I use when I'm up there—and the son of a bitch plays a hell of a game of tennis. But why all these personal questions?"

"I'll get to that. Do you have someone who provides you personally with security? Very rich people make enemies. You must have someone watching over you."

"I do. You might have noticed that I have security specialists all over the property, and the front of this house is full of cameras, pointing at every possible angle. Dylan saw who you were before you rang the doorbell. And nobody comes through the back because there is no back—we're built into the side of the mountain." He thought for a moment, then said, "I have a personal security guard at my office, too."

"Tell me about him."

"I suppose it wouldn't hurt. He's black." Zack waited for a shocked response from Sierra; when he didn't get one, he continued. "He was on the second All-America team when he played linebacker for Stanford. Everybody thought he'd go pro after graduation, but he didn't."

"Why is that?"

"Because he's gay."

Damn! Sierra thought. None of those who work at Mr. Zack's right hand seemed to fit the man who'd led the little girl into the men's room at the multiplex theater. Her mouth was dry, and she wished she could have accepted his offer of a drink. Now it was too late, and things were going to get sticky.

"Are you seeing anyone now, Mr. Zack? Steady girlfriend, or playing the field?"

"Are you planning to ask me what color my underwear is, or what I wear to bed?" he said, becoming irate. "I don't know what you want from me!" He downed the rest of his Scotch in one gulp, then gasped after the too-big swallow, his face turning red.

"I'm sorry," she said. "You've been remarkably cooperative with me so far. Just stick with me on this a little while longer."

"I don't have to. Unless I committed a crime and you're arresting me, I can demand you leave my home at once."

"You can, sir—but if I get answers elsewhere that you refused to give me, it'll be all over town—and all over the coast, too, from Los Angeles to the Mexican border, and every town in between." She flipped both hands, palms upward, and shrugged. "Your choice."

"No—it's *your* choice, Chief Bravo," Ken Zack said. "One word from me to the city council, and you're out on your ass."

"I'm not shocked. Your reputation for being a bully is well known. You don't scare me, Mr. Zack, not even a little bit. You can get me fired. You pushed for that before I even rang your doorbell. But I don't think you'll have me beaten up—or killed. Bullies only pick on those smaller and weaker."

"Easy for you to say," Zack responded, "while you're sitting there wearing a gun."

"That's my job. That's what I do. And another thing I do is investigate people who buy little pre-teen girls—buy them so they can fuck them whenever they want to—or until they hit puberty when they wouldn't want them anymore."

Dumbfounded, Kenneth Zack let his eyes grow larger and his jaw opened a bit. For almost fifteen seconds, he didn't speak—or couldn't. Finally: "Are you out of your goddamn mind?"

"No, sir. I'm—investigating."

His eyes blazed into her, almost white-hot rage. "How dare you investigate *me*?"

"Someone in Sundown Beach—someone with a lot of money—has bought a young girl." Zack began to answer, but Sierra held up a hand. "Let me finish. He didn't make the deal personally, and no names were exchanged. Apparently, it was one of his sidekicks—guys near the top—which is why I asked you about all your vice presidents."

"And you actually think I'm a—a—chicken hawk?"

Sierra tried not to laugh. "Chicken hawk? Where did you hear that?"

"I—don't remember."

"Well, Mr. Zack, unless you're actually talking about birds who fly around and swoop down to eat chickens, the term *chicken hawk* is most often used to describe older men who are sexually attracted to young boys. If you're thinking of an expression used in prison when older men prey on little girls, I'd suggest *short eyes*."

He sat there quietly for half a minute. Then he murmured "short eyes" and shook his head slowly. How come all police officers know shit like that? He poured himself a new drink with a trembling hand. "Listen carefully, because I'll only say this once," he warned her, "and if it leaves this room, for any reason, I'll make sure that you're not only fired but that you'll never in your life get another job with a law enforcement agency in this country. I own half this town, in case you didn't know—and if I wanted to, I could buy the other half with what I have in my pocket right now."

He sipped, then inhaled so deeply that Sierra felt the air in the room thin out. "My wife died a long time ago—when Dylan was about four years old. I loved her deeply. I know, lots of rich men have mistresses, but I never did." He closed his eyes for a moment. "I never stopped mourning her. I'm a tough, egotistical bastard and, as you say, a bully when it comes to business. But if you love someone as much as I loved my wife, remarriage or even dating never appealed to me in the slightest."

Another sip. "After about two years—and this is humiliating, but you're a cop and you've heard lots of stories like this—I did see high-class prostitutes at least four times, through escort services—and I met with them in hotels up in Los Angeles. You can't arrest me for that."

"If you hire prostitutes in Sundown Beach, you're going to jail. That's the law. But I can't arrest you for patronizing call girls fifty miles away from where we live."

"Well, *that's* good to hear—though it's been many years since I did that." He took a moment for remembrances. "They were beautiful, cultured women, too. Their conversation was as interesting as their sexual prowess—one of the reasons each visit cost me four thousand dollars. But to me it seemed like a silly, pointless thing to do with strange women who might be good actresses in their jobs, but they never fooled me into thinking they gave a damn about me, so I stopped. For the last ten years, I've had no interest in sex—not with women, not with men, not with children. My two priorities—my passions, if you choose to call them that—are my business, and my son, Dylan."

His chin rested on his chest, his eyes closed, breathing deeply, as though fresh air in his lungs was nutritious and energizing. Eventually he raised his head, and his eyes locked with Sierra's. "So investigate me all you want, Chief. You'll be wasting your time. And if one word—one single *word* about my sex life or lack thereof, or what suspicions you might have, gets any farther than the door to this room, I guarantee you'll be more than sorry you were ever born." He finished the rest of his drink and put the glass on the table beside him—loudly and firmly. "Now get the hell out of my home and don't ever come back. If you see me on the street, or anywhere else, don't say hello. Don't even look at me. Keep walking. Call it part of your job—for as long as you'll have it."

He stomped to the door of the library and flung it open. "Get out," he said. "Don't say another word. Just go!"

She felt the need to say goodbye, but that *was* another word, so she thought better of it and left quietly.

Outside the Zack mansion, Sierra breathed the unmistakable scent of the sea as she stared out at the municipality whose law enforcement she operated, and beyond to the dark, inscrutable Pacific. Not much traffic down there on the streets, but a few cars were on the move. The lights from the downtown area, where young people often went to drink and party, were bright and joyous, and if she tried, she could hear distant music spilling out from some of the taverns. A good town, she thought, especially for young people and artists. A decent town.

She nodded at the front door guard, drove past the gate and waved at the armed men there, then headed toward the town she policed, and beyond to the dark, inscrutable Pacific. Not much traffic down there, but a few cars were on the move. The lights from the downtown area, where young people were bright and joyous.

But there was someone in Sundown Beach who was not decent at all—someone she had to find.

She'd been lied to her entire career, as most cops had. Lying to a police officer was as natural for most people as breathing.

"*I only had one drink.*"

"*I put it in my pocket and forgot to pay for it.*"

"*It was an accident.*"

"*My speedometer wasn't working.*"

Over years, she'd learned how easily she differentiated between the prevaricators and the truth-tellers. It was in their movements, their facial expressions, their "tells" when they lied by playing with their hair or keeping their heads down, not making eye contact, blinking too much or letting their eyes wander all over. She was expert at discerning lies.

Which is why she figured that, big an asshole as he might be, Kenneth Zack was not guilty of pedophilia.

CHAPTER SIXTEEN

"My God!" Griffin Parrish said. It was the following morning, and once again, he and Sierra were in her office with the door shut, keeping their voices low. "You actually knocked on Zack's door and accused him of sexually abusing children? You've got more guts than I thought."

"I didn't accuse him," Chief Bravo said, "but I brought it up. That's why I went there in the first place, but I think I wasted my time. A gut feeling. A cop feeling. If I bugged him for nothing, I stuck my neck too far out."

"You sure as hell did, Sierra."

She shrugged. "I guess I'll be fired any old time now."

"That's what happens when you piss off somebody who's richer than God. If they're born with more than a million bucks in their family, they have a black platinum get-out-of-jail-free card for life."

Sierra nibbled on the skin surrounding one of her fingernails. "The good news is Ken Zack is probably not guilty—at least not guilty of what I thought he was up to."

"That won't help if he's truly bent out of shape. Where can you get another job?"

"In Uzbekistan, probably."

Parrish looked really sad. "This stinks—unless you find the real pedo and slap him in irons for several decades."

"For several generations," she said.

"You don't have to do it alone, either, Sierra."

"How do you figure that?"

"You poked around in Hemlock Hills. You had no jurisdiction except the people you rounded up to help you, and you lucked out that the U.S. Marshal's office was willing to lend a hand. But if there's a child predator in Sundown Beach, you have tremendous power—the entire department is here to work as you tell them to."

Sierra's smile lit up the room as the truth washed over her.

"What would you like us to do first?"

She didn't take long to decide. "Make a list of super-rich in this town—who are so obscenely wealthy that they'd shell out twenty-five grand or more to buy another human being."

"Got it."

"Find those people—Google them if you have to—who own big companies where more than a hundred people work. They must have a whole slew of vice presidents under them, wouldn't they? Find out who they are, especially their heads of security. Check into them first. And make sure you look for any Sundowner names that sound familiar."

"If we find one who's guilty, should we make the arrest?"

Sierra cocked her head and her eyebrows lifted. "That's what we cops *do.* Just make sure I'm along for the ride."

He smiled back and nodded. "You're the boss, Chief."

By the end of the afternoon, Griff, Nancy Flower and one of the female department clerks who'd searched the Internet all day had made a list. More than half of Sundown Beach's male resident citizens were either under-eighteen minors or married. Fifty-two percent of the adults were female. Sixty-four percent were Caucasian, twenty-three percent were Latino, and the rest were black. There were a few Asians, but not enough to make the list. Many immigrant Vietnamese had settled several miles north, in Huntington Beach.

Sixty-one millionaires resided in Sundown—not surprising because of the proximity to the ocean, a squeaky-clean, National Geographic-beautiful crescent beach, and easy freeway access to drive along the coastline. Their average age, as Nancy Flower deduced on her calculator, was 59.3 years old.

Danielle Tokes and Chris Fornadel were worth slightly over two million bucks each. Nice work if you can get it, Sierra thought, but not nearly enough dough to rule the world.

When it came to multimillionaires, the roster was a bit longer. The two remaining town council members, Eben Flood and J. Richard Stubblefield, were among the fifteen money mavens of Sundown Beach, though Ken Zack led the parade. There were a dozen more.

Now Flower and Parrish were back in Sierra Bravo's office, doors closed, as the working day edged toward its end. There are on-duty cops on all night, too, but the day shift generally clocked out at five o'clock.

Not on this day.

Sierra studied the list for a long time of those who were grotesquely wealthy. "Nancy," she said. "we need analyzing."

Nancy Flower nodded. "I wish the answer glowed in the dark, but we did the best we could on short notice."

"Let's take a few more minutes. Maybe the answer will glow." She clicked open a ballpoint pen. "I talked to Ken Zack personally last night, and for many reasons, he's not the guy we might be looking for. He's not completely off my shit list, but instinct tells me he's not our guy." She drew a line through Zack's name—lightly, in case she had to erase it later. "Two of these billionaires are in their mid-eighties. At that advanced age, pre-teen girls would probably not be their interest."

"With their bank accounts," Griff said, "they can afford all the Viagra they want."

"Eew!" Flower said.

"True. But at that age, they might be too tired out to spend all their time with an eleven-year-old. Let's face it, when there's a sixty- or seventy-year difference, they wouldn't have much in common. So—I'm lining out their names, too." She did so. "Now let's pursue. Five more of them are attorneys. Big-time law firms."

"Right," Flower observed, "and they have a crowd of people working for them."

Sierra said, "Lawyers who work under them, especially those who haven't made partner yet, spend sixteen hours a day at their desks, looking up stuff their bosses are too busy for. They wouldn't have time to drive to another town and purchase a child for sex purposes—not even for the schmucks who pay them."

"Why not?"

"Junior partners work their asses off to be where they are. They won't work for their boss forever, so why get involved in highly criminal sex perversion?"

"What about non-lawyers?" Griff wondered. "Secretaries, researchers, things like that."

"If you were the top lawyer in your firm, worth ten million dollars or more, and fought your whole life to be on top of the game, do you really think you'd entrust your highly illegal and completely disgusting perversion to someone who made maybe forty grand a year? They'd blackmail you for the rest of your life—and the only way to stop them is to kill them, which gets us into a different situation altogether. Fairly new lawyers move to the back of the line." Her face twisted into a frown. "Even Councilman Eben Flood."

"Are you sure about Flood?" Flower asked.

"I'm not sure of anything," Sierra said, "which is why I'm drawing a light line through his name, along with the other lawyers. That leaves us seven to go."

"Right," Griff said. "We have an art dealer, who has a glamorous and expensive gallery in San Diego—but he travels to Europe at least four times a year and stays there for several weeks each time. I can't prove it, but no way there is a child stashed away when the master predator is off in another part of the world. The person who really runs the gallery, the one who does most of the work while the owner is preening in Barcelona or Paris or Rome, is female."

"Not likely," Sierra said, lining the art dealer's name out. "Next?"

"You know the big spa and health club a block from the ocean?" Flower said.

"Sure."

"Ever been in there?"

"After a day at work," Sierra said, "my only exercise is pouring wine from a bottle into a glass. I guess most rich Sundowners go there, though—a good place to hunt around and find someone for a little whoop-de-doo after they both take showers."

"They have everything in that place," Nancy Flower said. "Trainers, experts in all sorts of things like bicycle spinning, yoga, a wine bar, and a fancy-shmancy cafe serving only vegan food. They have masseurs and masseuses and a full-time chiropractor. They even have a playroom you can park your kids in, and a babysitter to watch them while you sweat and grunt, toning your body—and paying them a hell of a lot of money. They've opened two more places like this—one in Cardiff-by-the-Sea and one in San Luis Obispo—and the word is out that they're planning another one in Scottsdale, Arizona."

"Are you trying to scare up customers for them, Nancy?" Sierra asked.

"Hardly. But the man who owns them is worth about thirty million bucks, and that puts him on our list, right?"

Sierra nodded.

"Except..."

"What?"

"He's gay."

Sierra Bravo put down her pen and leaned her elbows on the desk, running fingers through her hair. "Shit on a shingle," she murmured.

Parrish said, "Every other Sundown Beach multimillionaire is well-married and has their own kids, either in their teens or twenties."

"Uh-huh." Sigh.

"Except one."

"J. Richard Stubblefield," Nancy said. "He's been divorced for about ten years—no kids. His ex-wife took him for a bundle in court and went off to live in France. He owns some huge construction outfits—with an awful pile of employees."

"And from what I've been able to figure out, he has a highly paid security expert working out of his own office right here in town," Griff told her.

Sierra Bravo sat up rigid, straight, fingers clutching the edge of her desk. "Who is he?" she demanded. "The security guy. What's his name?"

"I don't know yet. I'll get it first thing in the morning."

Sierra took several deep breaths to slow down her heartbeat, extra-fast drumming in her chest near her throat. "Make damn sure you do that, Sergeant Parrish."

She probably shouldn't have invited Chet Quigley to visit her again that evening. She was too caught up in her job—in being close to the truth and finally doing something about it. He sat quietly, sipping his wine and watching her pace back and forth, glance out the window, check her watch, occasionally asking him if he were hungry, even though he'd told her he'd eaten dinner before he arrived.

After her second glass of wine, Sierra felt guilty. She had to say something soothe.ng to him. Guilt after their first intimate contact was what gave her the idea to contact him—not a booty call.

"Chet," she finally said, "I can't imagine why you hang around with me."

"Because you have a sexy ass," he said, "but that's not even in the top ten. Shall I start at Number One and work my way down?"

"It's just—I'm very hung up on this case."

"That's how you and I met in the first place."

She nodded. "But I shouldn't have called you tonight. I'm ignoring you—"

"You're not ignoring me, Sierra," Chet said, "but I know you're deep in thought about what you're doing. Don't worry—I enjoy looking at you when you walk around like a nutcase. As a matter of fact, I love looking at you no matter what you're doing."

"The flattery will do me in."

"You're a big girl, you can take it."

"Chet, I like you—but I keep hurting you, and I don't want to do that. When a cop wears stars on the collar, the job eats up time and energy they'd rather use someplace else. Someplace fun." She stopped pacing, turned away from him, and quickly shook her head. "If I still know you thirty years from now, maybe I can talk about it."

"Everyone has their preferences and intense dislikes. When you care for someone that much, Sierra, you adjust to the differences."

"Are you talking about love at first sight?"

He laughed, ducking his head, discomfited. "Not exactly. Lust at first sight is more like it. But I care for you more than I imagined I would—so I'd like to hang around on the edges for a while and see what happens."

She touched his face with her palm. "You're terrific, Chet."

"Terrific is over the top. I'd settle for 'pretty good guy,' if I can get away with it."

"So," she said, "the first thing I do with a pretty good guy is to throw him out of my bed and out of my condo. The second thing I do is ask him to come over again and ignore him while I think about what I'll do tomorrow, which is goddamn dangerous."

"And tonight," Chet said, "is the third thing."

She ran her fingers through her hair. "I shouldn't have called you. Tonight is not—well, I can't get my head around making love. I'm sorry."

"I'm sorry, too," he said. "So, can I suggest something a little bit different?"

Her brows lifted as she looked at him.

"When you're really crazy about someone—just cuddling them and falling asleep with your arms around them is every bit as good as screwing. I'd really like to stay the night without us tearing each other's clothes off and leaving a trail from the living room to the bedroom."

Sierra gave that a moment's thought. Was he bullshitting her? Would he try to change a cuddle into something else altogether? Should she trust him?

He *looked* trustworthy. And maybe, with everything falling down around her ears and a probably huge arrest , she probably *could* trust him.

Well—what the hell!

"Do you sleep in your underwear when you're not having sex?" she said.

"No. I have M.J. Hammer-type pants and a T-shirt I wear to bed. Otherwise—" He shrugged his shoulders and tried not to laugh.

She sighed again. "Damn," she said, holding her hand out to him.

CHAPTER SEVENTEEN

Judge Lawrence Klein was in his chambers in the local courthouse, sitting behind his desk eating a takeout lunch ordered from a nearby Applebee's. Black robes that judges wear reminded Sierra of the Grim Reaper without a scythe. At least American judges don't have to wear silly white curly wigs in court as they do in England. Klein's black robe was on a hanger behind the door, the window at his back was open to capture the breeze, and during this particular lunch hour he'd rolled up his sleeves and pulled his tie down to loosen the top button on his shirt. "I don't like dressing like a judge," he said between bites. "Especially on a day like today—sunny, warm, but not too warm. Damn it, this is a tennis day, not a judge day."

"I know the feeling, Your Honor." Sierra Bravo sat across from him, wishing that she, too, had ordered a takeout lunch, too. But the judge was not the most attractive man she'd pick to dine with. He was broad without being fat, short without being runty, and his gray hair was long everyplace—except on his head. His thick brows almost shaded his eyes from the sun, gray clumps sprouted from his ears, and one long hair amongst the many from his nose hung halfway down to his upper lip. Why he never noticed that single hair and plucked it out, or at least cut it, she had no idea.

"And when I do decide to step out from behind my exalted place in the courtroom and grab a quick bite," he said, taking a large swallow of a half-raw hamburger with many layers of lettuce, cheese, bacon, tomato and pickles, "here you come to spoil my lunch hour with some damn warrant you want me to sign."

"Yes, sir."

"I've heard all about your recent escapades and I don't like any of them, not one bit." Klein shook his finger in Sierra's face, as if he were a teacher and she a second-grader. "Everyone thinks you neglect your duties as chief of police because all you have is a hunch."

"It's more than a hunch. I've been investigating this case for some time now. I've even left town for a few days to continue it. Unfortunately, I had no jurisdiction in any other town. I got lucky with a terrific lead, and I put two police officers on a local search. That, plus a simple deduction, gave me one answer I was looking for, and several shitheels are going to jail for a long, long time. So, I need to check out this home, to see what I can see—and I'm asking for a warrant."

"And if it turns out you don't see anything, then what?"

"Then I'll continue looking elsewhere."

"After ripping someone's house to pieces?"

"We're not planning to kick in the door, tear the place up, open all the drawers, rip up the carpets, and cut open the sofa cushions. It's not that kind of a search."

He glanced at the warrant beside his paper plate as if it were part of a porn novel right next to his burger. "Who is this guy, anyway? I've never heard of him."

"He lives up in the hills. Keeps a very low profile."

"What if your search *does* find something?"

"We'll make the arrest—and investigate further, if we have to."

Judge Klein gulped from a bottle of Arizona ice tea, and put the bottle down harder than he needed to. "Then he'll probably wind up in front of me, right?"

"Probably, Your Honor."

He shook his head, fuming. "I'm busy enough as it is without a case like this in my court. Why would I sign this warrant?"

"Because a little girl has been abducted from a country far away and is used as a sex-traffic slave in our city. If that doesn't gross you out, I don't know what will."

"We don't have crimes like that in Sundown Beach."

"There are crimes like that everywhere," Sierra answered. "Human trafficking is a several-billion-dollar business all over the world. I've learned a lot about it in the past few days, but most people choose not to talk about it."

He stretched his neck as far as he could, making him appear like a very old vulture. "If you're right—if you make this bust—it'll hit national news. The whole country—half the civilized world—will consider Sundown Beach one of the worst places in America."

"I don't believe it. They'll consider Sundown Beach a great place with a conscience that has done something wonderful for a helpless child."

"And plenty of publicity for you, right?" Judge Klein was clearly contemptuous. "*The Today Show*, *60 Minutes*—hell, even a shot on the *Stephen Colbert Late Show* so you can sit there and trade jokes with him while your hometown begins to look like shit. You may be the prettiest cop in America, Chief, and you'll become a national celebrity. Someone might even ask you to run for Congress. And you'll win, too."

"If I'd wanted to be a member of Congress, I would have studied law, sir, and not law enforcement." Sierra was annoyed as well. "As far as being a celebrity—I assure you that never crossed my mind until you said it just now." She leaned forward aggressively. "I'm only doing it for a little girl."

"A little girl you've never laid eyes on."

"For any little girl—for any child, anywhere." Her fingers gripped the arms of her chair tightly, her knuckles turning white. "But if you don't sign that warrant, that child will continue to be a forced prostitute. Do you understand how that works, Judge

Klein? This is a little girl, ten or eleven years old—no older than that. Think about it. She'll live the rest of her life *not* playing with Barbie dolls and trying on her mother's lipstick, *not* hanging out with all the other girls and whispering with them that some boy or other is—cute. She'll be forced to have sex as often as some rich old white man in this town wants to—and when and if he gets tired of her when she reaches puberty, he'll sell her back to this vast network again, and she'll wind up in a horrible place in the Latin America or the Middle East, turning twenty tricks a day or more, and being beaten daily in places on her body that would never show the bruises. By the time she's seventeen, she'll look fifty, and probably be infected with AIDS. That means they'll throw her out on the street—if she's lucky. If she's not, no one will know what happened to her."

Now Judge Klein's voice was low, intense and threatening—a trick he'd used in court to intimidate thousands of lawyers. He put down his sandwich and leaned forward slowly. "Are you trying to bully me into signing this warrant?"

Sierra's tone was low and vehement as his. "Your Honor," she answered, "I haven't even begun to bully."

"If you fuck this up, Chief Bravo," he snarled, "if you nail someone high up in this town and the whole world knows about it, I'll get screwed in the press, too, if I sign my permission to let you do anything you want! Nobody is going to screw me, Chief Bravo—not even you! You're halfway out of my chambers right now. If you continue this bizarre investigation with no higher authority, you'll be outside looking in. I guarantee it. So I'll be double goddamned if I sign any warrant."

"You'd rather a child goes through the rest of her life as a piece of rotting meat to be thrown away like garbage than to pick up your pen and write your name, huh?"

Like some of those evil aliens on fantasy TV shows, Judge Klein's eyes widened and grew red. "You're a true drama queen, aren't you? Rotting meat? Jesus!"

Sierra Bravo pushed herself up out of her chair. "Since I'll be fired anyway, there's nothing stopping me from reaching out to all the TV news networks, the *L.A. Times*, the *San Diego Union Tribune* and even *U.S. World*, and let them know how you valued your own reputation over the life of an eleven-year-old girl." She opened the door to his inner chamber. "That's not a threat, Your Honor. It's a promise."

"I don't understand," Griff Parrish said as he and Flower sat across from Sierra in her office. "How did you get Judge Klein to sign this warrant? Everyone is terrified of him—especially lawyers."

"I batted my baby blues at him, and he melted," Sierra said.

"Why do we have to wait until tonight?"

Flower chimed in. "We usually check out of here at five o'clock. Why pay overtime? Let's drive there and get it over with."

"This guy has a job," Sierra told them. "He's at work now, not home, so kicking in his door might not help us—and if we don't confront him directly, it's pointless. Let's face it, we have no proof he's done anything wrong. He could be in church right now, waving his arms to the heavens and singing to the lord at the top of his voice. No, we've got to wait."

"What about those U.S. Marshals who helped you out in Hemlock Hills?" Griffin asked. "What were their names again?"

"Garfield and Blazek. I had to bring them in because I didn't have the jurisdiction to make an arrest in Hemlock Hills. Marshals can make an arrest anywhere in the country. I can't." Her grin was bitter. "Anyone with a *federal* cop badge can barge in anywhere they want to, take over everything, and make sure they get credit for the bust."

"Is that the way Garfield and Blazek are?"

"Blazek," Sierra said, "is female—Marie—and apparently she and Garfield don't go to their separate corners every night after work."

"Married?" Flower wondered.

"No wedding rings visible. No matter. This arrest will be made by the Sundown Beach Police—and you two will get credit on the arrest report." Sierra grimaced. "I don't want my name on the bust. Judge Klein accused me of being an attention pig."

Nancy Flower said, "You're even tougher than I thought you were, Chief."

"Okay, listen. Nobody gets shot—unless they come at you with a deadly weapon."

"Like a Scottish broadsword?" Griffin asked.

She ignored Griff's joke. "If you have to shoot, try not to kill him. Just stop him."

"Why?" Flower wanted to know.

"Because this guy is the middle man. If we don't get him, alive, we don't have a chance in hell to catch his boss—the one spending big money."

Griffin looked at his wristwatch. "I can't shoot a guy on an empty stomach."

"Well, let's get something to eat," Sierra said. "I'm buying."

"Or the city is buying."

Sierra said, "Dinner's on me tonight. If I submit *that* receipt to the city council, I won't have a job left."

"We won't have one, either," he said.

Sierra said, "You're so close to retirement, Griff, you should be packing up your stuff. If you want to back out, I'll completely understand."

Sergeant Parrish reached across the desk to squeeze Sierra's hand briefly. Then he let go. "When pigs fly," he said

At about 7:30, they were at the Dolphin Lounge, finishing their dinners. The orange ball of the sun had settled into the Pacific, leaving a beautiful Degas-colored sky. Nobody ordered dessert, as they were too tense, and they all drank ginger ale or coffee. They were still in uniform and wouldn't want to be seen imbibing booze of any sort, especially since they might have to draw their weapons later that night.

For Sierra, it was black coffee—her third cup during the meal. She knew she shouldn't drink coffee past three o'clock in the afternoon lest she be completely awake and getting up to pee once every two hours. In her previous job and in this one, she'd arrested so many people she'd lost count. Burglars, speeders, armed assaulters, pickpockets, drunk or stoned drivers, hookers, johns, domestic abusers, department store robbers, peeping Toms, a rapist or two, couples having sex on the beach in broad daylight, and even a middle-aged man caught jerking off in the back row of a movie theater while watching Jessica Chastain playing the role of Tammy Fae Baker.

But one who lived on child sex trafficking was a different story. Sierra had warned Parrish and Flower that no one was to be shot dead that evening, but a powerful part of her wanted it to happen—and that she'd get to do it herself.

She waved at the waiter to bring the bill, and paid it with her personal Visa card, leaving a twenty-five percent tip in cash, knowing as she did tips added to a charge card demanded tax payments from the waitstaff, whereas real money didn't.

When all was taken care of, she looked across at her two best cops. "Ready to go?"

Nancy Flower nodded.

In the parking lot, Sierra drove her chief's car; Parrish and Flower shared a squad car. It took them nearly half an hour, driving up into the hills on twisty roads, then halfway down the other side and out onto a relatively flat spread of land in the valley. Finally, in the distance, she saw the house. It was so removed from any other dwelling or even a business, one could stage a rap concert on the front porch with sound speakers cranked up to the highest level, and no neighbor would be able to hear it.

A few minutes later, both cars arrived via an unpaved dirt road to the front of the house. The three quietly checked their weapons before marching to the front door, Parrish and Flower standing behind Sierra, who leaned hard on the doorbell.

No one answered for a minute, but finally the door opened. The man standing in the frame was in his mid-forties, a G.I. crew cut, blue jeans and sneakers, a gray hoodie with the hood down around his shoulders, and a half-empty bottle of Samuel Adams in his hand. On a finger on his right hand was a large turquoise ring—what cops often referred to as a *punching ring*. He looked more than startled to see three police officers on his doorstep.

"I'm Chief Bravo of the police department. My associates: Sergeant Parrish and Officer Flower." She held up a sheet of paper. "We have a warrant here to search your premises." She tried not to smile as she watched the man's face blanch and tighten up—scared already. "Are you the owner of this house? Edgar Pratt?"

Edgar Pratt looked around in panic, hoping an escape would reveal itself to him, wishing he would become instantly invisible. "I'm Pratt," he stammered.

"Step aside, Mr. Pratt," Sierra Bravo said. "We're coming in."

CHAPTER EIGHTEEN

Edgar Pratt dug deep down for any testosterone left inside him and moved to block the entrance of the three police officers. "May I see the warrant first?" he said.

Sierra handed him the paper, which he scrutinized, his left hand still holding the beer. "How do I know this is a genuine warrant?"

"This is official Sundown Beach stationery, signed by Judge Lawrence Klein, and being served on you by sworn police officers. In case you don't think *we're* genuine, write down our badge numbers. We'll wait—but we'll do it inside your home and not out here on the doorstep—and though we have no malicious intent in mind, if we get cheesed off enough, we might leave your house looking like one that didn't survive a hurricane." She put both hands on Pratt's chest and moved him aside—not rough, but not gentle, either—and they soldiered their way into his home. Flower shut the front door behind her.

"Have I done something wrong?" Pratt asked.

"We're here to find out." Sierra checked out the living room. Decent furniture from a mid-expensive furniture store, probably in Long Beach—not particularly tasteful, nor was it placed at its best advantage. The sofa was on one side of the room with its back to the window that would have accorded a sweeping view of the nearby mountain had anyone thought to swing the furniture around. Fifty-five-inch flat TV on an otherwise bare table against one wall. There was no other art, photographs, trinkets, gewgaws, or accent pieces anywhere—like a motel room at a Holiday Inn Express, minus the bad paintings. It had no personality. A cheap dining room set, possibly bought used, was pushed into a corner of the main room. Two of the four chairs had been pulled out from the table and not put back; the other two chairs looked untouched. Beyond, in the kitchen, unwashed dinner dishes were still on the counter—two sets of dishes, and two empty glasses. One of them, not yet rinsed, bore the traces of milk.

"Do you own this home?" Parrish asked.

"Me and the Sundown National Bank," Pratt answered, trying to be amusing and failing miserably. He set his unfinished Sam Adams down on the coffee table.

"Live here alone?"

Pause.Too long a pause before he said, "Yes, I do."

"I'm told you're employed by Stubblefield Properties. Is that true?"

"I'm head of security."

"Security? Were you in the military?" Sierra asked, though she already knew.

"U.S. Army. I fought in Desert Storm in the early nineties."

"Officer?"

Pratt shook his head. "Buck sergeant."

"Do you have a gun in the house?" Sierra asked.

"No."

"Interesting," she said, "since you bought a Kel-Tec PF-9 seven-round handgun from a gun store in San Diego on October 17th of last year and registered the purchase with the state."

Pratt gulped hard, his eyes flickering, looking for an answer. "It's—not here. It's at work—in my desk. I mean, that's what I do."

"Shoot people, do you? Fascinating. But that's a pants-on-fire lie, Mr. Pratt."

"Either tell us where the gun is, *now*," Griffin said, "or we'll open every drawer in the house and dump its contents on the floor until we find it."

"And we don't supply maid service," Flower added. "You'll have to clean it up yourself."

Pratt sighed. Moving to a small foyer table at the front door, he removed from his pocket key ring, overburdened with many keys, found the smallest one, and unlocked the drawer. He removed a small gun safe and handed it to Sierra.

"Maybe you think I'm Supergirl," she said, fingering the combination lock, "but I don't have X-ray vision. Open the safe, please, and let me see the weapon."

"I don't see the point of this," Pratt whined.

"You don't have to." Sierra Bravo hit him firmly in the stomach with the safe—like a quarterback handing off the football to a running back. "Open it!"

Pratt sat down on the well-worn khaki sofa, put the gun safe on his lap, and began turning the dial. "I keep this here for protection," he said.

"Good thought," Griffin said. "So when a burglar or an attacker knocks on your door, he waits patiently while you unlock the drawer and diddle around with the gun safe combination so you can protect yourself. You're a pretty scary guy, Mr. Pratt."

"Which makes me ask," Sierra mused, "why you keep a loaded gun all locked up when there isn't a single other residence around. You say nobody else lives here but you. Of course, keeping a loaded weapon under lock and key would be mandatory if, say, a child lived here. We don't want children playing with guns, do we?"

His hands shook, not surprising to police officers used to innocent civilians getting the shivers when confronted by a badge and a gun. It took him a few tries, but eventually, he opened the safe. Flower and Parrish moved to either side of him, with hands on their weapons, as Pratt removed a loaded firearm.

Sierra slipped on a latex glove. "Give it to me, please—butt first." She examined it. "Small, lightweight."

"A little girlie gun," Griffin said.

"Don't be sexist, Sergeant." Sierra's tone indicated that she meant it.

"I haven't fired it in years," Pratt said.

She closed one eye and peered down the barrel. "It looks like you haven't cleaned it in years, either. Not smart. It might explode and blow your hand off. No holster for it?"

"No."

Griffin said, "He probably carries it in his purse."

"Sergeant!"

"Sorry."

Sierra took a clear plastic freezer bag from her back pocket and put the gun inside. "Show us the rest of the place. There's a barn and a small hut out back. Let's start there, shall we?"

"Fine," Pratt said, "but there's nothing to see." Sierra right behind him, he led them through the kitchen, Griff and Nancy bringing up the rear. A large pot soaked in the sink, the water tinted red from what was probably the remnants of spaghetti sauce. The smell of garlic hung in the air. The kitchen door was peeling paint.

No one could call this area a "back yard." There were no fences or markings, and the land seemed to disappear in the almost-dark, as it stretched for nearly half a mile and then around the corner of a hill. The barn loomed—also in need of red paint and patching, as several missing planks allowed sunlight in during the days. Pratt swung open the squeaky door and the three cops looked inside, flashlights playing about the place like lights on a pinball machine.

"It smells of horseshit," Nancy Flower said.

"I haven't had a horse here in years," Edgar Pratt said. "There was one who came with the purchase. I didn't know what to do with it, though. I don't farm here, so I didn't need a horse pulling a plow—and I've never ridden, so I got rid of him."

"Did you sell him?" Griffin wanted to know.

"He was an old broken-down horse, maybe seventeen years

old or so. Who the hell would want him?"

"So you sent him to the slaughterhouse?" Griffin's tone grew sharp and nasty.

Pratt shrugged. "I sold him to some guy who offered me fifty bucks for him. I don't know what happened to him after that."

"You're some wonderful human being, Pratt."

Nancy Flower added, "You probably haven't cleaned out the barn since then. A slob, aren't you?"

"Let's move on," Sierra said severely. "What's in the hut over there?"

"Nothing—just tools and stuff."

"Let's have a look."

"It's not a big deal. You're wasting your time, you know."

"It's my time," Sierra said.

"It's my time, too." Pratt teetered close to pre-K skittish, his hands twitching.

"Our warrant gives us all *your* time we need, so let's go. The quicker we finish, the quicker you'll get your time back."

They moved across the stretch of ground, not grassy but sandy, not amenable to planting anything, and choked with stray weeds. "I'm not sure I have the key with me," Pratt said.

"You'd better look, then," Parrish rumbled, "or else we'll kick down the door."

The house owner fumbled with his keys. "It's dark to see out here—"

Sierra shined her bright flashlight beam on his hands. "There. Better?"

Finally, he found the proper key and unlocked the large, tough-looking padlock on the hut's door, then stood back as Sierra and Nancy Flower went inside.

Their police beams threw broad, bright lights, and the two women looked carefully at what was stored in there. Shovels, spades, a rake. Big cans of white paint that had been opened before. A length of medium-weight chain hung from a rafter. Next to it dangled two pairs of handcuffs.

Handcuffs?

And what was the rest of the contents of the hut?

Toys.

Girls' toys. Two different versions of Barbie dolls in wrapping that had never been opened. Big fluffy animal dolls—a bear, a horse, an Angora goat, a dog doll as big as an Old English Sheepdog, a few other toy animals no one could identify. A baby girl doll, also never unwrapped—the plastic covering proclaimed that it blinked, talked and wet itself.

"I have no idea what all this shit is doing in here," Edgar Pratt said. "It was all here when I first moved in."

"Looks newer than that to me," Flower observed. "Like it was bought less than a month ago."

"The handcuffs were here, too, Mr. Pratt?" Sierra's voice as icy as were her eyes.

"They're—well, I bought those. I'm head of security, of course. These are just a couple of extras."

"Nothing like keeping a few extra pairs of handcuffs in a shed about a hundred yards from the house," Parrish said. "Let's search inside the house, shall we?"

"There's nothing to see!" Pratt protested.

Sierra said, "Then we'll be bored to death. Come along, Mr. Pratt."

As they trudged toward the main house, she thought about what she'd just said. *Come along?* That's something one might say to a kindergartener—or to a puppy. A hand over her mouth hid her smile.

Is that the way she considered every perp she'd arrested? Was she one of those cops who looked on every non-cop with distrust or contempt?

She hadn't been police chief in Sundown Beach long enough for her to meet too many people, although she truly cared for the two cops who now followed her toward the house. But the only two non-cops in her city that she cared for at all, and who cared about her, were the top-shelf lawyer and city manager Chris

Fornadel, and the assistant middle school principal she'd just started sleeping with, Chester Quigley.

Where could she find more friends? With her job, it wasn't easy. The checkout girl at Ralph's supermarket? The female Dolphin Lounge bartender? The eighty-year-old Asian woman—Chinese or Korean or something even more obscure—who worked at the dry-cleaning establishment, could barely speak English, and smiled all the time?

Screw it, Sierra thought, as Pratt led her crew back into his home to find—what? Was she closer than ever to meeting the little girl from the movie theater restroom?

When they all re-entered the home, Sierra Bravo said, "We've seen your living room and kitchen, Mr. Pratt. Are there any other rooms on the main floor?"

"Well, yes. My—office, I guess you'd call it. Office and TV room."

"Lead the way."

The room Pratt showed them was even larger than the living room. A large flat screen TV on the wall dominated everything else in the room, but the owner did indeed have a desk—the top totally clear except for a thick layer of dust, as if it hadn't been used in a year. A big bookcase covered another wall, and all three police officers noted the book titles. One third of them were about war and combat. Many more seemed science-fiction novels—none by famous writers like Ray Bradbury or Harlan Ellison, but all having tacky, *femme fatale* covers. The other books seemed to be porn lit. There were two shelves of DVDs that also appeared to be what used to be called "blue movies."

Nancy Flower picked up one of the books, entitled "Big Butt Teen," and had cover art to prove it. "Spend most of your time in this room, I bet."

Pratt snatched the book away from her. "You have no right—"

"Warrant!" Sierra snapped. "We can do anything we want, and you've got nothing to say about it. Warrant, Mr. Pratt!" She grabbed the book from him, flipping it open to a random page.

"His giant dick," she read aloud, *"repeatedly slammed into her mouth, banging against the back of her throat."* She closed the book, her eyebrows raised as she looked at Pratt. "Giant dick? Really?"

"Hmm," Flower said, "I think I missed reading that one."

"Then wait for the movie." Sierra smirked at her own joke.

"Hey, I purchased that legally!" Pratt protested. "It's not a crime."

"Of course it's not," Sierra said. "A fine upstanding religious man like yourself wouldn't do anything illegal, now, would he?" She walked to his desk and began opening drawers, riffling through them, making as much of a mess as possible without actually dumping the contents onto the floor. "Anything in here that's not legal?"

"Business stuff," he said. "Bank accounts, taxes, a checkbook. Nothing illegal."

"Let's see," she said. She opened his savings account book. "Interesting. You have one hundred sixty-one thousand dollars and change here in your savings account."

"So?" He waved his hand around. "I live frugally."

"Really? How much are you paid at Stubblefield Properties?"

He hesitated, "Two thousand a week."

"Saving for a rainy day, huh?" Griffin Parrish said.

"Something like that." Now Pratt was growing belligerent; the downturned corners of his mouth proclaimed derision of those who earned less than he did—including police officers. "Plus bonuses, of course." The braggadocio tone was not lost on his visitors.

"Bonuses for what?"

He lost some of his arrogance. "Uhh—various different things."

Nancy Flower suggested, "How about we look at his checkbook? See what 'various things' he writes checks for."

"And his credit card purchases, too." Sierra opened two more drawers before she found the checkbook, and more importantly, the transaction register. "He's got an eighty-two-thousand-dollar balance in his checkbook. I guess he gets lots of those 'bonuses.'" She studied the register. "Well, he pays his electric bill and water bill faithfully," she said. "Good for you, Mr. Pratt." She ran her finger along a line of writing. "And he writes checks to Master-Card and American Express, too."

Griffin said, "Is there a door to the cellar here?"

"Nobody has cellars or basements in Southern California," Pratt said. "Too many earthquakes. What are you, a new visitor?"

The sergeant didn't answer as Sierra noted the register of some checks Pratt had written recently. "Six hundred twenty-six dollars to a furniture company in San Diego," she said. "What was that for, Mr. Pratt."

"Oh, that was—I bought a new bed."

"Queen size?"

He shook his head. "Just a double bed. I sleep alone, as I've told you."

"This check for the bed was written not quite five weeks ago."

He nodded.

"What were you sleeping on before? The floor?"

"People buy new beds occasionally," he said, growing defensive. "It's not peculiar."

"We want to see this wonderful new bed, then."

Pratt's breathing grew heavier, and white showed all around his eyes. "Damn it, there's nothing up there! It's just my bedroom! Don't I have any privacy?"

"Take it up with the judge who signed the warrant. We're going upstairs."

Pratt paused for at least fifteen seconds, paralyzed by fright. Then he raced out of his TV room, and planted himself at the foot of the stairs opposite the front door. "You're not going up there!" he screamed, spreading his legs wide, his arms held out at his sides, blocking anyone from going past him—as if he thought that the perfect way to stop three armed police officers from doing what they wanted.

Sierra didn't rush, but strolled, followed by Sergeant Parrish and Officer Nancy Flower. "Get out of the way, Edgar," she said quietly. "Don't make this hard on yourself."

"This is my home! You have no right!"

The staring contest went on for too long. Then Sierra said, "Oooh-kay!" Reaching out, she grabbed Pratt's left ear with her right hand and twisted it. Pratt shrieked in pain as she dragged him off the step and out of the way.

"I don't want to tire out poor old Edgar having to walk upstairs," she said. "Officer Flower and I will go up. Sergeant Parrish, you stay down here with him. If he tries to come up after us—or if he even looks like he's going to run away—shoot him."

Pratt rubbed his sore ear and whimpered like a three-year-old.

"But don't kill him," Sierra went on. "That would be police brutality. Shoot him in the kneecap, that'll get his attention—and keep it for the rest of his life."

Griffin patted his weapon. "I'm on it, Chief."

Then she turned to Pratt one last time. "The sergeant's a good shot, Edgar—in case you're interested."

Sierra jerked her head at Flower, and they climbed the stairs to the second floor, leaving Pratt fuming as Parrish made it clear that he wasn't going anywhere.

There were three doors on the second floor, one on each side of the hallway and another at the far end. Nancy Flower said, "That one at the end of the hall must lead up to the attic."

"We'll check that out last." Sierra moved to the door on the left and turned the knob. Nancy stood next to her, right hand hovering over her holstered weapon. The door was thrown open.

Nothing.

It was just a bedroom. Double-sized bed, made neatly but casually with the kind of brownish-reddish bedspread only a man would choose. A chest of drawers, dresser, night table with a small lamp on it, an alarm clock-radio, a Spiral notebook and a ballpoint pen. An old sixteen inch TV with rabbit-ear antennas took up the top of the dresser. No art on the walls in here either except a calendar with raunchy photographs.

"Does Penthouse Magazine put out a wall calendar every year?" Sierra wondered. "Check the drawers." She moved to the bed, inspecting the headboard, mattress and frame. "This double bed looks like Pratt has knocked the shit out of it."

"Where then is the newer bed?" Flower wondered. She moved to the closet, hand on her gun butt, ready to draw and fire at a millisecond's notice. Throwing open the door, she found nothing more fascinating than men's clothes. Three low-end suits—one black, one blue, one gray. A line of well-hung trousers—dress slacks, khakis, two plaid and blindingly colorful golf pants, and four pair of faded jeans separating the suits from the dress shirts. A hook inside the closet door was where Edgar hung his ugly neckties. Several shoeboxes were stacked on the top shelf, and Sierra took them down and tossed them on the bed. When she opened them, all she found were shoes, size 11, sandals, two pairs of deck shoes, one white and one tan, and work boots. One shoebox, however, contained approximately seven thousand dollars in cash—fifties and hundreds.

Sierra riffled through the cash, not bothering to count it.

Flower closed the last of the drawers she'd searched. "All that's here are T-shirts," she said. "Polo shirts, not very well-folded. Socks in two different drawers—the dress socks and the casual socks. Several pair of exercise shorts, a few sleeveless shirts. One drawer chock full of underwear, all of them faded whitey-tighties, for God's sake! He's got money coming out of his ass, and he buys his clothes in a thrift shop."

"Let's go across the hall."

They both moved out of the bedroom to stand in front of the other door. Both drew their weapons, at the ready, and Sierra Bravo tried the doorknob.

"Locked," she said. "What's so valuable that Pratt has all locked up?" She moved to the top of the stairs and called down. "The door to this room is locked, Mr. Pratt. Bring up the key."

The women both heard Parrish mumble something, and finally Edgar Pratt called up, "I don't have the key. I lost it somewhere. It's just a storeroom."

Sierra and Nancy looked at one another. Then Sierra shrugged. "Whose turn is it this time? Shall we do rock-paper-scissors to find out?"

Nancy shook her head. "You do it, Chief. I'm an old lady."

"You're only four years older than I am!" Sierra said. Then she shrugged. "Oh, well." She backed up a step and aimed a bottom-of-her-shoe kick directly under the knob. It didn't give. It took three more violent kicks for the double lock to pull itself away from the doorframe. The door blasted open, and she and Nancy went in, gripping their service weapons with both hands.

Then they stopped.

It was another bedroom. The one window was completely blocked with wide wooden planks. The ugly shag yellow carpeting, probably a holdover from the 1960s, was fading but thick. Off to one side was a small bathroom, but Sierra noticed immediately that there was no doorknob, making sure no one could go in there and lock the door.

Cowering in a corner between the new-looking single bed and a large toy box filled with all sorts of playthings, was a little girl, wearing nothing but a pre-teen white nightgown. She was wide-eyed with dread, and when she saw the two police officers enter, she screamed with all her might.

Sierra smiled as best she could, speaking softly. "Shhh, sweetheart. Shhh. It's all right. We're here to help you. We're here to save you." She held out her arms, but the child was too frightened to run to her and be enveloped by gentle, loving hugs from a woman she'd never seen before. She could barely speak English, and had no idea what this strange person was saying.

It would be another fifteen minutes before Sierra got her calmed down enough to wrap her in a blanket she took from the bed and half-led, half-carried the little girl down the stairs, and ten minutes after that until she ultimately convinced Edgar Pratt to confess that the child's name was Ilinca.

Griffin Parrish loved to say his next line, one he'd used hundreds of times before. It always gave him a boost. "You're under arrest, Edgar Pratt. You have the right to remain silent..."

Pratt's face was white, his eyes big as saucers. One gasp to interrupt the Miranda warning, and then he turned and blasted out the front door and into the night. Parrish drew his weapon and started after him.

"No shooting!" Sierra handled the shivering Ilinca into Nancy Flower's outstretched arms. "Back me up, Griff—-but this one is *mine!*" Turning, she moved through the doorway at top speed.

In the darkness, Pratt had a twenty-yard head start, his serpentine run a throwback to his military days. He didn't even know where he was running to, but all he cared about was getting away from these three cops. The hills rose ahead of him, even though he could barely see them in the darkness—and having walked and hiked those hills before, he felt he knew a few places in which he could hide until they gave up on him and went away.

Sierra Bravo's legs were longer than Pratt's, though, and she caught up to him quickly, even when she stumbled after stepping into a hole she'd not noticed in the dark and limped slightly, for the last ten yards. She hit Pratt in the back and wrapped her left arm around his neck as they both fell forward, her elbow hitting the ground hard; she was fortunate to have landed on grass and not on the pavement.

She'd seen this takedown on television more times than she could count. The actors who play cops always seem to run faster than the perps. As Edgar Pratt struggled beneath her, she realized this was the first time in her life she'd ever chased and tackled someone trying to run away from her. Maybe she thought, smiling, that *Law and Order: SVU* would hire her in a minute.

Pratt half-rolled onto his side, far enough so he could punch her in the mouth, his turquoise ring splitting open her bottom lip.

Her answer was to tighten her arm-grip around his neck. His eyes bulged, and he thrashed around for a while until he felt himself losing consciousness from being unable to breathe. That's when Sierra let go his throat and while he was still face down beneath her, she ground his face into the dirt, hard. Then she twisted both his arms behind his back and handcuffed them—very tightly.

"Edgar," she panted, spitting out a mouthful of her own blood, "you gotta get more exercise. You're a fucking wreck!"

CHAPTER NINETEEN

When Sierra Bravo rolled into the police parking lot, she sent Nancy Flower back to the holding cells to lock up Edgar Pratt. Then she and Griff Parrish repaired to her office to set up an unusual system most often used in big cities like New York and Los Angeles. She called the main police stations in several nearby cities and asked them to keep Pratt for an hour, no more, then move him to another city for the same treatment. Torrance, Long Beach, Newport Beach, Balboa, Redondo Beach, and Harbor City readily agreed. If they kept him moving around from jail to jail for the rest of the night, he wouldn't be able to make his one phone call. He wouldn't call any lawyer, either, but would try getting in touch with his boss—and Sierra didn't want anything to spoil the boss's surprise.

At nine a.m. sharp, the chief of police reached Child Welfare in Long Beach, and the woman in charge promised to be there by mid-afternoon to take the child into custody.

She wasn't smiling when she hung up the phone, only partly because her lower lip was torn. Custody, she thought. An awful word, one step up from imprisonment. Ilinca would be in "custody" until she turned eighteen—a long stretch for a little girl who knew no one and couldn't speak English. Adoption would be difficult, considering she was both physically and emotionally damaged. A foster home, more likely a group home, was more possible, and while the thought of it made Sierra shudder, it would be far better than Ilinca returning to a sexual hell.

The woman at Child Welfare had said an effort would be made to return the child to her parents in Romania, but that was sure to be a problem. It would cost tons of money, and no Child Welfare Service had enough to go around. She might have been kidnapped from her home—but possibly her parents had sold her to a trafficker for enough money to carry them through the next three months. Sierra also called San Diego State University, trying to reach anyone there who spoke an Eastern European language so she could ask Ilinca questions—how long had she lived with Edgar Pratt? How had she been treated? Most importantly, less than two weeks ago, had she been taken to a movie?

She was grateful to have entered that room the previous night, leaving Parrish downstairs to make sure Pratt didn't stick his nose out the door. When Ilinca saw them, the relief in her eyes was almost too painful to look at. She'd never seen a cop in working blues before, so she didn't really understand who they were. All she knew was that no *man* was forcing his way into her room and her life.

Not this time.

Sierra rarely visited the holding cells. She had no desire for social amenities with her prisoners, but was anxious to check the condition and well-being of her newest capture, who'd taken the grand tour of every police station near South Bay before being returned. At ten o'clock she strolled down a long hallway, unlocked two steel doors with a heavy key, and stood in front of a barred entrance until a jail guard hustled to admit her.

"Good morning, Chief," he said.

"Morning. How's our prisoner doing?"

"He hasn't stopped whining since he got here."

"His federal cellmates will love him." Sierra followed him down a corridor to four cells and a holding pen. Nobody was in residence at the moment except Edgar Pratt, who paced the length of his small cell, eyes wide and terrified, perspiration dripping from his forehead and building up to Richard Nixon-like upper lip sweat. The skin on his face was still abraded from when Sierra ground it into the dirt.

He rushed to the front of his cell, two hands up on the triple-glass window that separated him from the rest of the world. "I get to make one phone call," he whimpered into the microphone in the middle of the glass. "That's the law. I get to make one phone call while you've got me here."

"We brought you in too late last night, Edgar. You'll get your phone call. Give us some time."

"You've gotta let me out of here."

"Compared to where you're heading, this jail is Club Med."

"I'm going nuts in here."

"Don't make me cry," she said, pulling a metal folding chair over so she could sit down.

"I swear to God, I'll do anything."

"We are talking, aren't we? Even though I'm already bored listening to it."

"I'll tell you whatever you want to know."

"I know," Sierra said coldly, "you're a disgusting pedophile." Her upper lip curled into something beyond contempt. "Don't pull the innocent shit with me. You've sexually abused that little girl for who knows how long. Do you actually think I'll unlock this cell and let you breeze right out of here just because you *talk?*"

"But I never fucked her! I swear to God!"

"The first thing you'd better do is quit swearing to God in every sentence. I've heard it a thousand times before."

"I never did! I—" He stopped before swearing to his deity. Then: "I told you it was my boss who bought Ilinca, not me. I'm the bagman, that's all—and the babysitter."

"A babysitter who makes the baby suck you off two or three times a day. Is that what you're telling me?" Sierra rose, turned, and began walking away.

"Wait! Wait, Chief!"

"I have no use for anything you have to say, Edgar."

"Wait! Listen, I know stuff."

"We all know 'stuff'—"

"Stuff about this organization!"

"What organization is that?" Sierra asked. "The Girl Scouts of America?"

Pratt took a deep breath. "Don't you know that sex trafficking is a major enterprise all over the world?"

"Of course I do."

"Well, where do you think my boss found Ilinca in the first place?"

Sierra turned to face him. Her eyes glittered like those of a falcon circling the skies who just spotted a squirrel for breakfast. "Edgar Pratt—you're beginning to interest me."

Pratt ran his hands through his messed-up hair. A half-smile teased the corners of his mouth, and a cynical look behind his eyes announced what a shit he really was. "Yeah? Then I want to make a deal."

"I don't deal, friend. I have a gun and a badge—I don't *have* to deal."

"You say that." Pratt leveled a pointing finger at her. "Okay, you got me. But I'm so far down the line that I'm like a pickpocket at a parade. You want names? You want big shots? You want to shut this whole operation down?"

She sat back down in the chair. "Edgar," she said, "I'm all ears."

A half hour later, Sierra was on the phone with Special Agent in Charge Leonard Beckman from the Los Angeles Federal Bureau of Investigation.

"You've apparently done a great job, Chief Bravo," he was saying. "Congratulations."

"It was our arrest, Special Agent," she interrupted. "Not the

U.S. Marshals and not the FBI. It was ours, in our town. But this is a federal offense, so I wish you'd send someone down here to take him into your custody."

"I'll have someone there later today." Beckman cleared his throat almost delicately. "So, does this wrap up your case?"

"Not quite. One more arrest to be made—also in our town. It's a big one—and it's our arrest."

"In that case, I have to inform you, Chief Bravo, that this child was taken from her home country against her will and brought to the United States. That makes it an international incident."

"Meaning?"

"Meaning," Beckman said, "that the Federal Bureau of Investigation and the CIA are much more well-prepared than a local police department to make this kind of arrest."

"That's a slap in the face, Special Agent."

"I didn't mean it to be."

"A *backhand* slap in the face." Sierra felt her nerves tightening. She was almost as angry with Beckman as she had been with Edgar Pratt and Marvin Dreskler. That which made her so tough when she was thirteen years old was creeping back to her, stiffening her backbone, giving her Popeye's spinach strength. Her voice grew raspy as she said, "I know lots of things you don't know, Mr. Beckman. Things that'll make you look good."

Now she hesitated. What she was about to say to the FBI was the same thing Edgar Pratt had said to her. She fiddled with a ballpoint pen on her desk, tapping its end on the pad of yellow paper, thinking. Considering.

Oh, well, she thought—the hell with it. "Okay. I'll make you a deal," she said. "This department makes the arrest today to go along with the one we made last night. We get the respect, we get the applause, we get the medals or framed certificates of thanks or trophy cups or anything else awarded to great solid cops. Your Bureau people show up here at four o'clock and I'll turn both prisoners over to you—and trust me, they'll both sing their hearts out—and you'll be able to move on and bust one of the biggest international sex traffic rings in the world. That'll make you look terrific, too. See, it's better to share things with others, Special Agent. Didn't you learn that in FBI kindergarten?"

Beckman didn't say anything for a long time.

"I'm no bully," Sierra said, "and don't want to become one."

"Then history is re-inventing itself." Special Agent Beckman had found his snarl.

"I hope so," Sierra said, "because with any luck we'll have two really evil guys for your people to collect this afternoon, not just one."

"I might make it down there myself." The tone was threatening, and Sierra Bravo didn't ignore it.

"You'd better bring several other agents," she suggested. "And a van."

She hung up, then immediately lifted the phone again to announce to the station house. "Sergeant Parrish to the chief's office, please. Sergeant Parrish."

Within forty-five seconds, Griffin was standing in her doorway. "Are we ready to go?" he said, his hand almost caressing the butt of the weapon in his holster. "I couldn't sleep all night thinking about busting this son of a bitch."

"Not quite yet. Edgar is pissing and moaning about getting his one phone call. We roll out of here as long as someone makes sure he doesn't touch a telephone until almost noon." Sierra pondered that for a while. "I guess locking him in my condo is a lousy idea."

"Beyond lousy."

"Here's a better one. Take three guys with you—tough guys. Drive Pratt back up to his place in the hills. Stick him in that shed out back, and use his own handcuffs to keep him there—and if he gives you any trouble at all, hang him from one of those rafters. Then leave the three guys there, and you return ASAP. After we make that arrest, have the guys bring him back by three o'clock, because the Fibs will show up here flashing badges and making demands. By that time, we can give them anything they want."

Griffin nodded. "I get your drift. If Dreskler and Pratt get their phone calls, they won't contact a lawyer, will they?"

"I hope not. After all, nobody wants to ruin a surprise party."

The "surprise" happened at about 11:45 a.m. when Chief of Police Sierra Bravo, Sergeant Parrish, Officer Flower, and three detectives in plainclothes, invaded the offices of Stubblefield Properties near the northeastern city limits of Sundown Beach, arresting the CEO and Chairman of the Board J. Richard Stubblefield for rape, kidnapping, sexual child abuse, and several international criminal charges that would be better explained to him when the Federal Bureau of Investigation came to pick him up.

His face turned to stone when Chief Bravo cuffed his hands behind him as several of his top-rung employees watched in awe, and read him his Miranda rights, but he was smart enough not to say anything that might be used against him in court. He was a disgusting, vile, pedophile rapist who didn't make his fortune on industrial properties by being stupid.

The look he bestowed upon Sierra Bravo, however, was the worst kind of hatred. When she finished the Miranda recitation, Stubblefield leaned forward, his mouth far too near Sierra's head, and quietly said, "Chief Bravo—you have stepped in shit."

She couldn't help moving a few steps back, as if his breath was foul. What kind of threat was that? He was guilty, and completely busted because they had Ilinca safely in custody and that the shattered, torn-down Marvin Dreskler had spilled his guts already when he ratted on Pratt, and that Edgar Pratt pointed the blame finger on him.

So what could Stubblefield do to Sierra Bravo from prison? He wasn't Al Capone or one of the Mafia guys who could run the entire gang without ever leaving his cell and order her death with a quiet whisper in the cafeteria.

Or maybe he could have her killed for a buck and a quarter. He *was* stinking rich.

As he stumbled down the stairs to the parking lot outside his multimillion-dollar headquarters, two officers on each side of him with a tight grip on his elbows and two more cops clearing the way in front of him, the last thing his shocked employees heard was him shouting, "Call my lawyers! Call my lawyers!"

In the fifteen minutes it took to get from Stubblefield Properties to the police station, lawyers had already arrived, all wearing thousand-dollar made-to-order suits—two representing Dick Stubblefield and two for Edgar Pratt. Sierra allowed them to meet with their clients in interrogation rooms that were rarely used. Both were under arrest, and there was no way Sierra would let them loose.

Half an hour after that, the local media—newspapers and TV stations—descended on the police department with cameras, field reporters and print journalists brandishing notebooks. Sierra had called in her graveyard-shift cops, stationing three of them outside the front door to keep them from crowding into the station.

SAC Leonard Beckman arrived with four other Fibs, all dressed pretty much alike, and he didn't bother introducing them to Sierra Bravo. After very few words, a cuffed Stubblefield was brought from his cell and marched out through the milling news crowd. Beckman actually paused to answer a few questions leveled at him by one of the sexy blond stand-ups, checking his tie, cuffs and hair before he stepped before the cameras, happy that Stubblefield was just standing there, hands cuffed behind his back so all the TV cameras could take pictures of him. Though Beckman took no credit for the arrests, he didn't deny it, either. Pomposity almost leaked out of his pores.

It was Griffin Parrish who guided Dick Stubblefield into the van. He wanted to smash Stubblefield's head against the car's roof, but despite a former president's suggestion he do so, there were police rules against it, so he regretfully refrained.

Almost the entire police department stood outside with the news workers, watching as the FBI vans roared into action and drove out of the parking lot and back toward Los Angeles. Some younger cops who hadn't yet learned the rules of decorum actually waved bye-bye as the vans turned the corner, heading for the northbound US5 freeway.

There wasn't an officer on the Sundown Beach police department who wouldn't have happily beaten Dick Stubblefield to death—slowly. There were few violent criminal acts committed in their vicinity, so it's rare a local cop had the urge to rain heavy blows on the head and body of a bad guy—but Stubblefield fit the bill perfectly.

Several reporters hung around after the mass departure, trying to interview the chief of police, jabbing microphones in her face (which annoyed the hell out of her), but though she didn't stick with a brusque "No comment," her answers were deliberately sparse, therefore not fascinating to those locally and all over the country who yearned for more sizzle and sleaze from an attractive youngish law enforcement chief of a beachside town who busted up one small pocket of the international human trafficking empire.

She was still angry with Ken Zack, who seemed to think she had mounted her entire interrogation as an easy way to become famous. Even though he was not the pedophile she'd thought he might be, he was a thorn in her side, and would probably push hard for her dismissal.

That's why the congratulatory phone call from Chris Fornadel got her to thinking.

"You're amazing, Sierra," he said. "The whole town is babbling about you—and from Los Angeles to the Mexican border, too. You'll be voted Cop of the Year."

"There's no such award," she said.

"Nobody could track down a vague idea, identify it as a big-time crime, and make it stick the way you did. It makes me proud I hired you. Big cheers for you, lady."

"Sure. And Ken Zack is going to be proud when he fires me."

"You think?"

"The other night he roared at me I should never darken his door again."

"Jesus," Chris laughed, "I haven't heard that one in about fifty years."

"I can't blame him, since I more or less accused him of being a baby-rapist. I knew someone rich in this town bought a pre-teen child for regular sex. Ken Zack, for me, was the most obvious place to start."

"Uh-huh. Not your best idea."

"Not as it turned out. However—just talking to him convinced me I was wrong, and he gave me an idea where I should look next."

"Maybe you ought to thank him for it."

"What?"

"Call him up," Chris said amiably. "Tell him he did you a great service—and thank his ass off. It'd be pretty tough for him to fire you after that."

"I'm not going to get Dylan Zack off the hook for him, if that's what you mean."

"The case you busted is a hell of a lot more important than tearing up a speeding ticket."

"I don't know, Chris," Sierra said. "I've got a bad back. It hurts too much for me to bend over and kiss somebody's ass."

Chris took a moment. Then he spoke slowly and sadly. "Sierra—you're like a tree. No matter how strong or tall it stands, when the wind blows hard, it bends. Otherwise, it will break. Don't let yourself break. Our town needs you—and without all the bullshit, you need us, too."

"I'm not going to apologize!"

"It doesn't have to be an 'I'm sorry' phone call. It'll sound better to him if you tell him it was he who unwittingly led you to the solving of this case. Then he feels like a hero, you feel like a hero, and most of the anti-Sierra shit in City Council dies down for a while." Chris stopped to take a breath. "Besides which, Stubblefield won't still be on City Council if he's in prison for the rest of his life, so they'll have to pick someone new—who probably shares your views on human trafficking."

"I—hadn't thought of that," Sierra said.

"Think about it. You've hit a home run, Sierra. Don't let it fall through the cracks."

She *did* think about it after she arrived home that evening. After taking off her gun and holster, removing the throwaway derringer from her right ankle, taking off her shoes and putting the extra-sharp nail file she carried in her left one along with all her other weapons, she spent five minutes in front of the bathroom mirror combing out her hair. Then she poured herself a glass of wine and dialed the home number of Kenneth Zack.

He sounded cranky on the phone. No big surprise.

"I thought we agreed you'd stay completely away from me," he growled.

"Actually, *you* said it, Mr. Zack, not I. You told me never to come to your home again, and if I saw you anywhere, even on the street, I'm not even allowed to say hello to you. But you didn't say anything about calling you on the phone."

Through the earpiece, ice cubes tinkled; Mr. Zack had already begun his single malt Scotch evening. "All right, then—what do you want?"

"To thank you."

"For what?"

"I'm sure you heard what happened today regarding Dick Stubblefield."

"Naturally I heard. Someone from his office called my office before you ever put him in the squad car. You better be damn sure he's guilty."

"I don't put people under arrest for the fun of it, Mr. Zack— especially members of the city council."

"All right, fine—but why thank me?"

"I knew that someone in Sundown Beach had—bought a child."

"How did you hear about that?"

That gave Sierra pause. She certainly couldn't tell Zack about how U.S. Marshals Garfield and Blazek, and Tyler, too, had physically tortured Kurt Wimblehart and Marvin Dreskler to make them talk. She sipped some wine and said, "Confidential informant."

"I see. And did this so-called confidential informant of yours say I was innocent?"

"I was told to realize that anyone having enough money to *buy* another human being had to be very wealthy."

Angry, now: "So you thought of me first, is that it?"

"You are the richest man in town, Mr. Zack. I'm sure you're quite proud of that."

"You're goddamn right I am!"

"When I talked to you at your home, you were more than willing to be open about those who work for you. That's one point for you." Sierra inhaled deeply. "You were honest speaking about feelings for your late wife and your—subsequent adventures. That took guts to say, especially to someone like me. But not to worry—all you told me stays between you and me and goes no further. That's a promise."

He didn't answer.

"All things considered, I'm certain you had nothing to do with this investigation—so you are no longer a person of interest."

The sound Zack made might have been a laugh. "That's good to hear. I've never been on a shit list before."

"Don't kid yourself," she said. "You're some sort of American baron. You have to know there's a busy bustling crowd out there, working their asses off trying to make it from one paycheck to the next, that all hate your guts."

"Interesting way to thank me," he said.

"No, I thanked you at the start of this conversation. Frankly, if being a complete asshole was a felony, you'd be locked up with Stubblefield."

Sierra heard Zack breathing. Finally, he said, "So nothing's really changed with us, has it?"

"You actually answered my call, which is a step up. And I thanked you. Otherwise, I guess we're still at loggerheads."

"You're not going to give my son a break even though I helped you?"

"Your son is an adult," Sierra said. "He didn't help me, Mr. Zack. You did. Lawbreakers are not patted on the head by the police and told to be more careful, even though their parents are the most wonderful human beings on earth."

"Then my threat to you from the other night still stands."

Sierra didn't respond for at least twenty seconds, too busy biting down hard to keep from screaming. Finally, before she hung up, she simply said, "Then just bring it!"

CHAPTER TWENTY

Sierra Bravo should have been exhausted. Difficult days—the invasion of Marvin Dreskler's headquarters to the arrest of Pratt, to the head-butting showdown with Ken Zack and the eventual capture of J. Richard Stubblefield and watching him being hauled away by the FBI and the high-falutin', look-down-his-nose-at-you Special Agent in Charge, Leonard Beckman.

It hadn't sapped Sierra's strength but stimulated her. She needed to know more.

It had felt good sharing her adventures with Chris Fornadel. He really was a good buddy, making her realize she didn't have enough friends.

Her talk on the phone with Chet Quigley was a relief, too—informing him of what had transpired since she first marched into his office and asked about missing little girls, although she made it clear that this was no night for festivities at all, including cuddling.

Instead, she corked the wine bottle and put it in the refrigerator, made a quick dinner of a peanut butter and jelly sandwich—always crunchy, never plain—and washed it down with coffee. She wanted to be certain she didn't fall asleep before she found what she wanted. She sat at the table, open her laptop, and began.

Checking her Google for "child sex trafficking," she found several sites detailing with the horrific reports of adolescent girls being sold by their poverty-stricken parents to prostitution centers, many in Cambodia. Others were about American children who have disappeared without a trace only to be found in brothels clear on the other side of the world. Abuse of the worst kind—rape, beating, torture, starvation, and eventual abandonment. Sierra shuddered more than once—but she knew most of this information already.

It took her more than an hour to discover some names—mostly Cambodians, but some in far-flung places like Romania and Estonia. There were a few Americans, too—all arrested for pimping kids on a massive scale. Interpol made most foreign busts. The American men, plus one woman, were captured by U.S. Federal Marshals in Toledo, Ohio, in Brownsville, Texas, and on the outskirts of Miami. There was little information on the Internet regarding how long they'd been in business, but all were multimillionaires.

How many others were still at it? How many other obscenely rich people all over the world have amassed their ill-gotten gains forcing small children into sexual slavery? Who, for instance, was truly behind the disappearance of Ilinca from her home country—to be shipped to Hemlock Hills and then taken, kicking and screaming, to the lovely, sun-kissed waterfront town of Sundown Beach and installed in the remote, off-the-beaten-track home of Edgar Pratt for the enjoyment of J. Richard Stubblefield, who'd paid twenty thousand dollars for her?

Sierra took a moment to rest her chin on her hand, staring sadly at another heinous crime reportage post. Twenty thousand dollars seemed like a lot of money for a little girl. New *cars* cost more than that. Is this what America has become? Were humans worth less than some inanimate *thing* with a bloated price tag? Was selling a child into sex simply a profitable idea so many extra bucks could change hands.

What the hell was she *doing* in a job like this, anyway?

She plugged her printer into her computer and spent the next hour printing out all the things she'd need to know for her call the next morning. Another twenty minutes reading it again on paper, underlining certain words to make sure she'd mention them, and feeling the anger and strength within her, banging on the inside, fighting to get out.

She wouldn't go to bed—she couldn't imagine closing her eyes and drifting off to sleep. Eventually she put on a jacket, went downstairs to her car, and headed for the beach. She was a cop, not stupid enough to stroll around unarmed in a dark, lonely place, so she tucked her police weapon into the waistband of her jeans. People sometimes get hassled while walking on the midnight beach, even in Sundown, and after what she'd gone through in the past few days, it sure as hell wasn't going to be her.

She made her way across the foreshore and onto the pier, where she sat on a bench, her jacket zipped up to her throat, and gazed out at the ocean. The plashing of the waves breaking onto the sand did not soothe her as she hoped it would. Little girls like Ilinca, who were now, sadly, in Child Service Custody, had been dragged from their homes and families and shipped across this very ocean by plane or boat to be the vaginas owned by grossly rich white men.

It wasn't only a foreign problem. Children of both genders went missing every single day in the United States of America. Sometimes they were rescued and survived. Other times, they were never heard from again.

She couldn't change the world—no one could. Given her circumstances, she did a hell of a job, saving two little girls and putting four execrable human beings behind bars. Yes, the children were now "in custody," and the four loathsome men were all lawyered up—but still, she felt she'd done a pretty good thing all the way around, considering it wasn't part of her paying job.

Sierra felt rather than saw movement to her left. She looked up to see a uniformed cop approaching her. It was dark out on that pier, so he got within fifteen feet of her before she recognized him as Sundown Beach patrolman Pat Russo—Pasquale being his given first name. Close to her age, early forties, he always worked the graveyard shift, so she hadn't been able to fully acquaint herself with him.

"Chief Bravo!" He hadn't recognized her either. "This is a surprise."

"Hello, Officer Russo," she said.

"I didn't know it was you. I was about to run you in for either loitering or hooking."

"Just getting some fresh air," she said. "Had problems sleeping." To show him she wasn't completely unprepared, she pulled up the bottom of her jacket. "I'm armed—I'm always armed."

"Good. Women aren't always safe all by themselves in the middle of the night."

"Men either," Sierra said.

He hitched up his belt. "You made some outstanding busts all by yourself, today." He looked at his watch. "Well, technically, it was yesterday."

"Not by myself. Some of our people with me."

"Were you by yourself in Hemlock Hills?"

"No. The only thing I like doing alone is sitting out here on the pier, listening to the waves."

Pasquale Russo pushed his cap back on his head. "That's a subtle reminder for me to take a hike, isn't it?"

"I didn't mean it that way," Sierra said. "I've got a lot on my mind right now."

"You'd feel better with some shuteye, Chief. I'll walk you back to your car."

Nice guy, she thought as he escorted her across the sand to where she'd parked. It reminded her to make more of an effort getting to know most of the graveyard shift cops. Her new hero reputation was all over the precinct. Dick Stubblefield, being the bad guy in this scenario, everyone in Sundown Beach knew about it before she got him from his office to her jail.

When she got home, she realized Russo had also been correct

suggesting she get some rest. She went into her bedroom, removed her jacket, kicked off her shoes, and took off her hip holster. Face first across the coverlet, she was fast asleep within ninety seconds.

"You look tired, Chief," Nancy Flower said, bringing Sierra Bravo her black coffee as soon as she arrived the next morning. "Take a few days off and get your breath back."

Sierra shook her head, squirming around in her chair. She'd donned her holster quickly that morning and it was digging into her hip, and the raspy side of the sharpened nail file was rubbing a blister on her ankle. "I've had too many days off already—and City Council won't pat me on the back, no matter what I've done. You were in on both Sundown Beach arrests, too, Nancy."

"Just the back-up."

"Don't call yourself *just*. Cops like you save lives."

"I didn't save your life."

"Not this time—but you might have."

Flower shrugged. "Okay, then—I guess I'll have to follow you around every minute for the rest of your life so nobody threatens you."

Sierra laughed. "You'll bore yourself to death."

"There are worse ways to go." Nancy Flower moved toward the door. "Let me know when you need another coffee."

Sierra did catch-up paperwork until ten a.m. Then she took the sheaf of papers she'd printed off the Internet the day before, spread them out on her desk, and called U.S. Marshal Cass Garfield.

When she read him the list of names she'd discovered, he spoke kindly to her, but firmly. "Chief," he said, "we have better apps and programs than you do, so we know all those names already. So does the FBI, whether you like them or not. Both of us, by law, deal with American crime. We can't go storming down doors in Asia or Africa. Neither can you."

Sierra clenched her free hand so tightly that her fingernails made indents on her palm. Then she said, "What should I do, then, Marshal? Join the CIA?"

"They don't mess with this stuff, either. Chasing sex criminals throughout the world falls under the Interpol umbrella, and not to a police chief from a California coastal town."

"You mean I'm helpless?"

"Those silver stars mean you're a far cry from helpless. But if you decide to go off to Abu Dhabi or Sofia on a hunch, you wouldn't keep those stars for long."

Her voice came out low and strained. "Then I'm fucked."

"You endangered your job, arrested six sex traffickers, and saved the lives of two little girls," he said. "You're nowhere near fucked—you're a hero. Sit back and enjoy it."

And enjoy it she did—reluctantly and more than a bit embarrassed.

Part of her satisfaction was knowing Marvin Dreskler, Dick Stubblefield and Edgar Pratt will have hearings in the Federal Court in Los Angeles. She'd be asked to testify against them, and she hoped her pride, rage and passion would affect the hearing judge to hold them without bail until their trials, which would occur in the autumn. Heavyweight attorneys—Stubblefield's were from New York and Pratt's from Los Angeles—had been quickly brought on board to defend the perverts. They'd made handsome livings by keeping pedophiles and child molesters out of jail, and now Stubblefield's money would keep *them* in luxury for several years. Big money always skates unharmed from horrific crimes, and that might be the final outcome of the men she'd arrested. Well, she thought, with the assistance of Griff Parrish and Nancy Flower, she'd done her job to the best of her ability. The rest was in the wheels of justice, which turn slowly and sometimes—*only* sometimes—efficiently.

Her sexual couplings with Chet Quigley settled into a pattern. They saw each other two or three times a week, usually in the evenings. The times together were pleasant, the sex was more than that, and all in all, it was a good relationship. She was fond of him, and he respected the hell out of her.

On occasion, though, she fretted that this gratifying twosome was inching closer and closer to something else. She guessed Chet Quigley might want to get married again and would eventually propose to her—but marriage was the last thing in the world she'd want.

Marriage was never easy, she figured. The romantic beginnings, the boxes of candy, the flowers, the thoughtful gifts, the fantastic sexual experiments, gave way to an everyday repeat of the day before. Money problems arose, the careers would get in the way of the ardor, and then children came, puking and pooping and drooling and crying all night, chipping away more than three quarters of the relationship that got the couple-in-love to the altar in the first place. The boredom haunted the home, and adultery often followed.

Please, Chet Quigley, Sierra thought silently, even when they were having a great time together, a terrific dinner, a walk on the beach, a wake-up that goes from cuddling and stretching to eroticism—*please don't even think about getting down on one knee to ask that question. If you do, I'll have to say no, and then what would happen to the romance?*

She worked at her job for the next weeks, as no major crimes occurred in Sundown Beach. The local media and even a few TV network news bureaus had been all over her with questions and even offers, but other than pedophile busts, she'd done nothing else to make her an international Facebook rock star, so they moved on to fresher meat. Occasionally, when she was at lunch or dinner in a restaurant, fellow residents of her town would glance over, smile and nod, or bestow her with an enthusiastic thumbs up.

As for Dylan Zack's speeding ticket, neither Dylan, his father, nor Danielle Micaela Tokes had bothered Sierra about it anymore, apparently because Ken Zack had lost a close friend, and Danielle had a City Council co-member yanked away from her.

Dylan lost his driving license for one hundred twenty days, and was fined five hundred dollars by Judge Klein, which was paid by Papa Zack. A full-time Zack chauffeur was ready and waiting if Dylan had to go anywhere.

When the evening arrived for Sierra to address the Chamber of Commerce, she had a time deciding whether to wear one of her classiest going-out-in-the-evening dresses or her Chief's uniform. She finally chose the dark blues with stars and badges, which evidently was what everyone wanted to see. She'd had five different uniforms made when she first checked in as chief, and she chose the one she'd only worn three times at other semiformal events. Her makeup was subdued, little more than lipstick and a dab of rouge, and she made sure her dark hair was pulled back tightly so it wouldn't show while she wore her cap. She also brought the personal weapons she wore every day, because they actually made her feel more complete—the Glock in her holster, the throwaway gun at her ankle and the sharp nail file in her left sock—but her Chamber audience would be unaware of all that.

She'd never been to a Chamber of Commerce meeting before. They met monthly, lunchtime in a private dining room at the Dolphin, but this one was their special twice-a-year dinner meeting. The faces looked familiar to Sierra—restaurant and bar CEOs, those running small businesses like real estate and office temps and ad agencies, proprietors of retail outlets downtown, insurance agents, and elected managers of local, county and state government offices. There were five animal clinics in Sundown Beach, and vets all attended these Chamber get-togethers. There was also a small hospital and two Crisis Care clinics; doctors, head nurses, and fussy bean counters showed up for the semi-annual dinner, too. The business "suits" actually ran the hospital and never failed to check how many towels and Band-aids were used each week so they could bitch about it to those who actually cared for their patients. Two Catholic priests showed up, one elderly man who forgot many things each day, and one with a cheery suntan who looked as if he spent more time in plaid golfing pants than his black vestments and turned-around collars. Six Protestant churches peppered all the residential neighborhoods, and their ministers arrived, too, happily gathered around the cash bar the Dolphin Lounge set up for the occasion.

Walter and Grace Lyons appeared. They rarely attended Chamber of Commerce meetings because he was a mid-level government worker with no voice and no power, but he made sure he'd be there to cheer noisily for Sierra Bravo, who'd become a hero and made him, by association, a kind of third-rank hero, too.

Chris Fornadel was there with his wife—rarely seen in public together, since he spent most of his evenings with his girlfriend. Apparently, Mrs. Fornadel knew about it and didn't give a damn because he made a lot of money, and she could spend it faster than he could earn it.

There was no sign of Eben Flood, Danielle Tokes, or J. Richard Stubblefield. Ken Zack didn't come, either.

After dinner, when Sierra took her place behind the podium to give her talk, she was glad those people hadn't shown up. They all hated her, or so it would seem—and it would have been tougher giving a speech while the most important people in the room glared at her and wished she were dead.

She spoke for about half an hour. She hadn't written out a speech or even made notes ahead of time, figuring her listeners had no real idea of what a chief of police did during the day anyway, so whatever she said was off the top of her head.

She asked, then, if anyone had a question. The first four she'd expected, ones she could answer by rote. The fifth one, however, was a biggie.

The questioner ran a private real estate investment company and was known from Long Beach Harbor through Newport Beach and Balboa, Laguna Beach, and clear down to Dana Point. Homely was a kind description of him—a broad nose rosy from drinking too much, a silly-looking comb-over to disguise the bald spot, and reddish bruises on his hands, caused by his daily intake of Coumadin for a heart murmur. Sierra vaguely remembered his name as Frank Chapman.

"We've all read about your recent heroic antics, Chief," he said, "but from the news and TV reports, you began this investigation away from your law enforcement job instead of doing your regular duties. Why was that?"

"When a child is in danger, most people don't care whether it's in their hometown or not." She cleared away a frog in her throat. "And my arrests happened right here."

"Naturally," Chapman said. "But now Sundown Beach has a crappy reputation we'll all have to live down. That'll keep visitors away and definitely change the minds of those who consider living here. As a result, Sundown Beach will suffer economically."

Sierra's eyes narrowed, and each side of her jaw visibly jumped as she gritted her teeth. "I'd hate to see Sundown Beach suffer economically," she said, icicles hanging from every word. "I guess I should have ignored pre-teen children being forced into prostitution before they'd even begun menstruating. Two little girls should be way less important than this town missing out on a few bucks. Have I got that right, Mr. Chapman?"

The crowd gasped. Chapman looked around, furtive, humiliated. He finally stammered, "That's not what I meant—"

"It's okay," she said. "I got it the first time." She made a big production of looking at her watch. "Well, I see my time is about up. Thank you for inviting me. It was a great dinner, too. Good night, folks, and sleep tight."

As she made her way through the crowd, she glimpsed Walter Lyons staring at her. He put his palms together in front of him as if he were praying and mouthed a "Thank you" as she brushed by him.

It was Chris Fornadel who stopped her before she left the Dolphin Lounge. He took her hand in both of his, sucked in a gallon of air, and shook his head regretfully. "If you ever decide to write a book about good manners, Sierra—-I probably won't buy it."

"Sorry, Chris. Maybe I should run back in there and apologize to Mr. Chapman—just before I tell him to go fuck himself."

Driving home, Sierra Bravo's heart beat hard. She knew she'd offended not only Frank Chapman, but all business-minded people whose profits were more important than anything. Replaying the speech, she could have said something milder—but damn it, she was *not* a politician, nor an ass-kisser. She was chief of police, and she said and did what she believed was the law and was moral and right.

Saving one child from a lifetime of nightmare beat hell out of *any* profit to anyone. Collateral damage happened in war but shouldn't occur in the process of doing business. Sometimes it happened to kids in the one place where they should feel safe—their home—and as it did too often, Sierra's memories leaped out of her subconscious and bit her.

Damn Frank Chapman, she thought as she pulled her car into her condo's garage. If this confrontation would hurry her termination, so be it. She'd leave town with shoulders back and head high—and if she couldn't land a job anywhere else, she'd switch professions altogether. Nobody could make her crawl.

She put her cap on the passenger seat so she wouldn't forget it the next morning, got out of her car, closed the door with a purpose, and walked out of the garage. Then a hard blow on the back of her head made the pain explode. It unfocused her eyes, made her knees as wobbly as overcooked spaghetti. Another impact in the same spot—it wasn't a fist, but something hard like a blackjack or even a length of iron pipe—sent her into the darkest of darkness she'd never known before.

CHAPTER TWENTY-ONE

Moving.

Hurting. Inside her head, on fire.

Was this what migraines were like? This one started in the back of her head, behind her right ear, sloshing through her brain and settling behind her eyes. She wasn't sure her scalp was bleeding, but it felt like it. Something was thrown over her head like a black hood to block off her vision, and her wrists were fastened together by duct tape. More tape had bound those hands to a bar or railing on the inside of a van. The chill of the uncarpeted metal floor burrowed its way through her blue police uniform pants and made her knees and thighs numb from cold. Her brain throbbed. She could neither see nor stand, and she thought the knockout blow she'd suffered might have caused a concussion.

Football players got concussions, she knew. Boxers who'd been knocked off their feet and counted out got concussions. Chiefs of police, whose main jobs are shuffling papers, issuing orders, giving dinner talks to boring businesspeople and their irritated wives, and presenting themselves as the face of the department don't often get concussed, because none of them seemed anxious to hit her on the head.

What the hell had she gotten herself into?

She bit the inside of her cheek, and the pain forced her to stay conscious and aware. She rummaged around her memory. Never had she been truly hurt before. Some arrestees had kicked her, one threw a punch she turned away from, taking it on her shoulder rather than her face, and Edgar Pratt had managed to punch her in the mouth and make her lip bleed before she ground his face into the dirt—but in her police career she'd never really been injured as an adult by another human being.

This was a first. She wondered if it would be the last.

Her ankles hadn't been tied or taped; she couldn't go anywhere fastened inside of the van. But the weapon at her hip and the one strapped to her ankle had been taken.

Voices from the front seat—two men speaking quietly. She couldn't understand them because their radio was playing loud hip-hop music.

Smell. The ocean—salty and fishy. Wherever she was being driven, the Pacific was close by, the aroma coming from the right—meaning she was heading southward. Useless information, since she had no idea how long she'd been comatose in the van. Were they near Newport Beach now, or close to the Mexican border? She couldn't know.

There was another odor, too, that hung inside the van as if its windows hadn't been opened for a long time. It was the odor of human sweat—the stink of fear.

Her own.

She'd been abducted, all right—but by whom? She knew the Zacks and Danielle Tokes were furious with her, but that was all in the recent past, and the slap-on-the-wrist punishment applied to Dylan Zack was certainly not a reason for an attack, abduction and kidnapping. As for Dick Stubblefield and Edgar Pratt, they'd been carefully tucked into a federal lockup in Los Angeles until they received a trial and were taken away, hopefully to decay and die inside a prison—and neither had a family looking for revenge.

Then why?

How many people had she busted in her career? Until arrests of the co-perverts in Sundown Beach, none of the crimes she'd snuffed out had been really major. Speeding, fighting, robbery, domestic abuse and a couple of date rapes—and all the takedowns in Sundown Beach were executed by her efficient police force, and not by her personally.

Fame, however fleeting—triumphs over Stubblefield, Dreskler and Pratt already fading from public view, could be dangerous. No matter how brave and noble is the heroic effort that creates fame in the first place, there's always a roiling cadre of batshit-crazy panty-sniffers who hate your guts for it. Yet here she was, neck-deep in that danger, and not knowing whether she'd be alive when the sun came up the next morning.

Her eyes kept closing whether she wanted them to or not, and she fought with every ounce to stay awake. Concussion victims shouldn't be allowed to sleep for a while, she knew, and somehow, she understood she was concussed.

Who would be crazy enough to snatch her for ransom? There'd be no one with a huge amount of money to bail her out from the current frightening situation. Besides, until work the next morning, nobody would realize she was missing. If she wound up in Tijuana, just over the international border, or maybe even further into Mexico, she would probably be gone forever, no matter what would happen to her there.

Her fight against sleep lasted for another forty-five minutes until she felt the van slowing down and turning off the freeway. It hadn't halted for a conversation with border patrol officers, which made her believe she was still in the United States. That was something, she thought. Then she realized she was a helpless captive, no matter what country she was in.

Another few minutes driving through ordinary streets, stopping frequently for what she believed to be stop signs and red traffic lights, the car turned right into what felt like a driveway heading upward, halting briefly while a garage door raised by remote control, then moving out of the air and into the musty, oil-smelling confine. Then the garage door creaked shut, the radio turned off, and the car's engine silenced.

The doors opened and closed on each side of the van. Footsteps. Then the rear door was yanked open. Someone crawled in and roughly freed her arms from the railing to which she'd been fastened without easing the pain of the tape wrapped around her wrists, and shoved her roughly out of the van. "On your feet, cunt! Walk!"

An agonizingly strong grip on her elbow steered her up two steps, through a doorway, then up five more steps, and in all probability, she was inside a house, one that smelled as if it were scoured for cleanliness daily. She half-walked and was pushed through a room, then heard a door being opened. She was led down another flight of steps. The scent changed. The air pressure was different, the carpet on the steps were different—a strange kind of carpet. She sensed she was in a basement. There was still soft carpet beneath her feet, but a different kind—thinner, and less luxurious-feeling. Herded into another room with no carpet at all, the person who'd gripped her elbow now pushed her in the chest so she sat down hard on what felt like a toilet. Then her feet were pushed together and trussed with duct tape at the ankles, during which time she heard another male voice say one word: "Tight," making her wonder how long her legs would last bound that tightly before they lost feeling altogether.

The hood, or whatever it was covering her face, was yanked off, and she squinted hard against the light, the bruise on the back of her head throbbing painfully. Opening her eyes wide enough, she saw she was in a small bathroom—closed toilet on which she was sitting, and a small basin in which no one could wash anything but their hands. Two men stood in front of her, and she tried vainly to remember if she'd ever seen either of them before.

One was big, wearing a black windbreaker over a T-shirt and casual black jeans—well-muscled but going to fat, looking like a high school football star now in his forties and recalling what a gridiron big shot he'd been at seventeen. The other man was older, near sixty, wearing a pewter-colored pullover cashmere sweater with a starched white dress shirt beneath it, and rimless John Lennon-style glasses tinted a subtle gray. His formal three-hundred-dollar black shoes were mirror-shined. He had a small mustache with a space in the middle.

"Good evening, Chief," the older man said. "I'm glad to see you're awake. Welcome to my humble home. I hope your trip wasn't too uncomfortable."

"Who the hell are you?" Sierra demanded.

"My name isn't important to you—and you'll never get the chance to use it. Let's just say you've fucked up my business—royally." She heard the faint remnants of a foreign accent, but she couldn't place it. European, she thought. Eastern European.

"I gather your business is not selling Ferraris."

He sighed. "My business encompasses the entire west coast of this country—and you have sabotaged my Southern California branch." He leaned against the tile wall. "In case you're wondering, I frankly don't give a damn about Richard Stubblefield and Edgar Pratt. Pratt was Stubblefield's errand boy—and Stubblefield was one of many twisted shits to whom my organization caters. No, it's the fate of my local supervisors that bothers me."

"Supervisors?"

He nodded. "Marvin Dreskler was my top man in your—" He frowned, wrinkled up his nose, searching for a word. Finally: "—your California neighborhood. Any requests or orders from the Mexican border up through Sacramento were Dreskler's responsibility, and Wimblehart was his second in command. But you," and he pointed a neatly-manicured finger at Sierra, "captured Dreskler and handed him over to the FBI. It's entirely possible he'll sing his ass off, possibly mentioning me. You also caused Wimblehart to be injured so badly that he left the country to scrounge around for work in Abu Dhabi with those who operate a similar business there." He frowned sadly, pursing his lips for one moment. "You, of all people, should realize your powerful nation is built on profit. Not patriotism. Not creativity. Not the faith of a god no one has ever actually seen. Just—profit."

Sierra said, "Why kidnap me and drive me this far from Sundown Beach? You plan to kill me, right? Why didn't you do it back there and save yourself all this trouble?"

He touched his mustache with the tips of his fingers as if to make sure it was still there. "You know about public relations?"

"Of course."

"I have a reputation to sustain—in my circles. People respect me. Fear me. Nobody messes with me, and I like to keep it that way. That's what I mean about public relations."

"I don't even know your name," she said. "You threw a monkey wrench into how I make my living."

The crushing headache knocking around in Sierra's skull was not going to be this asshole's only payback to her. She shivered.

"I thought first of sending you off somewhere," he continued, "maybe to some ghastly brothel in Cambodia, where, trust me, you wouldn't survive six months. In spite of your good looks, you're too old to whore. So we're going to kill you—but that isn't enough. We must send a firm, definitive message out there— what happens to anyone who gets in the way of the human trafficking business. So." He rubbed his hands together as though it were cold. "We'll break many bones in your body. Slowly— fingers, toes, arms, legs, ribs. We'll beat your face so badly that your own mother won't recognize you. We might even cut off your nose."

He made a scissor movement with his second and third fingers.

"When you're dead," he went on, "we'll leave you someplace public near Sundown Beach, wearing your uniform like you are now, right downtown so everyone knows it's you when they head in for work. You'll be a message to anyone on the west coast who thinks they can fuck up my business."

"Selling off babies for sex?"

"I traffic in human beings."

"You think the FBI will just ignore you?" Sierra said.

The man snorted back a laugh. "The FBI is so busy tracking

Muslim terrorists that hardly exist in this country that they won't give *you* a second thought. So is the CIA, except they strictly operate outside the United States. As for Interpol—they don't pay attention to a murder around here unless it's a foreign diplomat, an ambassador, or a visiting head of state. I'm afraid, Chief Bravo, that you're screwed."

"Fucked," his companion grunted. His vocabulary needed a brush-up, as that was the only word he'd uttered so far.

"We'll wait until everyone is asleep. Then in a secluded place—not in this house, but outside somewhere—we'll take our time killing you. You deserve that. Meantime, you sit here all night and think about it." His smile defined evil. "Thinking of what we'll do to you is almost worse than us doing it. Almost."

Sierra looked up at him. "You're even sicker than I thought you were."

He laughed. "I'm not sick. Top drug dealers don't use heroin or crack themselves, as that would be stupid and get in the way of making money. Well, I sell children all the time—but I don't fuck them. Doesn't that make you like me a teensy bit more?" He moved a few steps toward the door. "I'm not going to tape your mouth shut," he said, "so you can breathe more easily. Don't bother screaming—no one can hear you. But if you do, if your screaming bothers me—" and here he jerked his chin toward the younger man, "he'll come and knock all your teeth out, one by one. I'm sure you don't want that."

The younger one opened the bathroom door and walked out. The mustache man paused. "Remember your life, Chief Bravo. Cherish the good memories, and shit-can the bad ones."

And then he was gone.

Sierra Bravo sat quietly on the toilet for several minutes, thinking not so much about her past life, as the mustache man suggested, but about her immediate future, which made her mouth dry and her shoulders shake.

It wasn't that she was afraid to die. All cops know, from the first moment they pin on their badge, their profession brings danger and violence with it. But she knew her death would be soon, and deliberately agonizing—something she didn't want to think about.

She was a police officer—and no cop anywhere quietly sits back and waits for the inevitable. They do something about it, even if they'd been taped down, relieved of all their weapons, and plunked onto a closed toilet seat to wait for torture and death.

She was no movie superhero, but she was tough. Two law enforcement decades taught her to be mean and efficient. But she felt naked now, and vulnerable. After the long ride in the van with her legs doubled up beneath her, she wasn't even sure she could stand.

She had no idea where she was. South of Sundown Beach was all she was sure of, but it really didn't matter. Her main priority was to get the hell out of there.

For the next twenty minutes, she sat quietly, head down, chin on her chest, thinking. Staring down at her feet, which were becoming numb from the tight binding. She tried to wiggle her toes inside the shoes to get some life back into them.

And then—the nail file! The metallic nail file she always carried in her left sock—just in case, for protection. It was still there.

After a few minutes of thinking and figuring, Sierra took a deep breath and gritted her teeth. Tucking her feet under, she pressed her knees tight together and as far as she could to the right, giving her the access to her highly polished left shoe. Grunting with the effort, she bent low, force her fingers inside the sock as far as she could.

It wasn't easy—almost impossible to get two fingers in when her wrists were bound so close together. And after the vicious blow to the back of her head, bending over for that long made her not only wobbly from the pain, but nauseated. Several times, she stopped to sit up straight and catch her breath. Finally, sweat-soaked and exhausted, she managed to get two fingers around that metallic nail file and scrape it up out of her sock.

She slumped back against the toilet tank, closing her eyes for a few minutes, worn out but clutching the file between her two hands and trying to think now that she had it, what was she going to do with it. The point of it was sharp—she'd honed it down against a rock several years ago—but its sides had no cutting edge.

There was no way she could slice through the several layers of duct tape around her wrists. The angle was wrong. She couldn't get proper leverage—and she couldn't release her hands by holding the file between her teeth while she sawed away.

Again, she bent over, picking away at the binding around her ankles with the point of the file, concentrating on where several layers of duct tape covered her Achilles tendons, straightening up every few minutes when dizziness almost overcame her.

She wasn't sure how long it took—at least half an hour—but finally she felt the tape part behind her heels. Careful to ensure if anyone came in and looked down, it would appear she was still trussed up around her ankles, as her hands were of little use. She wore a wristwatch, but her captors had taped over it, so she couldn't tell what time it was.

She calculated they probably wouldn't be hauling her out of there to take her out to abuse and kill her for at least another two hours. They wouldn't want anyone awake and riding around so they could be seen accidentally. She had a while longer to create a plan that might save her life.

She had another idea, too. Her struggle, bent over to get two fingers into her left shoe, had caused her great discomfort in her crotch area. The pepper spray was still there. It'd be a shame to waste it.

She managed to hold the sharp file between her teeth while she awkwardly tried unzipping the front of her pants, and somehow, with both wrists tied together, work her way down into her panties and remove the pepper spray.

The spray can was in her left hand, the nail file in her right, so it was hopeless for her to pull up her zipper. She relaxed, working through her pulsing headache. Then, ready as she'd ever be, she took a deep breath—and began screaming at the top of her lungs, as loud as she could, considering duct tape covered her mouth.

Her own bellowing deafened her in that small, enclosed space, but she still heard the heavy footsteps of someone rushing toward the basement—maybe the big guy, the nearly silent one, whose job it was to remove her teeth if she made any noise. She hoped so. If they both showed up at the same time, she'd be in trouble.

Big trouble.

Terminal trouble.

She kept screeching as she gathered her legs under her, the footsteps now on the thin carpeting of the basement, coming closer. The click of a key in the lock, and the door was flung open. The high school athlete barged in, his evil mouth twisted half in hatred and half in expectation.

"You were told to keep your fucking mouth shut, bitch!" he roared, striding near her, looming over her, legs about twelve inches apart for better balance, and raised his hand to backhand her across the mouth. If he had, it might have knocked her head halfway off.

But he didn't get the chance.

She jerked both her bound hands, squeezing a big shot of pepper spray right into his face. He raised both hands to his eyes, screaming, but she dropped the spray bottle, and drove the sharpened file through his trousers and into his testicles.

He howled, stumbling backward, his crotch spurting blood. She leaped to her feet, took three long steps toward him, and plunged the now-bloody nail file into his throat, drawing it from one side of his neck to the other.

The look on his face was instantly transmogrified from anguish to total shock. He tried to speak, but the sound he made through his slashed throat beggared description. He bounced off the bathroom wall and into the larger part of the basement and fell hard, just outside the doorway.

His body wriggled for a few seconds, and Sierra was astonished at how heavily he bled.

And then he was dead.

She took a mini-second to realize that she'd never killed anyone before in her life—but she'd worry about that later. The Mustache Man must have heard the commotion and would come down those stairs momentarily.

Not wanting to leave gruesome footprints for him to follow—she'd already stepped in the other man's blood with both feet—she kicked her shoes off, stepped over the bloody corpse, and ventured out into the basement.

Nicely appointed, she thought as she glanced around quickly. A man-cave. There were several sofas and easy chairs, a full-sized pool table, a gigantic curved TV set mounted on the wall, three huge Mac computers—one on a desk, one on a sofa end table, and one at the corner of a bar at the far end of the basement.

High on the wall on one side were several short but wide windows, looking out at above ground level. An air conditioner hummed, keeping the room temperature comfortable. There'd been no cooling in the bathroom, and her clothing dripped perspiration.

There was also a large clock on the wood-paneled wall telling her the time was 1:47 a.m. Her life would probably end horribly within the next three hours, but now, at least, she had a fighting chance.

The Mustache Man was running down the stairs. "What's going on, Bubba?" he shouted. "What's happening down there?"

Bubba, she thought ruefully. Now she must live forever with the knowledge that the only human being whose life she'd ever taken was named Bubba.

With her hands tightly taped together, the nail file would be of no use at all against a man who most likely had a gun. She ducked behind the bar, crouching down so as not to be seen, dropping the nail file at her stockinged feet.

Mustache Man blasted into the basement, weapon in hand, and from where Sierra could peek out, she saw at once that the gun was the police-issued Glock he'd taken from her. Stopping in mid-stride, he spotted the blood-drenched Bubba sprawled half in and half out of the bathroom. "Oh God," he whispered. "Oh my fucking God."

His face turned steel gray, like a storm just before a rainfall, and his mouth became one thin, tense slash across his face. He bent halfway over, alert, nervous, aware his foe was somewhere in the vicinity. He held the gun in front of him with both hands the way he'd seen every TV cop hold theirs, and he spoke softy, his voice quivering with emotion—and fear.

"Where are you, Chief Bravo? Show yourself."

Sierra didn't answer him, nor make a sound. Frustrated that she couldn't manage to pull her hands apart because of the tight wrapping of the duct tape, she looked around desperately, hunkered down behind the bar, for something with which she could defend herself. Then it struck her, bringing on a half-smile that no one else could see. She wasn't on defense. He was a high-ranking international criminal, and she was a cop—which means a cop is always on the offensive. That made all the difference in the world.

The Mustache Man looked at the high windows to see if one was open, but they all seemed locked as usual. Besides, they were too small for anyone, even a female, to squeeze through. There was no way she could have reached them, anyway. Seeing her shoes with bloody soles, kicked off in the bathroom, he knew she wouldn't be running.

"Come on out, Chief Bravo. It doesn't have to end like this. We can make a deal—"

Sure, Sierra thought bitterly. *The deal is that I tell you where I am and then you kill me.* She heard him pull the sofa away from the wall in case she was hiding behind it.

"Ah," he said. "I think I know where you are. Come out and play." He jerked open the door of a closet, then made a disappointing sound almost like a groan.

From her crouch, she looked desperately around. Like most commercial cocktail lounges, the top-shelf liquors were on the back bar, in front of the mirror, but below the bar itself and next to a steel sink, was the cheap no-name junk—vodka, of course, because few people drank vodka straight and there'd be no point in watering down the expensive stuff—and a half-empty bottle of Jack Daniels. Sierra quietly lifted the vodka bottle from its perch, grasping it with both hands.

And waited.

"You killed poor Bubba," the Mustache Man said loudly. "I don't know how you did it, but you'll never be able to run from it. Come out now, let's get this over with. It won't be as bad as I said now. It'll be quick. Merciful."

She heard his feet on the thin rug, moving closer to her.

"Give it up, Chief Bravo," he said, and then she saw his hands clasping the weapon in front of him, reaching around the open end of the bar.

She swung hard, bottle shattering against his wrists, knocking the gun loose and drawing blood.

"Fuck!" he howled, as Sierra stood straight up, fast, now less than two feet away from him, and drove the broken vodka bottle into his face.

And twisted it.

As he screamed, too shocked to even move, she dropped the now-shattered bottle and swung her bound hands, which had turned into fists, at the side of his head, striking him just below the ear. He went down hard and stayed there, blood pumping from several gouges on his wrists and face.

Gasping from relief, she leaned weakly against the bar, taking time to look around the basement to see what wrath she'd committed. She was safe, for the moment—but her hands were still bound together, she was shoeless and car-less, and Bubba was dead. The Mustache Man was alive but completely unconscious, his hands and face bleeding freely. She forced herself to slow down and let her mind think.

She bent and picked up the gun—*her* gun. On a table next to one of the easy chairs was a stack of magazines. She had to examine three of them before she found an address label. Her captor's name was Dieter Krotzge. She picked up the magazine and searched the room for a telephone, finding one atop the table, behind the sofa. She dialed 911—with difficulty.

"Officer," she barked into the phone, "I'm at 3680 Horizon Lane in Cardiff-by-the-Sea." This was an extremely wealthy community that was part of the larger, more urban Encinitas to its west and south. "This is Police Chief Sierra Bravo from Sundown Beach. I need an ambulance, a coroner, and armed police officers at this address ASAP." She licked her dried lips. "I've killed one man here, and maimed another one. I need help."

CHAPTER TWENTY-TWO

It took Sierra Bravo ten minutes to massage her wrists and shake her hands back into circulation. The Encinitas police suggested taking her to the nearest emergency room, but she insisted she be driven to Sundown Beach, as Griff Parrish and Nancy Flower waited for her at her office, along with a very concerned Chris Fornadel. All she wanted was to veg out in her own bed and sleep for a week, but her friends insisted she be transported to the hospital immediately. She argued with them hotly, but to no avail.

The ER doctors kept her there for the rest of the night, and for thirty-six hours after that to give her a thorough check-up, though she threatened to shoot them all if they didn't release her. Her concussion, they told her, was slight, but they kept a keen eye on her for safety's sake.

Finally, though, she was taken home to enjoy the large bouquets delivered to her condo, ordered by the cops under her command, the City Council—or what was left of them, Eben Flood and Danielle Tokes. On Chris Fornadel's bouquet, he'd obviously visited the flower shop personally and had scrawled on the gift card: "Wow! You're Supergirl! xoxox."

Chester Quigley had sent flowers too, and the largest one of all was from Kenneth Zack and his son Dylan, who'd been furious with her just a few days earlier. Touched by the thoughtful generosity, Sierra could barely find enough vases and table-tops to display the flowers, but she still felt she was in the middle of a Tarzan-in-the-Jungle movie.

Despite her eagerness to return to work and a normal life-style, she needed a few days to decompress, so other than calling a locksmith to install an extra police lock on her door, she lounged around in pajamas and robe, drank spring water and decaffeinated tea, and ate organic foods. She had no trouble falling asleep at night, and half-hour daytime naps didn't hurt her, either.

She'd already had two sessions with a psychologist, and more to come, on orders from Chris Fornadel. The Sundown Beach Department was far too small for an Internal Affairs Division, so the Encinitas cops had their Internal Affairs guys investigate before they'd give Sierra Bravo back her gun.

On her first Saturday at home, Chris came by to tell her news-papers in Los Angeles, San Diego, Sacramento, Arizona and Nevada had picked up on her harrowing adventure and were writing about it at length.

"I don't want publicity," she said wearily. "I'm a cop. I do my job."

"You killed a man," Chris said, "and caused the federal arrest of someone so high up in human trafficking on the West Coast that you majorly crippled the entire operation. You'll be famous, Sierra—and not just in Sundown Beach."

"Movie stars are famous, Chris. Quarterbacks in the NFL are famous—assuming they don't get intercepted eight times in every game and they stick around for more than a year or two. Serial killers are famous. Not cops." She slumped in the recliner while he was ensconced on one end of the sofa. "A little bird whispers you're the city manager who's gently come to tell me I'm not a cop any longer."

His eyes bugged out in surprise. "You think you're fired? You're nuts! Everyone is planning a big dinner in your honor, and to present you with some plaque or trophy—we'll decide that later—and funnel all the money to the charity of your choice."

"I don't want any trophy, I don't want to be guest of honor at anything, and I sure as hell don't want a damn dinner!"

He laughed. "I don't know how I can stop it. You don't realize how much respect everyone has for you now."

"Respect—until next time an officer writes a speeding ticket for some millionaire Sundowner. Then I'll be Mussolini with tits."

"Ken Zack told me after you did what you've done, he feels like a total asshole for the way he's treated you. And Danielle actually called and asked how you were doing and could the two of you maybe have lunch when you're feeling better."

"She'll try to feed me a poisoned apple."

"Don't look on the dark side, Sierra, because there isn't one. You can stay chief of police forever, if that's your choice."

She ran both hands through her hair, getting it out of her face, and took a moment to think. She liked Chris and appreciated his help and his favors, but she wished he would go home.

"Take a few more days off," he continued, "to put this all into perspective so you won't be frightened anymore."

It took her about two seconds to process that. Then she sat up perfectly straight in her chair. "I beg your pardon?" she asked, a scalpel edge to her tone. "I beg your goddamn *pardon*?"

"I said—"

"I heard what you said. 'So I won't be frightened anymore?' Really?"

"I know what you went through."

"You don't have the foggiest idea of what I went through." She pushed herself into a standing position, hovering over him. "I was knocked unconscious and driven halfway to Mexico. My hands and feet were tied, and two men told me, before the night was out, they were going to torture me to death. I was so 'frightened' that I killed one of them by stabbing him in the balls and cutting his throat, and just about destroyed the other one— mangled his face and hit him so hard that he didn't wake up until he was handcuffed in the back of a cop car. That's how fucking *frightened* I was."

"I didn't mean—"

"I speak English! I understand what you mean. I'm a cop, Chris. Cops either get tough, or they turn in their badge and gun and become a night watchman at a toy factory. Maybe a rookie is scared the first time he pulls over someone who looks suspicious when he writes up a traffic citation. But I've been a cop twenty years, and I haven't been scared for nineteen of them. I can shoot better than you can, I can run faster, and longer, and because all you've done for those twenty years is sit on your ass typing out legal briefs, I can kick the crap out of you with one hand tied behind me." She swallowed air, which made her body feel stronger. "I stopped being scared the moment I killed the first guy. So don't worry about me being frightened."

Chris Fornadel's eyes were saucer large. "Wow!" he breathed. "Please sit down again, Sierra, because now *I'm* frightened."

"Then be frightened at your girlfriend's house." She smiled. "I need to wash my hair and put on some big girl panties so I'll be back at my desk Monday morning—and I'll *not* be frightened."

After he left, she showered and shampooed, put on khaki slacks and a dark blue long-sleeved T-shirt, and applied her usual makeup. Even on more formal occasions, her makeup was barely more than minimal; it wasn't her style to slop it on with a trowel. She wondered why all female TV police officers looked, at their worst, like fashion models.

She spent more time than usual in front of the full-length mirror in her bedroom, but she really wasn't examining herself for faults or mistakes. She was instead thinking of what she'd said to Chris Fornadel about not being frightened anymore.

More truth to that than she'd realized.

Ever since she was nine years old, she'd always been afraid of something. Becoming a cop, going through rigorous cadet school training and strapping a holster around her hips helped her ignore her dread, making her a highly efficient law enforcer in the bargain—but those dreads had always lived right under her skin, battling to get out.

They were rare frights in her police experience, but subcutaneous memories went with them, threatening to break out.

She'd been sent information a day earlier, along with a short letter signed by FBI Special Agent Leonard Beckman. The man she killed, known only to her as "Bubba," was really Willard Anthony Brownley, a Mississippi native who'd spent twenty-two years in prison for the rape and sexual abuse of minor children. Mustache Man was German native Dieter Krotzge, who began his human-trafficking career in Bulgaria and Romania and earned a small fortune, letting him move to the elegant seaside town of Cardiff-by-the-Sea in California to continue making big money by selling young girls to the disgustingly wealthy and living in luxury. The medical report Special Agent Beckman included stated that Krotzge's right wrist was slashed deeply and badly broken, and the scars on his face from Sierra gouging him with a broken bottle were severe enough that only highly expensive plastic surgery could make him look like himself again—and that kind of medical treatment was not available in a federal prison he'd be sent to after his trial.

Beckman's letter was brief. *"You've done a magnificent job, Chief Bravo, despite many pitfalls along the way. Keep up the good work. The Bureau is proud of you."*

It was signed, "Leonard."

Cass Garfield sent an email instead, signed by Marie Blazek, too. *"Chief: you're one scary bad-ass! WTFG!!!!!"*

Way to fucking go. That was fine, Sierra thought. Two federal guys who can do anything they want to, telling her what a good cop she was. Neither offered her coming to work for them—and she was relieved about that. She was happy where she was, at least until the city council got mad at her again and waved a pink slip. Whatever new business she got herself into, there would be an enormous amount of new training involved, and she had neither the time nor the inclination to submit to it, nor would she ever wrap her mind around having to call her supervisors "Sir." She was already in her forties—too old to be starting out with the U.S. Marshals or the Federal Bureau of Investigation.

And from what little she knew of the two men who'd written her congratulations, one was a tight-ass and one was a cowboy. She was closer to being a cowboy than a tight-ass, but being a beach town police chief fit her like a glove. A gnawing ambition to be Police Commissioner of a huge metropolitan area like New York or Los Angeles had never crossed her consciousness.

She puttered around the condo, dusting and vacuuming, spent an hour or so reading out on her small terrace, actually watched *The Price is Right* TV game show for the first time in many years—it still bored her and seemed silly—and took in a half hour of TV local news from San Diego, thinking all the time. At length, she tucked her legs under her on the sofa and called Chet Quigley.

"Are you feeling better, Sierra?" was his first question.

"Raring to get back to work," she said. "How about you?"

"Other than worrying about your health, I'm as good as can be expected."

"Are you free tonight?"

"No," he said, "but I'm reasonably inexpensive."

"Can you come by at 8:30? Have dinner first—I'm not cooking for company."

"Love to."

"We have to—talk, I guess."

"'We have to talk' always sounds ominous."

"Come casual—I'm not dressing up."

"If we know each other well enough to dress casual," Chet said, "that's a good sign."

"I hope it is," she said.

For the next two hours, she thought carefully about what she would say to him. It was odd she'd never had a serious conversation with any lover before—about her own background, her life. She was a private person—to everyone.

Now, though, she planned honesty and truth. Maybe, she considered, she cared for Chester more than she'd imagined.

No wedding bells rang in her fantasy. To her, marriage was slow-moving suicide, nor did she want cohabitation—sharing living space with anyone for the rest of her life. Since leaving her parental home, she'd always lived alone, and she liked it that way. Her passion for Chet was just that—passion. A fling, if you will—a romance, an enjoyment of sex. No commitment. No love involved.

Or maybe it *was* love, she thought. She had no idea what love felt like. Her previous relationships had ended with a yawn rather than a whimper. They'd never been anything close to a "love" affair. So what did she now feel for Chet Quigley? And more importantly, what was he feeling for her?

What man would could love a woman who had deliberately killed another human being—one who straps lethal instruments to various parts of her body and goes out every day with the unspoken fear that she might not come back at all?

Who could base a loving relationship on a beautiful woman who realized poking gaping holes in the vicious business of child sex trafficking was all that interested her? What man could enter into a long-term relationship with tremendous sexual hang-ups his woman wouldn't tell him about?

One way or another, there were several six-hundred-pound gorillas in the room. They'd have to be discussed, or else tucked away in a closet. Sierra might not be able to hide those things forever.

She stared out the window, chewing on her thumbnail, until Chet Quigley rang the doorbell. She hesitated for fifteen seconds before answering it.

There was no kiss, no passion on Sierra's part. Just a quick hello hug, the kind of greeting to a spinster aunt not seen for an entire year and arriving for Thanksgiving.

"You want a drink, Chet?" she said when he'd sat down on the sofa.

"Whatever you're having."

She turned both palms upward. "I'm not having anything."

"Okay—I won't have anything, either." He smiled. "You look beautiful—as ever."

She didn't respond, but sat in her recliner opposite him. He said, "Can't we share this couch?"

"It's hard to talk sitting next to each other and twisting our heads around."

"Twisting our heads around?" Chet frowned. "This must be serious."

"Chet, my job *is* serious."

"It's a great job."

"It always has been—but things changed recently. I killed a man."

Chet leaned forward, elbows on thighs. "Everybody knows that, Sierra. It was all over the national news. It made you a hero." He wanted to reach out and touch her hand, but he was too far away. "I think you're a hero, too."

She chose to ignore it. "It's going to be different now."

"Why?"

"This whole case was about child sex-trafficking, Chet."

"It wasn't a 'case.' We met when you dealt yourself into a non-case to begin with."

"Call it whatever you like—but it won't be the last situation I'll be looking into."

"Is there another one?" Chet asked.

"Thousands of children—in the United States and all over the world—disappear every week. Most of them wind up working in disgusting brothels in some third-world country and then dying. I can't let that happen. It might get rough for me, like last time. I can't start up a relationship with you and every so often leave you to go off on another wild chase that could get me hurt—or killed. It's not fair to you."

"Sierra," he said, "law enforcement all over the country do that every day. The FBI, U.S. Marshals, local, state, federal cops..."

"If there were a million of them, it wouldn't be nearly enough."

"But why you?"

"I have my reasons—one of which is why you and I got off to a rocky start."

"I accepted that, Sierra. But that has nothing to do with you spending the rest of your life chasing down sex traffickers."

"It has everything to do with it."

"Why?"

Sierra looked down at her feet, regretting not having several glasses of wine before Chet had arrived. She did owe him an explanation, though, one she'd never offered before to anyone. Finally, looking anywhere but at his face—studying the wall behind him, the lamp, the doorway to the kitchen—she took a deep breath, and with a voice she struggled not to quiver, made him the first to ever hear her story.

Her childhood didn't relate to those 1950s sitcoms they show today on Nickelodeon—Mommy in a dress and pearls as she mopped the kitchen floor, Daddy wearing a suit and tie to dinner at home and later reading the newspaper. From her earliest remembrances, her mother was her father's doormat at home and a religious fanatic to the rest of the world—detached from everything in her quiet little universe except church on Sunday and praying morning and night the other six days of the week. Her husband was a full-blown alcoholic who lived in constant rage and anger. When he was drunk, which was often, sense, ethics and morals went right out the window, and when he stumbled home from a night at the tavern, he looked for release, desperately needed in order to go to sleep satisfied.

From the time she was six years old, whenever he returned from the local gin joint, her daddy would search out Sierra and pull down her panties and finger her private parts while he masturbated. She'd whimper from the pain—even more from humiliation. She'd sometimes cry so loudly that he would smack her, hard, to keep her quiet. He never penetrated her vagina with his penis— only with his fingers. When she turned nine, the abuse grew from drunken groping to forced fellatio.

At nine years old in a small town, she'd never heard of a woman taking a man's dick into her mouth. The taste of semen made her vomit until she forced herself to get used to it.

Did her mother know it was happening? Sierra was never sure. But Mommy never said peep about it. That's not what motherhood was supposed to be like. As time wore on, Sierra found herself hating her mother even more than she despised her father.

The oral sex continued for at least twice a week, if not more often—until she grew into a tall, athletic thirteen-year-old. She was in the kitchen one evening, washing dinner dishes, when her bitter, sizzled father reeled in, studied her lasciviously, and told her she had grown so much and was now beginning to sport breasts and pubic hair—"tits and cunt hair" is what he actually said—and that it was time for him to bust her cherry. She knew the meaning of 'busting her cherry,' so when he unzipped his fly and exposed himself, demanding another warm-up blow job, Sierra refused, which she hadn't ever done before. Enraged, he grabbed her by the back of her neck, forcing her head downward. She struggled with him—slapping, punching and eventually poking him in the eye with her finger. When he roared in pain and let go of her neck, she grabbed a heavy cast-iron frying pan from the drying rack and smashed his face hard, flattening his nose and gouging at his eye. The bones shattered into splinters, which never healed properly, so his face remained twisted and ugly, and he lost seven front teeth. His left eye, now much weaker than his right, remained permanently bloodshot.

He never touched her again, not sexually or even in anger, nor did he speak to her or meet her eyes with his own. It was as if she lived in a sleazy rooming house without knowing the names of her co-tenants. Her mother took him to the hospital a dozen times for reparation of his face, but it never worked, and he remained looking grotesque until after high school graduation when Sierra left home for good.

She never glanced back once.

During her few romantic relationships as an adult, the memories always tormented her. She'd always eschewed oral sex. She couldn't imagine doing it again if her life depended on it.

When finished unearthing her retentive memories aloud for the first time, Sierra subsided into dark silence for more than a minute, her breathing labored. Chet Quigley eventually said, "God, I feel like such a complete shit for asking you—that. Sierra, I'm so sorry."

"That was a story you didn't need to hear. I won't get bent out of shape if you said goodbye right now."

Chet remained silent, too, sighing. Finally: "I'm not saying goodbye."

"You should. Now you understand why I started this off-the-books investigation in the first place."

"I know," he said, "there's sex trafficking all over the world—"

"I've always known it—but it seemed so foreign, so out of my league, that it never truly bothered me before. When I suspected it happens right here in Sundown Beach, it got me off my ass for the first time."

"That's good, Sierra."

"I neglected my job, pissed off the people who hired me, and would've been dead by now if not killing the bad guy who was going to kill me."

"And the whole world thinks you're a paladin—a knight in shining armor."

"I'm no paladin, Chet—whatever the hell that is. But an investigation like this won't be the last time."

Quigley had trouble swallowing. "Why? Nothing like that happens in town now."

"Maybe not—but it happens someplace else. There's a group in Hemlock Hills, Chet, whose sole purpose is to save children from a nightmare of a life."

He frowned. "What's that got to do with you?"

"All they have to do is pick up the phone and call me—and I'll be there."

"In Hemlock Hills?"

"Wherever I'm needed."

"That could cost your job here."

"Then I'll get another job."

"In some other town? You'd leave here?"

She sighed again. "If I have to."

Chet leaned all the way forward, resting his arms on his thighs. Eventually he said, "I can't take off and move somewhere else, Sierra. Sundown Beach has been my home for decades."

"I know. But if we were together, I'd be running off somewhere, putting my neck on the chopping block. You couldn't handle that."

"I could."

"You couldn't! You'd have to move on because you couldn't take it." Sierra tried a smile that didn't work. "You're a teacher, Chet. You love it. You understand pre-teens—that's what you do. But your so-called girlfriend—me—being threatened with death and killing other people? I don't think you'd understand that at all."

Quiet. No one said anything. They both looked at their feet, frowning, as seconds ticked by for at least three minutes. Then Chet Quigley said, "Sierra."

She looked up to meet his eyes.

"I'm—I can live without oral sex. I understand your—story—and my heart aches for it. What we've had has been great and I love that. But I can't seem to process—"

"What?"

It took him thirty seconds before he could answer. "Death," he finally said. "I can't deal with death—yours, or some bad guy's that you caused."

She nodded.

"I know old people die. They all do. But that's a different kind of dying."

"Young people die, too," Sierra said. "Diseases. Accidents. Being kidnapped and sold as slaves." She took a deep breath and hung onto it for a while before exhaling. "Cops die, Chet."

"Not police chiefs. That's a safe job. You hang around the office, make decisions, you get to sign stuff..."

"I'm not planning on 'hanging around!' The people in Hemlock Hills—who live to save children—they have my phone number. They can call me anytime. Any place in the country could call me. And they will."

There was another prolonged silence, Sierra looking at Chet, him staring fixedly at his own knees. At length she said, "Our evening has gone about as far as it can go, Chet."

Chet, looking downward, shook his head. "I guess so." Then he leaned toward her, reached out and took her hand in his. "I'm desperately sorry. I still want to be your friend, Sierra."

Friend. Sure. Why not?

After Chet Quigley went home, it saddened her. Losing someone to occupy the other side of a warm bed was one thing—but unless love really hit the heavens, lovers can always be replaced.

She didn't have many real friends. Griffin Parrish and Nancy Flower proved themselves friends. Chris Fornadel? He was mostly a friend—and occasionally a pain in the ass. As for the city council—or the two thirds of them still left? It would be hard for them to forget it was Sierra who burned down their council partner, J. Richard Stubblefield, even when the rest of the city—even the country—considered her a glory-seeker.

You can applaud a hero, she thought—applaud, admire, and respect one. But it's far too difficult for anyone to become real friends with one.

When she returned to her job—truly embarrassed that all the police officers gave her a standing ovation when she walked in, even the night shift who'd hung around to celebrate the moment of her return—she tried to put everything behind her, including

Chet Quigley, the petty infighting of the city council, and the violent night she had spent in Cardiff-by-the-Sea with Dieter Krotzge.

Dylan Zack had to go to court regarding his driving indiscretion and his possession of too much marijuana—and Daddy naturally bought him out of it. Kenneth Zack's best buddy, Danielle Micaela Tokes, didn't like Sierra any better, but was wise enough—for the moment, anyway—to tiptoe around when a national hero in her town donned a badge and silver stars. Sierra and Chris Fornadel remained on friendly terms, though they spoke less frequently; he did invite her to a cocktail party at his home, where both his wife and his mistress were present. Awkward—but for Sierra it was pretty damn funny, too, and she glanced from one woman to the other, comparing faces, bodies, smiles, and patience.

She dined at the Dolphin Lounge one Saturday with the Anaheim Chief of Police and his wife, who were taking a weekend getaway at Sundown Beach. Anaheim was home to the original Disneyland and the baseball team that kept changing its name—Anaheim Angels, Los Angeles Angels, until finally it became the California Angels. The wife spent her days sitting on the Sundown sand in a rented chair reading romance novels and drinking mimosas while he fly-fished in the surf. At dinner, the Anaheim chief treated her as if she'd won the Medal of Honor. She hated every moment of the dinner and twisted mightily in discomfort.

Her office work was much the same as it had always been—supervising, signing things, reading police periodicals, and fighting for the summer replacement of the vintage air conditioner that kept failing at the most inopportune times.

Then one morning on the week following Thanksgiving Day, her cell phone rang. Few people had the number, and usually a call for her at the station came through the landline. She closed her eyes momentarily. Was it another millionaire calling to save the ass of an incorrigible kid busted for doing something stupid?

She pressed her lips together and picked up the phone. The Caller ID read "Unknown."

"Hello, Chief Bravo," came a familiar, raspy voice. "Tyler Calhoun here. How're you feeling? Listen, can you take a day off on, say, Thursday—and drive on over here to Hemlock Hills? We've got something that might interest you."

ACKNOWLEDGMENTS

I lived in Southern California for a quarter of a century. To my knowledge, there are no towns or cities in California called Sundown Beach or Hemlock Hills. They are fictional, created in my imagination.

My heartfelt salute to the FBI and to the United States Marshal Service. Sure, they spar sometimes over who gets the credit, but when the chips are down, they are the best organizations in the country.

My eternal thanks to Police Chief James T. McBride (retired), who patiently explains every question I ever asked about police procedure. He is a scholar, a published author, a gifted poet, a brilliant cop, and a bagpipe player extraordinaire.

A deep, tearful bow to the many organizations throughout the world that relentlessly battle the buying, selling, enslavement, and sex trafficking of children and adults.

My love and thanks to next-door neighbor Amy Schneiderman, now known as "Aims" for her kindness and understanding.

My enormous adoration, as ever, goes to Holly Albin, for her love, support, editing, and inspiring input. Without her, I'd live in a remote wilderness somewhere, eat leaves and sticks, and carve my next novel into the wall of a cave.

LES ROBERTS came to mystery writing by winning the very first "First Private Eye Novel" Contest, which gave him his literary. Prior to that, he worked in Los Angeles for a quarter of a century, writing and/or producing more than 2500 half hours of network and syndicated television. A Chicago native, he has lived for the past 31 years in Northeast Ohio.

On the following pages are a few
more great titles from the
Down & Out Books publishing family.

For a complete list of books and to
sign up for our newsletter,
go to DownAndOutBooks.com.

Midnight in Delhi
A Jonathan Brooks Thriller
A.C. Frieden

Down & Out Books
November 2024
978-1-64396-375-4

On a flight from Sri Lanka, attorney Jonathan Brooks is jolted from his seat by a sudden commotion. He rushes to assist an unconscious passenger, initiating CPR. But as the plane diverts to Oman, a second medical emergency grips the cabin. Moments before landing, the control tower issues a chilling order: the pilots must reverse course over the Arabian Sea. With fuel running low, Jonathan's flight is redirected again. to a remote airbase near New Delhi to impose a full-scale quarantine.

But Jonathan soon discovers evidence that a sinister plan is unfolding...

Agatha and Derringer Get Cozy
Thirteen Tales of Murder, Mystery, and Master Detection
Gay Toltl Kinman & Andrew McAleer, editors

Down & Out Books
November 2024
978-1-64396-382-2

In *Agatha & Derringer Get Cozy*, thirteen of today's cleverest mystery and suspense authors get cozy with mystery fans in thirteen original mysteries written exclusively by Agatha and Derringer Award-winning authors. In some of their most creative and cunning cozy stories yet, these modern masters of suspense—John Floyd, Barb Goffman, Tara Laskowski, BV Lawson, Robert Lopresti, Kris Neri, Alan Orloff, Josh Pachter, Stephen D. Rogers, Shawn Reilly Simmons, Marcia Talley, Art Taylor, and Stacy Woodson—have meticulously planned for mystery enthusiasts a full docket of murder, mischief, and mayhem.

Mickey Finn Vol. 5
21st Century Noir
Michael Bracken, editor

Down & Out Books
December 2024
978-1-64396-386-0

Mickey Finn: 21st Century Noir, Volume 5, the fifth volume of the hard-hitting series, is another crime-fiction cocktail that will knock readers into a literary stupor.

The eighteen contributors, including some of today's most respected short-story writers and new writers making their mark on the genre, include: K.L. Abrahamson, Alan Barker, Michael Chandos, Caleb Coy, Eddie Generous, Nils Gilbertson, James A. Hearn, Hugh Lessig, Sean McCluskey, Tom Milani, Bill W. Morgan, Alan Orloff, Travis Richardson, Andrew Welsh-Huggins, Robb T. White, Sam Wiebe, Joseph S. Walker, and Stacy Woodson.

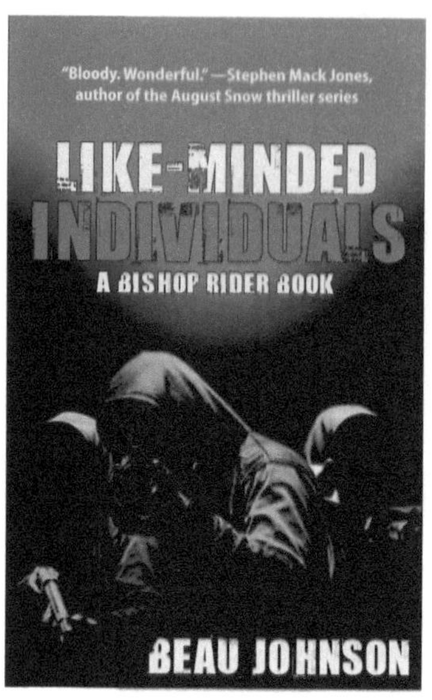

Like-Minded Individuals
A Bishop Rider Book
Beau Johnson

Down & Out Books
February 2025
978-1-64396-387-7

Bishop Rider may be dead but the mission lives on.

Jeramiah Abrum, the son of the man who murdered Bishop Rider's mother and sister, picking up the mantle of the man who would not stop and running with it in ways Bishop Rider never could. Involving bigger moves, bolder plays, and if he's lucky, an army who comes to understand that saving people or stopping them, the choice has never been clearer.

In *Like-Minded Individuals*, the endgame begins. Come see how they make them burn.